TRANSNATIONAL CHINESE

Transnational Chinese

Fujianese Migrants in Europe

FRANK N. PIEKE, PÁL NYÍRI, METTE THUNØ,
AND ANTONELLA CECCAGNO

STANFORD UNIVERSITY PRESS

STANFORD, CALIFORNIA

2004

Stanford University Press
Stanford, California
www.sup.org

Library of Congress Cataloging-in-Publication Data

Transnational Chinese : Fujianese migrants in Europe / Frank N. Pieke . . .
[et al.].
    p. cm.
    Includes bibliographical references and index.
    ISBN 0-8047-4994-9 (alk. paper)—ISBN 0-8047-4995-7 (pbk : alk. paper)
      1. Chinese—Europe—History.   2. Europe—Emigration and immigration.
3. Europe—Ethnic relations.   4. Europe—Emigration and immigration.
5. Fujian Sheng (China)—Emigration and immigration.   6. Globalization.
7. Chinese—Europe—Social conditions.   8. Fujian Sheng (China)—Economic
conditions.   I. Pieke, Frank N.
D1056.2.C55 T73 2004
304.8'4051245—dc22   2003019110

Printed in the United States of America on acid-free, archival-quality paper.

Original Printing 2004
Last figure below indicates year of this printing:
13 12 11 10 09 08 07 06 05 04

Designed and typeset at Stanford University Press in 10 / 12.5 Palatino.

Contents

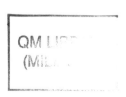

Illustrations and Tables

Preface

This book presents the findings of a three-year (1999–2001) research project on Fujianese migration and transnationalism in Europe that was funded by the British Economic and Social Research Council (ESRC) as part of its research program on transnational communities (grant number L214252012). Although I was the grant recipient and coordinator of the project, the book presents a genuinely collective effort of all four authors. In addition, the efforts of a fifth scholar, our fieldworker in Fujian, who wishes to remain anonymous, were absolutely indispensable.

At various points along the way, the project and the book benefited from the support and comments of many colleagues. In particular, I would like to thank Gregor Benton, Ulf Hannerz, Khalid Koser, Rana Mitter, Aihwa Ong, Ron Skeldon, Sarah Spencer, Steve Vertovec, and two anonymous reviewers for Stanford University Press. We are also grateful to the participants in two ESRC user group workshops: Tim Bridges (London Metropolitan Police), Haibin Xue (Chinese Information and Advice Centre), David Tan (Westminster City Council), Wahpiow Tan (Thomas Andrew & Tan Solicitors), Frank Laczko and Ling Li (International Organization for Migration), Angelos Pangratis and Ana Gonzalo (European Commission), Martin Wood and Nic Carlyle (Home Office), Claudio Loiodice (Turin municipal police), Monika Lazar (Hungarian Interior Ministry), Derk van der Zee (Rotterdam municipal police), and Richard McKee (Immigration Law Practitioners Association). None of them can in any way be held responsible for any factual mistakes or flaws in the arguments presented here.

A shorter version of Chapter 2 will be published in the *International*

Migration Review by Mette Thunø and Frank Pieke under the title "Institutionalizing Recent Rural Emigration from China to Europe: New Transnational Villages in Fujian." Parts of Chapter 5 are based on Pál Nyíri's article "Chinese in Hungary and Their Significant Others: A Multi-sited Approach to Transnational Practice and Discourse," published in *Identities: Global Studies in Culture and Power* 9 (2002): 69–86. Finally, several sections from my own report for the International Organization for Migration, "Recent Trends in Chinese Migration to Europe: Fujianese Migration in Perspective" (Geneva: IOM Migration Series no. 6, 2002) were used in Chapters 1, 3, and 6.

Electronic copies of all case files, interview notes, and fieldnotes referred to in this book have been made anonymous and lodged with the ESRC's Qualidata (http://www.qualidata.ac.uk/), from which they are publicly available for research purposes. With the exception of public figures, throughout the book all personal names are pseudonyms.

FRANK PIEKE

Oxford, January 2003

Currency Exchange Rates

The exchange rates used in the book are listed here.

1 British pound (£) = 1.5 US$
1 euro (€) = 1.0 US$
1 German mark (DM) = 0.5 US$
1,000 Italian lire (L) = 0.5 US$
10 Chinese renminbi (RMB) = 1.2 US$
10 Hong Kong dollars (HK$) = 1.2 US$
100 Hungarian forints (Ft) = 0.3 to 0.5 US$, depending on the year

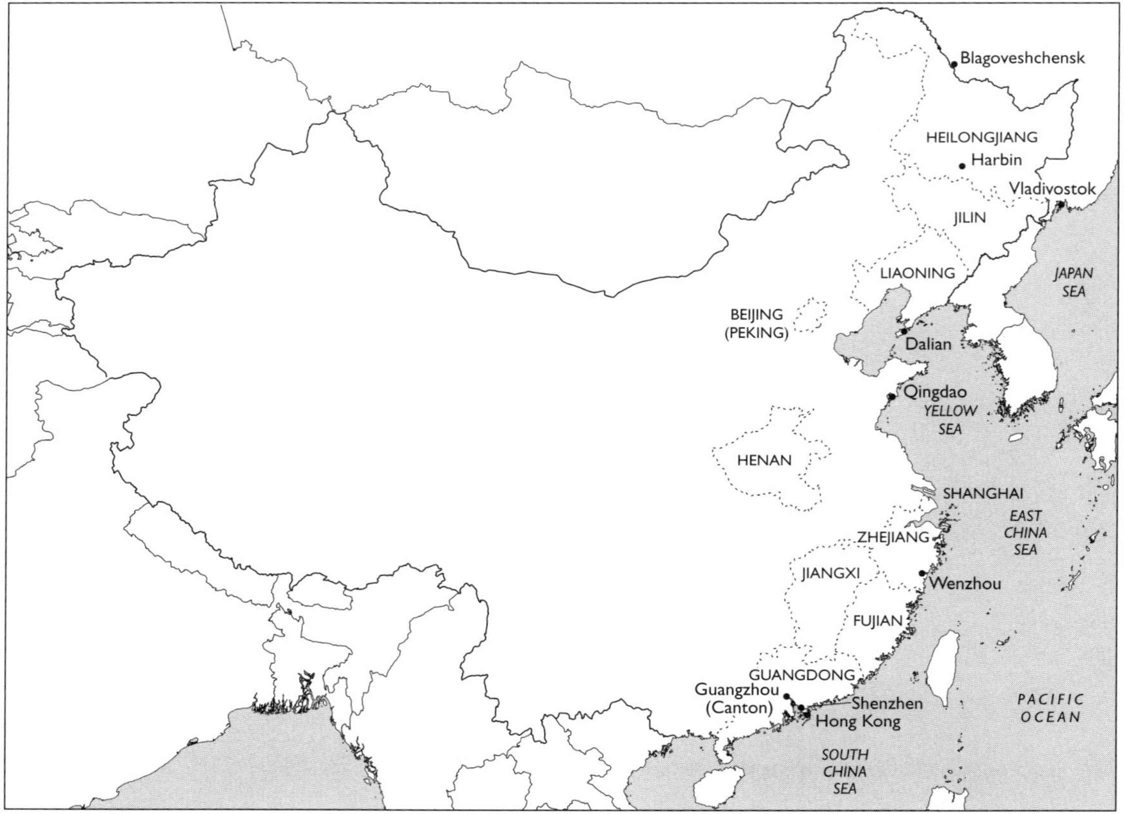
Blagoveshchensk
HEILONGJIANG
Harbin
Vladivostok
JILIN
LIAONING
JAPAN SEA
BEIJING (PEKING)
Dalian
Qingdao
YELLOW SEA
HENAN
SHANGHAI
EAST CHINA SEA
ZHEJIANG
JIANGXI
Wenzhou
FUJIAN
GUANGDONG
Guangzhou (Canton)
Shenzhen
Hong Kong
PACIFIC OCEAN
SOUTH CHINA SEA

MAP 1. China

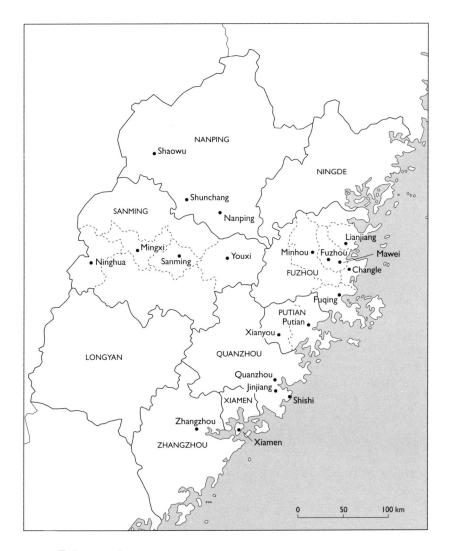

NANPING

Shaowu

NINGDE

Shunchang

SANMING

Nanping

Lianjiang

Mingxi

Minhou • Fuzhou • Mawei

Ninghua

Sanming

Youxi

FUZHOU

Changle

Fuqing

PUTIAN

Putian

Xianyou

LONGYAN

QUANZHOU

Quanzhou

Jinjiang

XIAMEN

Shishi

Zhangzhou

ZHANGZHOU

Xiamen

0   50   100 km

MAP 2. Fujian province

MAP 3. Europe

TRANSNATIONAL CHINESE

CHAPTER 1

Introduction: Conceptualizing Chinese Migration in a Global Age

CHINESE IN EUROPE have come and gone for well over a century. Hailing from many different countries, including those where Chinese often are only one of several ethnic groups, Chinese in Europe have many different nationalities, attachments, and migratory histories. Chinese migration to Europe thus consists of many different flows, and the vast differences in the timing and especially the volume of these flows make the Chinese community in each European country a unique configuration. Furthermore, since the late 1970s, Chinese immigration in Europe has undergone a fundamental change. Not Hong Kong or Southeast Asia, but the People's Republic of China itself has become the chief source of Chinese immigrants.

Among the new Chinese migrants in Europe, in the 1990s the Fujianese rapidly became a small but prominent group. Part—albeit by no means all—of Fujianese migration is irregular. Fujianese migration facilitators or "snakeheads" (*shetou*) have rapidly become the most visible expression of some of the changes taking place in Chinese migration worldwide, and not the least in Europe.[1] Although Fujianese are only a recent migratory flow and account for a relatively small minority of Chinese migrants to Europe, they have become in many ways emblematic of the changes taking place in Chinese migration at large. A better understanding of the dynamics of this flow will also highlight some of the most salient issues and current and future policy choices confronting the governments of sending and receiving areas alike.

To migrants, the many forms of "legal" and "illegal" migration constitute a continuum of alternatives rather than activities that are very different from each other. Which side of the boundary between legal and illegal movement and residence migrants find themselves on, and to what extent they employ the services of paid migration brokers, varies greatly from individual to individual. Legality or illegality is also influenced by the locality the migrant sets out from and by the immigration regimes of destination countries, which have changed over the ten-plus years of large-scale migration from Fujian to Europe. Migration of Fujianese between individual European countries and over time has varied considerably. In Germany, for example, asylum seekers who lodged their applications between 1997 and 2001 were not permitted to work, resulting, according to our informants, in the departure for the United Kingdom of a large number of Chinese migrants without residence permits. The Netherlands, unlike Britain and Germany, does not detain or deport anyone claiming to be an unaccompanied minor; such migrants are provided accommodation in flats and education. At the same time, jobs in the Chinese restaurant sector in the Netherlands are scarce. Thus, at least until some recent changes in enforcement, many Chinese migrants who applied for asylum in the Netherlands claimed to be unaccompanied minors.

Europe provides an important point of comparison for the study of Chinese international migration and the overseas Chinese, a field that has tended to focus on the older, larger, and better-known Chinese communities, particularly those in North America. The great variety in immigration regimes within a small geographic area, the newness of immigration, particularly in eastern and southern Europe, the rapid changes forged by the fall of the Soviet bloc and the unification of the European Union, and the highly contentious nature and fluidity of immigration policies make Europe a virtual laboratory for the study of Chinese international migration. From a Chinese perspective, the northern, eastern, and southern parts of the continent present a vast frontier of highly developed economies, where they nevertheless face little competition from established Chinese communities. These frontiers are either directly accessible through the former Soviet Union, or indirectly accessible by way of the old and relatively large Chinese communities in the metropolitan areas of northwestern Europe, which themselves continue to attract significant numbers of newcomers. Furthermore, Chinese migration to Europe is rapidly diversifying, both in the areas of origin of Chinese migrants and in the number of student, business, and professional migrants. It is following patterns similar, but not identical, to changes in Chinese migration to North America two decades ago.

Finally, work on migration to North America, and particularly to the United States, tends to reflect the attitude of many Americans and migrants alike that the United States is everybody's destination of choice, that all other destinations are second best, or perhaps just steps along the way. Western European studies of migration often display a similar attitude, though usually slightly more qualified. Furthermore, both North American and western European studies tend to perceive international migration as a relatively straightforward process that attracts people from peripheries to the global cities (Sassen 1991) that are centers of the world: New York, Los Angeles, Miami, Vancouver, Toronto, Berlin, London, and Paris. Yet the recent nature of much Chinese migration to Europe and the importance of peripheral or formerly peripheral areas in southern and eastern Europe as destinations make it a lot more difficult to ignore the fact that, worldwide, most migration, including that of Chinese, takes people to places that seem, at first glance, curiously nonobvious.

When we first started thinking about conducting research on the Fujianese in Europe in 1997, we were very much influenced by the literature that was then beginning to appear on illegal Fujianese migration to the United States, following the rude wake-up call provided by the grounding of the *Golden Venture* in New York harbor on June 6, 1993, with 286 illegal Fujianese migrants on board (K. Chin 1999; Kwong 1997; N. Liu 1996; Smith 1997; Xinjing 1995a, 1995b, 1995c). That literature highlighted the commercialization and criminalization of migration and the abuse, extortion, and suffering of migrants during transit and after arrival at their destination. We assumed that Fujianese in Europe were either castaways abandoned by migration facilitators on the way to the United States, or else people who could not afford the more expensive passage to that country. In short, we expected that the world was the snakeheads' oyster and ignored the relevance of the agency of migrants and the specific dynamics of individual migratory flows.

Transnational Ethnography

This book presents the findings of a three-year research project on Fujianese migration to Europe.[2] Although the project's research methods were broadly ethnographic, combining informal conversations and participant observation with formal interviews and a household survey, our topic compelled us to pioneer new ways of carrying out a global and multi-sited ethnography. The newness and breadth of the phenomena we wished to study, coupled with the speed with which they changed even during our project, required much more than a serial conventional ethnography of more than one place carried out by the same fieldworker, but involved five researchers working simultaneously in different localities. Furthermore, each main locality of research, both in Europe and in China, was visited several times by the same or different researchers in the course of just three years. These two features of our research enabled us to study the connections between the processes of migration, settlement, and transnationalism up close and almost in real time as they unfolded simultaneously in different sites.

In January 1999, we began gathering basic information about immigration, through-migration, and employment patterns in selected European countries: Britain, Germany, France, the Netherlands, Italy, Spain, Hungary, Romania, and Russia. Subsequently, we carried out exploratory research in Fujian province. During the second phase of the research, from September 1999 until April 2001, the project focused on three countries in Europe—Britain, Hungary, and Italy—that were selected on the basis of the exploratory research of the first phase. While acknowledging that each European country is unique, we chose Britain to represent the core countries of Chinese settlement in northwestern Europe, Italy to stand for the southern frontier opened up in the 1980s, and Hungary as the hub of the new eastern frontier of the 1990s. Each in its own region plays a key role in the new Chinese migration, and each is therefore a prominent point on the Fujianese map of Europe. Britain, with the oldest and one of the largest Chinese communities, had become the destination of choice for many Fujianese in the 1990s, also because of its close links with other Anglophone countries, such as the United States and Australia, that are major destinations for Fujianese migrants. Hungary occupies a pivotal place in the exploration of eastern Europe by Chinese migrants in the wake of the fall of the Soviet bloc in 1989–90. Hungary is also a gateway to southern and western Europe. Italy became the main Chinese destination country in southern Europe in the 1980s, also attracting many Fujianese in the 1990s and providing a template for future developments elsewhere in what to Chinese migrants is the European periphery.

The second phase of fieldwork in Europe entailed systematic interviews with more than one hundred migrants in Moscow (Russia); Budapest, Szeged, Nyírbátor, and Szombathely (Hungary); Mainz, Stuttgart, and Freiburg im Breisgau (Germany); Amsterdam, Rotterdam, Sneek, and Tilburg (the Netherlands); Paris (France); Oxford and London (Britain); Madrid and Valencia (Spain); and Rome, Prato, Terzigno, and San Giuseppe Vesuviano (Italy). These interviews were supplemented by interviews with employers, landlords, police, lawyers, employment agencies, community workers, and others professionally involved with Fujianese migrants. Simultaneously, detailed ethnographic research was carried out in two sending communities in Fujian. These two villages had likewise been identified during the first phase of research. They were selected because they were located in areas that, more than other localities in Fujian, specialized in migration to Europe, namely Fuqing municipality south of the provincial capital Fuzhou, and inland Mingxi county in Sanming prefecture. In total, 106 interviews were completed with officials and villagers. A questionnaire was administered to half (81 of the 162) of all emigrant households in the fieldwork village located in Mingxi county (equal to 26 percent of all households in the village). In March 2001 we also carried out exploratory research on the Fujianese in New York City, which, as the hub of the overseas Fujianese diaspora, foreshadows and has an important impact on many developments in Europe. We completed all of the field research for the project in June 2001.

In addition to the observations, interviews, and more informal conversations that are the mainstay of ethnographic research, we systematically read Chinese newspapers published in Europe and Fujian. Although we gathered statistical data from government agencies and officials in China and Europe where and when we could, we found most of these data of limited value.[3] Many records were incomplete, included only legal migration, or applied categories of analysis that were unsuited or simply too broad for our needs. Gathering our own quantitative data proved almost impossible owing to the illegal nature of much Fujianese migration. In only one of our study villages in China did we manage to conduct a village survey. Although we also explored the possibility of conducting a survey in one or more European countries, we abandoned the idea when we found that it would be impossible to construct a reliable sample population. For these reasons, this study regrettably cannot provide reliable numbers of migrants from Fujian to Europe; we have resisted the temptation to present our own or our informants' estimates, figures that in our experience are often mistakenly cited as authoritative facts in the literature and in policy documents.

Ethnographic research is therefore the most appropriate way of researching a topic like ours that is largely unexplored by previous research and that involves activities and sensitivities that cannot be confronted using more formal and intrusive research methods. Our work on "problems that manifest themselves in intensely local forms but have contexts that are anything but local" (Appadurai 2000: 6) is as much about the details of local places and communities as it is about the networks and connections linking these places to a transnational social space. A "global ethnography" (Burawoy 2000) such as ours presents specific challenges for ethnographic methods as conventionally used in anthropology and other social sciences. Traditionally, ethnography takes place in a particular field site and assumes a particular locality, community, and culture. The challenge of ethnographic fieldwork that wishes to map a particular transnational social space is not merely that it almost certainly must be multi-sited; this is in itself nothing new in anthropological fieldwork (Marcus 1995). The real challenge of such fieldwork is to recognize that place and community do not unproblematically exist out there awaiting the ethnographer's gaze. As Gupta and Ferguson put it, "Instead of assuming the autonomy of the primeval community, we have to examine how it was formed as a community out of the interconnected space that always existed" (Gupta and Ferguson 1997). In other words, place and community are products, and the object of ethnographic research is to elucidate the social processes that imagine, produce, and challenge specific places and communities, ranging from Benedict Anderson's nations to humble villages in the countryside and marginal migrant groups in the global cities of western Europe and North America.

Ethnographic work in and about transnational social space is much more than a choice of methodology and procedures; it is also a matter of the questions the fieldworker takes to the field: ultimately, the ethnographer's field site is not just the place where research happens to take place; instead, its existence as a place of belonging is the key problem to be investigated. In what way, to what extent, and under what circumstances is a migrant from a particular village in Fujian a member of a local Chinese or Fujianese community in a European city or country? Conversely, when do the same migrants imagine themselves to belong to a "transnational" community of fellow villagers or fellow Fujianese dispersed across Europe or North America, or both? When and for whom does the village or area of origin, or China as a whole, become the focus of a sense of belonging? What are the biographical and political mechanisms and implications of such belonging, and what are the culturally constructed conceptions of place, community, and belonging that inform such choices and processes?

The trail of Fujianese migrants led us to many different places in China, Europe, and the United States and involved close cooperation and coordination among five researchers based in as many countries: China, Denmark, Italy, Hungary, and Britain. Most of the fieldwork in Europe was carried out by Pál Nyíri. From his home base in Budapest, Nyíri undertook short visits of between two and four weeks each to the European countries selected for the first and second phases of research. In March 2001, Nyíri also made a similar field trip to New York City. In Italy in the first half of 2001, Antonella Ceccagno carried out an additional twenty interviews with Fujianese in Prato, a central Italian city that is a center of Chinese enterprise in the country and where she has worked with the local Chinese community. Apart from the interviews, Ceccagno's contributions to the book also draw on her long-term research on the Chinese in Italy and her knowledge of the Chinese in Prato.

Research in each European country was never an independent undertaking. Names of people to interview in other countries were always actively solicited, and a few informants were even interviewed in more than one country after they changed residence. Nyíri also joined several highly mobile informants or their family members as they traveled from place to place or country to country for business or in search of work. We also tried to trace emigrants in Europe who belonged to families interviewed in China, but this strategy had to be abandoned because families in China were reluctant to provide information about their relatives, who often resided illegally abroad; and they became very suspicious of our intentions when we pressed politely for the information.

In China itself, an exploratory field trip was undertaken by Nyíri in the summer of 1999 following an earlier trip by Mette Thunø in 1998 before the formal start of the project. These two trips made it clear to us that it would be impossible to carry out detailed field investigations ourselves. Because the issue of illegal migration (*toudu*) was so politically sensitive both nationally and internationally, foreign researchers had great difficulty gaining access to the sending villages. We decided that the only practical way forward was to ask a local researcher to carry out the fieldwork for us as a part of his own research on the over-seas Chinese in Fujian. Subsequently, Thunø undertook to train this fieldworker in ethnographic methods and interview techniques, closely supervising and monitoring his fieldwork from Fuzhou city or her home base in Copenhagen by means of daily or even more frequent e-mail exchanges and telephone conversations. After the fieldworker's return from a field trip, Thunø would receive full field notes in Chinese, which she and the researcher discussed in detail in preparation for sub-sequent field trips.

This method worked remarkably well, in large part because the local researcher was keen to learn what he saw as modern Western methods of social research. He quickly became a skilled fieldworker who began to ask probing questions himself. However, suspicions of any kind of research ran so high that even this local researcher had difficulty gain-ing prolonged access to emigrant villages. He could also investigate the issue of emigration only indirectly, which is why he has chosen not to be named in any publications or reports that include data that he gath-ered for us. Fortunately, we had decided to work in two emigrant vil-lages rather than just one: one located in coastal Fuqing county (munic-ipality), the other in inland Mingxi county (see a later section for more details about our field sites). In Mingxi the local authorities were, on the whole, proud of their achievements in opening up the overseas Chinese "market" and saw the research as an opportunity to gain recognition for their efforts. Only in Fuqing, with its long-standing and intensive involvement in emigration, did the sensitivity of illegal migration have a significant impact on the quality of the information that could be col-lected, and even there our fieldworker was able to piece together a rea-sonably complete picture of the deep embeddedness of migration in the local society and culture.

Research in such a broad range of sites across three continents and involving fieldworkers in four different countries poses considerable challenges of cooperation and coordination. Frank Pieke's role was to manage the individual team members and maintain the thematic co-herence of the project. E-mail was indispensable, supplemented by face-to-face meetings with individual team members and among the team as a whole. Almost all interviews conducted for this book were held in the interviewees' own language. All interview and field notes were typed out either in English or Chinese, the two languages known by all members of the team. Through routine e-mail contact, all Euro-pean team members filed their field notes with Pieke, who forwarded them to the other European members of the team (apart from a brief visit to Fuzhou by Pieke in 2000, contact with the Chinese team member ran almost exclusively through Thunø in order not to arouse suspicions in China). Pieke and the other European team members read all of the field notes and also provided feedback, suggesting further lines of inquiry and explanations based on their own experiences.

An additional important coordination tool was a list of originally dozens of research questions and an outline of the monograph that we undertook to write together. We frequently consulted and revised these questions and the outline to ensure that our fieldwork adhered to a common agenda and to check our progress in getting at some of the answers. In this way, all of the team members had clearly defined tasks both during the fieldwork and in drafting the chapters of this book. Having five experienced researchers acting as a critical sounding board for each other over a period of three years has helped us focus the mind, tease out conclusions, and most important, complete a project well beyond the capability of an individual researcher in a relatively short period of time. The project and this book thus represent a genuinely collective effort. For this reason, we decided not to attribute principal authorship to the chapters, despite the fact that the first draft of each one was prepared by a particular team member.

Conceptualizing Chinese Globalization

The new Chinese migration of which the Fujianese are a prominent part is one of the most visible exponents of the increasing globalization of China. The term *globalization* captures a great number of processes that transcend and redefine regional and national boundaries. The ever freer flow of capital, information, goods, and people makes its impact felt not only on the world's economy, politics, and population, but equally on culture, religion, and education, reshaping the world we live in (Castells 1996). Yet it is easy to get carried away with the idea of globalization. The much greater interconnectedness of even distant parts of the world shapes a new reality as much as it reconfigures and reproduces established social forms, such as the nation-state, the family, class, race, or ethnicity. In our use of the term *globalization*, we therefore heed the advice of Held and his coauthors and try to avoid the pitfalls of the two extremes in the debate—the proponents of which they respectively dub hyper-globalizers and skeptics—but view globalization as a range of open-ended transformative processes (Held et al. 1999).

A case in point—now often made in discussions on globalization—is that globalization is not simply a one-directional process in which hegemonic impositions from the Western, capitalist center obliterate cultural differences. Globalization and localization go hand in hand, spawning "creolized" cultural forms that are as much locally rooted and unique as they are variations on global themes (Hannerz 1987, 1988, 1992, chap. 7). Yet the challenge of globalization studies is not only to delineate the twin processes of universalization and localization of cultures, networks, capital, and population flows. Such an undifferentiated focus on the global and its counterpoint, the local, fails to appreciate two points. First, in as far as globalization is a homogenizing force, it works in both directions: as non-Western cultures and societies become more global and Western, these globalizing non-Western cultures also insert aspects of their own, globalizing cultures into the global melting pot. Second, and more pertinent to the topic of this book, globalization needs to be seen as taking place in multiple centers beyond the traditional centers of the capitalist world system. Globalization has not created a unified playing field for all social actors, but consists of a great many separate social spaces that are entangled and disentangled in multiple and complex ways. Globalization thus provides a new mode for the expression and production of difference.

In this book we describe the fractured, open-ended, and interlocking nature of globalization from the perspective of Chinese migrants to Europe. In discussions on globalization, China and the ethnic Chinese routinely feature as the prime example of a group, culture, or civilization that has successfully risen to the challenge of a global modernity originating from and dominated by the West. China from this perspective is different and even more exciting than its "Confucian" neighbor Japan. China combines continental size, rapid economic growth, and increasing integration in the world system with large, proactive, affluent, and widely dispersed diasporic communities. China, moreover, had largely cut itself off from the world during the more radical Cultural Revolution years of the Maoist era (1966–76). Consequently, after the onset of the reforms in 1978, China had to reenter the global community almost from scratch. The short time frame and sheer massive scale of Chinese globalization throw into especially sharp relief not only how China itself is becoming more global, but also, and equally important, how Chinese people, ideas, capital, and goods find their way across the globe.

Various concepts have been proposed to capture part or all of these exciting developments, including "greater China," a "Chinese commonwealth," the "clash of civilizations," "Chinese capitalism," and "Confucian values."[4] These terms point in important directions, yet do not provide the analytical tools that are required. Most important, they tend to obscure the fact that the globalization of Chinese business, society, and culture is by no means an established and uncontested fact. The global involvement of China has not settled in unambiguous and stable structures or patterns, but is an ongoing process that is constantly on the move. We propose here to explore the usefulness of the more open-ended and processual term *Chinese globalization*, which we conceptualize as multiple, transnational social spaces straddling and embedded in diversifying smaller regional or national systems on the one hand, and, on the other hand, as a part of a unifying global system. In our view, this reading conceptualizes globalization as an ongoing, never complete, and contested process that (1) is created and takes place in multiple centers and peripheries, (2) produces new forms of inequality and competition, and (3) encompasses a multiplicity of developments that are distinct yet at the same time interconnected. This reconceptualization of the global as an arena for competing and complementary processes aims to strip the teleological gloss from the term *globalization*. What we want to highlight here is that globalization consists of a range of contested, fragmented processes that do not necessarily result in a more homogeneous, integrated, or even more interdependent postmodern world that has transcended the shackles of the conventional modern world order consisting of discrete nation-states.

Even globalization research that agrees with many of the preceding observations often continues to rest on a powerful assumption of "common civilizational references in a world where the market is absolutely transcendental" (Ong 1999: 7). The image of an undivided world market inhabited by unqualified "cosmopolites" unfettered by political or cultural boundaries, while the rest of the world remains, for the time being at least, stuck in parochial lives, presents only a partial picture of the condition of "late modernity" (Giddens 1990). Yet we are very much in agreement with globalization theorists who argue against rival theories that see the world divided into spheres of influence, cultures, or civilizations that are fundamentally at loggerheads (Huntington 1998). Such a picture of the world, we should add, is by no means a matter of polite academic argument alone, and originates as much from the "periphery" as from the "center" of the world system, a realization driven home most forcefully by the events of September 11, 2001.

Our research and this book were guided by the desire to explore the

dimensions and ramifications of the new patterns of Chinese globalization that became apparent during the last twenty years of the twentieth
century and continue today. Chinese globalization manifests itself in a
broad range of contexts and forms, such as China's increased diplomatic and military prowess and role as an emerging regional or even
world superpower, the massive flows of capital and commodities to
and from China, the much greater prominence of Chinese language and
culture outside China, and the spectacular growth and much greater
heterogeneity of migration from China.

Without claiming that Chinese globalization is new and unrelated to
China's long history of global involvement and indeed prominence,[5]
we recognize that the new Chinese globalization has opened up a range
of transnational social spaces that combine "transnationalism from
above" and "transnationalism from below" of a variety and scale that
truly are unprecedented (Guarnizo and Smith 1998). This book endeav-
ors to explore the ramifications of the new Chinese globalization by
mapping the transnational social spaces opened up by the mobility,
work, settlement, and political involvement of a particular category of
Chinese international migrants whose migration is one of the most visible results of the new Chinese globalization. In this research there
should be at least two caveats. First, although work on Chinese international migrants arguably looks at globalization by starting with
"transnationalism from below," we should not lose sight of the fact that
this is intimately connected with the full range of global and transnational practices and spaces. Chinese globalization and the transnationalism that it has spawned do not exist in isolation, but are part of and
constrained by the structures of a world system still dominated by
Western capitalism and Western nations.

Second, transnationalism is best thought of as one aspect of observ-
able phenomena rather than as a phenomenon in its own right. It is
tempting to assume that transnationalism or even transnational communities exist simply because people move across international borders
a lot. Partly because of this, discussions of transnationalism, or "occupations and activities that require regular and sustained social contacts
over time across national borders" (Portes, Guarnizo, and Landolt 1999:
219), tend to get bogged down in claims that it is either a new social
form spawned by the new globalization of the "network society"
(Castells 1996), or that there is nothing new under the sun, and all that
scholars of transnationalism do is pour old wine into new bottles. Alejandro Portes has dealt conclusively with the latter claim by observing

that critics of the concept of transnationalism have fallen victim to what Robert K. Merton called the "fallacy of adumbration": "In science, it is a common occurrence for a significant finding to be preceded by a number of observations that pointed to the phenomenon in question, but failed to note its significance" (Portes 2001: 184). Like Portes, we find queries about the newness of transnationalism unhelpful, but would like to take the further cautionary step of refusing to reify transnationalism by a priori giving it the status of a separate social form, unless of course genuinely compelling empirical arguments can be presented to do so for a particular social group or phenomenon (as, for instance, seems to be the case with the Dominicans in the United States; see Levitt 2001). Instead, in this book we simply treat transnationalism as an empirical issue by constantly asking ourselves a more modest question: Which implications of phenomena become apparent when we interpret them in the context of sustained cross-border social relationships among their main protagonists?

By thinking of globalization as a multiplicity of processes (never a final state) that create a plurality of emerging and mature social spaces, we also do not want to repackage the nineteenth-century ideology of the world consisting of a mosaic of bounded nation-states; neither do we want to resurrect Cold War images of a world carved up into discrete spheres of influence. Lived-in spaces of social action created by Chinese globalization intersect and interact in a larger global system that is more than the sum of its parts. Fujianese migrants in New York, for instance, live in a major hub of a social world that they share with Fujianese across the globe that also includes other hubs such as Fuzhou city, Xiamen and Shenzhen Special Economic Zones, Hong Kong, Tokyo, Honduras, London, and Budapest. Many (but definitely not all) of these places are of major importance to the Fujianese because they also are cosmopolitan centers of the world system, global cities that are sites of the interaction among interdependent transnational social spaces and other globalization processes.

Yet in our research we also found ample evidence of the active involvement of agents of the Chinese state in the life of Fujianese migrants. This confirms the observation of Basch, Glick Schiller, and Szanton-Blanc in *Nations Unbound* that transnationalism has by no means relegated the nation-state to the rubbish bin of history. Nations that are the real or imagined home of diasporic populations actively extend their influence across the diaspora. Transnationalism has spawned new forms of "deterritorialized" nation-building in which "the idiom of the autonomous nation-state remains intact even though the geographic boundaries of the state no longer can be understood to contain the citizens of the nation-state. . . . The new construct of the 'deterritorialized' nation-state is a hegemonic construct representing the interests of the dominant sectors within each nation" (Basch, Glick Schiller, and Szanton-Blanc 1994: 260; see also Glick Schiller, Basch, and Blanc-Szanton, 1995).

As Gupta and Ferguson have pointed out, globalization constantly creates new connections between spaces and places (Gupta and Ferguson 1997: 39), or, phrased differently, generates and maintains the independence and interdependence of a range of social spaces and identity discourses across many sites the world over. However, one must take note of an important caveat here. Processes that generate and create transnational social spaces are contested, involving multiple hegemonic claims from, for instance, nation-states, local governments, ethnic groups, international organizations, and nongovernmental organizations. Applying this insight to the processes that we wish to capture brings into sharper relief the competitive nature of Chinese globalization. The ongoing rivalry between the People's Republic of China (PRC) and Taiwan is just one example of this. Equally important are the efforts of ethnic Chinese in North America and Southeast Asia, and increasingly in Europe itself, to divest themselves of the claims to their loyalty made by the PRC or Taiwanese government and to construct local *and* transnational identities, networks, and organizations relevant to their own lives and interests (see, for instance, McKeown 1999; Ong 1997; and the essays by Lee 1994; Tu 1994a; G. Wang 1994; L. Wang 1994; and D. Wu 1994).

We emphatically do not wish to conjure up an image of a systematic PRC campaign to carve out and fully dominate a separate Chinese world that wishes to unite all Chinese in competition with a similarly separate Western world (or with Indian, Muslim, Latin American, and other worlds). Yet we do wish to argue that the increasingly prominent flows of capital, goods, knowledge, and people to and from the PRC are beginning to be connected in new ways that strengthen the role of China (although not necessarily its government) as a central node. The gradual shift in the center of gravity of the world system forged by this process of Chinese globalization has profound consequences for all organizations, governments, and individuals who wish to or have to engage things Chinese. This is most clearly visible in the case of recent migrants from the PRC such as the Fujianese, who are the subject of this book; but we at a minimum wish to present as a hypothesis worth testing that the ramifications of Chinese globalization also reach people, networks, and identity constructions that wish to sever all ties with China. China as a distant "fatherland" may indeed no longer have any relevance to them. Yet the global presence of China, rather than a dimly remembered and faraway place, is rapidly integrating itself into the fabric of their daily life.

This conceptualization of the process of Chinese globalization will, we hope, help us better understand the creative tension that exists between plurality and homogenization on the one hand and integration and competition on the other: the tensions and synergies created by the meeting and meshing of flows are far more important and interesting than defining their putative boundaries. Speaking of "Chinese globalization" within the "world system" draws attention to fundamental reconfigurations of the relations of power, inequality, and exploitation that are intrinsic to globalization processes, but because of its focus on practice rather than structure, does so without assuming a clear, unified framework of centers, peripheries, and semiperipheries. Globalization, in other words, is as much specifically Chinese as it is universal, entailing particular Chinese versions and visions of modernity, parochialism, and cosmopolitanism that only partially intersect with their European, North American, South Asian, Middle Eastern, Latin American, and Japanese counterparts.

Operationalizing Chinese globalization as an empirical issue for the purposes of this book requires that we distinguish among three analytical levels. The first level is that of transnational social spaces proper: individuals, events, institutions, practices, and phenomena. At this level, we scrutinize trade, financial and migratory flows, transnational communities, business corporations, religious organizations and movements, native-place and lineage organizations, trade networks, diplomatic relations, scholarly and educational exchanges, media and the Internet, and consumption patterns that create specific social spaces that tie specific people together in a specific way and context.

The second level is that of how and to what extent these separate transnational phenomena come together at one location to create a distinct local social space, a local South Asian, Hispanic, or Chinese world set off from and interacting with its social surroundings by virtue of the people operating in it and the patterns of social action that pertain to it. It is at this second level that the local and the global meet, and also where currently fashionable theories of globalization and transnation-

alism encounter (i.e., inform and are informed by) older work on ethnicity, minorities, and race relations.

Analysis at the first two levels looks at processes and structures per-
taining to the economy, diplomatic relations, migration, education, culture, and religion that are verifiable: they are directly experienced and
thus amenable to empirical research. The people one studies are aware
of them because they involve transnational and local social spaces that
constitute their immediate social environment. Research at these two
levels should, following Portes, clearly separate out the local and
transnational processes that are often lumped together, thus leading to
conceptual confusion and analytical muddles (Portes 2001; Portes,
Guarnizo, and Landolt, 1999: 220–23). Yet *after* we have successfully
done so, we should proceed by analytically (rather than casually) putting the pieces of the jigsaw puzzle together again, lest we permanently
lose sight of the bigger picture only for the sake of greater analytical
clarity.

This brings us to the third and still largely unexplored level of analysis of globalization: to what extent and how the many transnational
spaces and local worlds add up to global processes that encompass and
transcend the individual phenomena of the first two levels. Analysis at
this level is more a matter of analytical objectives or preoccupations,
and even taste. To turn to our own ethnography, only relatively few
Chinese migrants are sufficiently cosmopolitan to experience Chinese
globalization in more than one or two transnational or local social
spaces and thus forge direct links between them. Yet what is more important than the number of people involved or the frequency and density of communication is the fact that some circumstances have the potential to create or activate ties between people, organizations, and
places operating in different Chinese local and transnational social
spaces on the basis of shared identities, interests, or social ties. In our
view, understanding Chinese globalization at this more encompassing
level should therefore not be a search for fixed and enduring structures.
The most fruitful way to gauge how the world is *also* becoming a Chinese place is by conceptualizing Chinese globalization as a process that
joins fields of interaction. Chinese globalization is a potentiality. It is
forever emerging and becomes tangible only in the observed impact
that seemingly disparate Chinese social facts have on particular events.

Searching for evidence that a "greater China" or "Chinese Commonwealth" does or does not exist is therefore, in our opinion, fruitless. To
what extent China should be viewed as more than a bounded nation-

state, national culture, and national economy depends on the phenomena one chooses to study and the information one deems relevant to the analysis. In other words, the question whether an imagined place named "China" forges connections between several Chinese transnational and local spaces and places across the globe can only be answered with a qualified yes or no. For some phenomena, Chinese globalization is indeed a significant factor; for others, hypothesizing the existence of such a Chinese globalization adds little to one's understanding and may in fact lead the analysis in unproductive directions.

In sum, Chinese globalization is not something that can be proven to exist or not to exist before and external to the events it impinges upon. Nevertheless, we maintain that an increasing range of phenomena can only be fully grasped against the background of a greater interdependence of seemingly disparate Chinese transnational processes. A comprehensive review of all such phenomena would require a monograph in itself. Worse still, such an effort would by necessity be subjective and selective and would inevitably run the risk of reifying a "Chinese world" or "Chinese world system," presenting it as an actually existing, objective structural fact, rather than as emerging, processual, and existing only in and as an aspect of many highly disparate phenomena.[6] Instead, at this point we will merely explain how we should reconceptualize several issues in Chinese migration and settlement directly relevant to the subject of this book against the background of the increasing significance of Chinese globalization processes. We first discuss how we propose to apply our understanding of Chinese globalization to the analysis of migratory flows. We then turn our attention to the "greatest of . . . apparently stable objects" in "a world of flows" (Appadurai 2000: 5), the nation-state in its encounter with globally dispersed migrant populations. Finally, we discuss how processes of Chinese globalization mean that Chinese affairs in China itself and abroad become increasingly interwoven, making it impossible to understand the dynamics of Chinese international migration and Chinese communities abroad without firmly embedding them in developments taking place in China.

Migration and Locality

In an earlier essay, one of us concluded that migration studies is a field of research predicated on the assumption that migration is a social phenomenon in its own right that can and should be studied sui generis.

Yet "migration" covers a very wide variety of phenomena that ultimately have in common only the spatial mobility of the people under study. Arguably, from the perspective of macroeconomics or population demography, spatial mobility may indeed be the most relevant fact about migratory flows, but from the perspective of sociology, anthropology, or political science, spatial mobility by itself begs many more questions than it answers (Pieke 1999).

The increasing transnational nature of Chinese migration and its embeddedness in Chinese globalization processes make it even more inappropriate to think of migration, including that of Fujianese, simply as the transfer of human beings and their labor from one place to another. Fujianese migrate in the context of dense networks and as part of careers of ongoing spatial and social mobility that do not start when the decision to move has been made or end upon arrival at the destination. In the Fujianese context, most people are involved in migration, regardless of whether they themselves move. Furthermore, a migrant's biography does not go through clear stages from local resident to migrant and settler. To many Fujianese, migration is an open-ended experience and process rather than a simple move from one place to another: transnational, migratory, and localizing practices mutually condition each other and cannot be treated as separate factors. Migration is a profound biographical event that ingrains in many migrants a new cosmopolitan attitude: their life, social environment, and aspirations will never again be limited to just one place. Once on the move, many migrants, even those who have returned home, never reach a final destination, but can always move on if the conditions are right. Fujianese migration is therefore a constantly evolving process as new areas of origin emerge and as migrants find new ways of migrating, new countries to go to, and new things to do in these countries.

Wherever they are and whether or not they themselves have experienced spatial mobility, to Fujianese migration is not a singular event, but has become a way of life. In order to get a conceptual handle on the diversity, scale, and social embeddedness of Chinese international migration, settlement, and transnationalism, in this book we continue to use the conventional terms *origin*, *destination*, and *transit*, despite the fact that we are fully aware that these categories are relative and tentative. We have done so chiefly to divide the ongoing process of Fujianese mobility into manageable bits, thus gaining an analytical handle on the many interrelated phenomena that mobility involves. Yet by treating each locality as potentially a sending, a transit, and a destination area at the same time, we again assemble these bits into the larger jigsaw puzzle of Fujianese mobility.

A more systematic perspective on the connections between the different aspects of Fujianese mobility is provided by the twin concepts of migration configuration and migration system, which are both each other's opposite and each other's complement. The term *migration system* has been around in migration studies for some time (see, for instance, Mabogunje 1970; Massey et al. 1998; Zlotnik 1992). The concept describes how migration from or to a particular area or country is composed of a collection of separate migratory flows to or from other areas or countries. Such separate flows are a system or structure not as far as individual migrants or migratory flows are concerned, but only from the perspective of the particular area (or its government or employers) chosen by the researcher as the system's focal point. We find this concept useful because it helps us describe how flows of Fujianese and other migrants to and from particular areas are causally and structurally connected. For instance, the concept describes how the flow of migrants to Italy from a field site in Mingxi county in eastern Fujian has been enabled by migratory flows of farm laborers from even more remote places into Mingxi and other flows of Mingxi residents to other areas in China. Similarly, it also helps describe the connections between the inflow of Fuqing migrants in Italy and other flows of Fuqing migrants in and out of Italy and to and from other destinations.

"Migration configuration," in contrast, describes the connections between the total sum of social institutions and practices in areas of origin, transit, and destination that produce and sustain a particular flow (or, more commonly, a set of closely connected flows) of migrants. A migratory flow cannot be studied as an institution or social group in isolation from its environment, but should rather be understood as an aspect of other institutions and communities, business and employment strategies, migration flows, and discourses of exclusion and inclusion.

A migration configuration constitutes a field of interaction that is much more than just people living and moving between locations, including flows of information, goods, money, and other resources. Institutions and networks within a migration configuration shape interaction across different sites. Examples of such institutions are kinship groups, friendship and home community networks, emigration and immigration officials and commercial migration brokers, other ethnic groups at a particular destination, airlines, railways and shipping companies, law firms, human rights groups, and even anti-immigration activists and politicians.

Analyzing Chinese migratory flows in terms of migration systems and migration configurations helps us in this book to tackle the complexity of Fujianese migration. However, this approach's focus on the process of migration itself only very partially captures the broader context and ramifications of Fujianese migration in the areas of origin, transit, and destination. In fact, such a focus on migration itself may obscure the fact that mobility is only one aspect of migrants' lives. Understanding the relationship between migration and processes of localization and settlement require that we embed migratory practices within other nonmigratory aspects of Chinese globalization, beginning with the state.

Globalization, Migrant Communities, and the State

With the onset of the reforms in 1978, China's chief diplomatic objective became to gain respectability as a partner of the West in world affairs. The 1990s, by contrast, witnessed the paradox that a further opening up of Chinese society and economy, renewed efforts to join the international community and organizations, and the global spread of Chinese people, institutions, and culture went hand in hand with heightened Chinese nationalism and a more assertive attitude of the Chinese state in international affairs. Yet this paradox can be readily explained. As pointed out above, globalization is a multiplicity of processes; as such, it can also be a mode of competition between nations for the loyalties of dispersed populations. China's continued globalization in the 1990s changed it from a marginal participant in the Western-dominated world system to a focal point of Chinese globalization processes, enabling China simultaneously to step up its participation in the global system and to distance itself from a Western hegemonic influence that in the 1980s had still appeared natural and inevitable.

Rather than dissolving the nation, "competitive globalization" changes the equation of rivalry between nations. Nations are still firmly rooted in core areas, but reach out throughout the global system by following, shaping, and imagining their own globalization processes (Basch, Glick Schiller, and Szanton-Blanc 1994). Although the Chinese state does not levy taxes or other forms of nonvoluntary contributions as some other nations with large emigrant populations such as the Philippines and Eritrea do, Chinese transnationals and cosmopolites find the Chinese state nevertheless increasingly interested in their life, loyalty, and above all, contribution to Chinese modernization. Unless they wish to sever all ties with China—which is not always an option—they are never totally free from the gaze of agents of the Chinese state. This usually is not effected through direct interference in the affairs of overseas Chinese communities, but rather through the organizations, schools, and networks of the overseas Chinese community of residence, in addition to the home community of origin.

First, in the world beyond China's national boundaries the Chinese state obviously cannot and does not want to claim total sovereign power over people that it does not consider its full subjects, but neither does it let go altogether. Very briefly, China's policy toward overseas Chinese gives Chinese citizens or people of Chinese origin who themselves or whose family live or have lived abroad the special status of a category of people who are neither wholly foreign nor wholly Chinese. To reap the maximum benefit from this category of people and minimize its liabilities—that is, in order to eat its overseas Chinese cake and have it too—the PRC encourages naturalization of overseas Chinese, thus turning overseas Chinese citizens (*Huaqiao*) into ethnically Chinese foreign nationals (*waiji Huaren*). Consequently, the PRC does not allow dual citizenship, but still claims a more nebulous and residual loyalty by calling these naturalized ethnic Chinese foreign nationals "our family and kin" (Nyíri 2001a; Pieke 1987; Thunø 2001).[7]

State power in the context of external populations is not a matter of all or nothing; it is partial, negotiated, and shared with other states. In fact, as in other contexts, it is misleading to think of the Chinese state as a unified corporate actor. The Chinese state, like any other state, consists of multiple actors: regional governments, specific state institutions, and even individual officials (Lieberthal and Lampton 1992; Lieberthal and Oksenburg 1988; Shirk 1993). In the context of overseas Chinese communities this is brought out very clearly, because here the national Chinese state meets local Chinese states of the overseas Chinese home areas, the Taiwanese and Hong Kong state, and most important, the various levels of the state of the country of residence.

A focus on the state in the context of Chinese globalization requires us to rethink local Chinese communities as arenas of and subject to *multicentered state power* (Pieke 1999: 21). Competition among the states and agents of the state in these arenas does not necessarily have to be a zero-sum game, and we do not want to conjure up suspicions about an alien fifth column that so often informs the perception of overseas Chinese, particularly in Southeast Asia. To limit ourselves to the national Chinese state (although that does not necessarily speak with one voice either), its involvement in Chinese globalization has various objectives that are themselves partially contradictory and changeable. Some of these objectives are overtly political, such as limiting Taiwanese diplomatic influence, containing possible political dissent and heterodox religious movements such as the Falungong, and most important, preventing material or diplomatic claims from overseas Chinese that may interfere with PRC diplomatic interests. Others tie in with long-term economic reform, such as de facto promotion of emigration and securing a flow of China-bound overseas Chinese investments. Yet other measures seem to cater to a long-term policy of attaining a more active role in the formation of the Chinese global culture, such as extending its own standardized reading of Chinese culture and language through Chinese education, or facilitating the setting up of remarkably standardized native-place organizations of overseas Chinese (see Chapter 5; also Nyíri 2001a; Thunø 2001).

In a global system made up of intersecting, competing, and symbiotically coexisting processes of globalization, nation-states are still prominent among the key players. Yet their rule over populations (like their recognition of citizenship) is no longer a matter of all or nothing. In many European countries, for instance, this reality is imperfectly catered to by allowing noncitizens voting rights in local, but not in national elections. In Germany a recent debate on dual citizenship addressed many of the same issues. States must more pragmatically select the objectives of their rule over specific population groups in competition with other states, and decide on policies and administrative measures accordingly.

The interweaving and meshing of Chinese globalization processes is by no means limited to what the Chinese state(s) condones, engineers, or encourages. As China reaches out into the world, its internal and international affairs become increasingly connected. Even modest villages in remote areas of China often have profound connections with the world outside, ranging from outmigration to foreign trade and investment and (increasingly) to Chinese investments abroad.[8] Yet much more is at hand than the obvious strengthening of ties between China and the world beyond. Processes taking place in China and as part of Chinese globalization increasingly share characteristics requiring that we analyze them as part of the same macro developments. Capital accumulated by private or collective entrepreneurs in one area is no longer restricted to its place of origin as it was in the 1980s, but may flow to other areas in China or be invested in Hong Kong, the United States, or Europe. Joint ventures in China now often involve two or more Chinese partners rather than a Chinese and a foreign partner. In fact, international investment often becomes a mere supplement to domestic business transactions: in order to take advantage of tax breaks available only to foreign investors, Chinese entrepreneurs often route their capital back into China through a foreign company specifically set up for this purpose. The progress of political and legal reform and the formation of a unified market have made China an increasingly level playing field that transcends the parochialism of local communities. Similarly, and more pertinent to the topic of this book, some Chinese migrants move to the cities and richer rural areas in China itself; others end up in London or New York. What is more, migrants often consider international and internal migration alternatives to each other, or use one to support or generate the capital for the other.

From Fujian to Europe

Although central Fujian was the source of a respectable flow of emigrants around the turn of the century, there was little cause to expect this area to become the source of the most globally distributed and the most visible, even paradigmatic, new Chinese migratory flow in the 1980s and 1990s. As we will detail in Chapter 2, between 1978 and 1984 the human smuggling networks and emigration orientation that grew in central Fujian have been crucial in creating, perpetuating, and intensifying migratory flows. As in other parts of the world, once established, patterns of migration became one of the main causes of further migration.

However, migration from the area is not as market-driven as the commodification of migration services might lead one to expect. To be sure, perceptions of potential earnings play an important role in migration decisions, and migrants frequently change their destination when they hear reports that earnings elsewhere are higher. Yet potential migrants do not simply book passage to the place where they expect the highest earnings, but tend to go to countries and areas where an established community from their village or wider area of origin already exists, a finding entirely in conformity with the general migration literature on the relevance of social capital and migrants as active social agents in sustaining and directing migratory flows. As Massey and his colleagues put it:

> Recognition of the complexity of international migration during the last quarter of the twentieth century reveals multiple insufficiencies in traditional theoretical approaches. Migrants clearly do not respond mechanically to wage differentials, if they ever did; they are not homogeneous with respect to tastes and motivations; and the contexts within which they make their decisions are not the same.
>
> Recognition of these problems has led to a renewed interest in the nature of migrant decision-making, a reconceptualization of the basic motivations that underlie geographic mobility, greater attention to the context within which the decisions are made, and more informed efforts to identify the specific social and economic dimensions that define this context. (Massey et al. 1998: 15)

This programmatic statement by some of the leaders in the field of migration studies served as a guiding principle of our own research. In the Fuzhou region, certain areas and villages tend to specialize in certain destinations, ignoring others. This realization led us to consider Fujianese migration to Europe as more than simply a spillover from the major migratory flows to the United States, and New York City in particular, but to think of Fujianese migration to Europe as a separate phenomenon, albeit one with strong connections to U.S.-bound flows. In particular, we found that the areas we focused on originally (Changle and Lianjiang counties and Fuzhou city itself) on the basis of our reading of the American studies actually sent relatively few people to European countries, with the exception of Changle, which had a sizable presence in Britain, albeit not on the continent.

Apart from the flow of migrants from Changle to Britain, two counties in particular were important, namely coastal Fuqing in Fuzhou prefecture and, surprisingly, inland Mingxi in Sanming prefecture. In each county we subsequently selected a village with a large migrant population in Europe for intensive fieldwork by our Chinese researcher (see Chapter 2).

Fuqing and Mingxi counties are two very different sending areas (for their precise location, please refer to Map 2, Fujian province). The social and economic differences between Mingxi and Fuqing have yielded distinctive migratory configurations that follow from very different histories of previous forms of mobility. Fuqing city / county[9] is located along the coast in the southern tip of Fuzhou prefecture in central Fujian. The Fuqing area has a history of more than one hundred years of migration to Southeast Asia. At this writing in the early twenty-first century, the international migration flow from this area is part of elaborate, highly diversified, and long-standing trade and smuggling networks and migratory practices that include family reunification and contract labor circulation to Singapore and Macao; irregular migration to and study in Taiwan, Latin America, Europe, and Japan; irregular or regular through-migration from and to any of these areas; and also labor circulation to cities in China itself, such as Fuzhou, Xiamen, Shenzhen, and Beijing.

In contrast, Mingxi county is located in Sanming prefecture in the mountainous interior of Fujian province. Mingxi is a newcomer in the emigration market, but emigration from there is intimately connected with Sanming's earlier role as a destination area of mainly state-initiated in-migration from elsewhere as part of the ill-fated "Third Front" policy of the 1960s that aimed to relocate China's strategic industrial base to remote and inaccessible areas in order to render China invulnerable to a Soviet, American, or Taiwanese attack (Lyons 1998; Naughton 1991). Resident natives from southern Zhejiang and urban state sector workers in Mingxi spearheaded emigration to Europe in the late 1980s. Many of them or their parents had moved to Mingxi from elsewhere in Fujian or even farther away in the 1960s and 1970s.

Whereas Fuqing emigration to Europe is the result of a revitalized migratory orientation and practices that earlier had focused on Southeast Asia, the Mingxi migration configuration had to be built from scratch. Yet despite their real and continuing differences, in both Mingxi and Fuqing emigration is the most profitable locally accessible opportunity for employment or entrepreneurship and an opportunity to invest resources (remittances from earlier migrants, family or individual savings, loans, and gifts) in a venture that potentially will pay back many times the original investment. Potential migrants have only limited information about destination countries at their disposal, and the information they have has a strong positive bias. Nevertheless, they generally know full well that their sojourns (very few contemplate permanent emigration at this point) will likely entail considerable financial and personal risk and great hardship, particularly during transit and the first several years abroad.

In Europe, Fujianese immigrants live at the interface of the local economy, its ethnic Chinese sector, and a transnational Chinese labor market. On the one hand, migrants arriving in an area compare their possible earnings in jobs or enterprises there with similar opportunities elsewhere. This transnational fragmentation of the global labor market shields immigration from the direct impact of the balance between supply and demand for labor globally and in the destination country. Chinese immigrants therefore rarely compete with non-Chinese for jobs, although they do frequently compete with other locally resident Chinese. Often developing or strengthening Chinese economic sectors, they constitute a net gain to the European economies. Examples are the Chinese restaurant trade in much of western Europe, leather and garment workshops in Italy, and the import, wholesale, and retail trade in eastern Europe. All these sectors would either never have emerged without the Chinese, or would have all but collapsed in the absence of fresh Chinese entrepreneurship and labor.

The flip side of this is that the level of Chinese immigration remains independent of the general supply of labor in the destination country and is adjusted only indirectly and partially to the extent that the local Chinese economic sector and labor market are integrated in the economy of the destination country. Furthermore, migrants send much of their earnings back home to repay debts incurred to finance their emigration and to support their dependents; those remittances are used to build ostentatious new houses and on other forms of conspicuous consumption. We have found only limited evidence of successful investments in the home areas. The chief economic benefits of migration for the source areas are a reduction of unemployment and underemployment, a higher standard of living, and a general boost to the local economy provided by increased consumptive spending.

On the other hand, neither the Chinese ethnic sector nor Chinese immigrant labor operates in isolation from the local economy. First, and most obvious, the ethnic Chinese sector is part of the local, not the Chinese, economy. Demand for Chinese transnational labor and entrepreneurship is driven by demand for the services and goods provided by local Chinese enterprises, which operate in an environment crowded as much by other Chinese as by non-Chinese competitors (Indian curry houses, Hungarian retailers, Italian *pronto moda* producers), suppliers, and customers. Second, in recent years Chinese entrepreneurs in Europe, much like their counterparts in the United States, have begun to turn to even cheaper non-Chinese immigrant laborers (such as Bangladeshis and North Africans) for the most menial tasks in their enterprises, the same positions that are normally filled by new Chinese immigrants. Third, Chinese migrants themselves are beginning to find employment outside the ethnic Chinese sector, in factories and construction, for example.

This second development is very recent, and our fieldwork has not generated sufficient data to say anything more about it. These changes may be the first indication of a trend toward a stronger and more complex integration of Chinese enterprises and labor into the local economy. However, they are unlikely to reduce the importance of the transnational connections that we describe in this book. Chinese migrants, even the most recent ones, have never lived in a Chinese world isolated from the societies surrounding them. Rather, the way and degree of the local integration of Chinese migrants, together with the increasing global presence of China—its language, culture, capital, and goods, as much as its diplomatic and military might—will together determine the shape and direction of future trends in Chinese globalization.

Conclusion

As China participates more in the world economy, it also becomes the focus of a distinctly Chinese pattern of globalization. Globalization does indeed break down the old borders, but China's integration in the world system can only be understood against the background of processes taking place in China itself. As China's influence and people expand around the globe, they do not simply join processes whose ground rules have already been well established elsewhere. Both in building up its own pattern of globalization and in its participation in more general global processes, China also exports its home-bred logic and patterns of capital accumulation, investment, migration, cultural production and consumption, and even religious proselytizing, just as it necessarily imports many of the same things from elsewhere in the world.

We recognize that Chinese globalization covers a great number of processes and people, whose differences should not be glossed over. Without wishing to say that the wave of migration from Fujian is in any way typical of Chinese globalization, we do believe that focusing on a group of recent migrants such as the Fujianese highlights the distinctive nature of these processes. Migration moves people. With people move capital, goods, and ideas around the globe. A study of migration therefore helps unravel the complexity of many interdependent globalization processes. From very modest beginnings, Fujianese migrants have spread around the globe in an extraordinarily short period of time, often overcoming seemingly impossible odds. In many respects, the Fujianese are the best illustration and epitome of the still raw and unfinished processes of Chinese globalization. The Fujianese sudden global presence opens up new social spaces and challenges received wisdom, well-established structures, and firmly entrenched interests. To understand Fujianese migration better is also better to grasp a world that China is fast becoming a vital part of.

The Luo Family: Workers in Italy, Market Traders in Hungary

THE LUO SIBLINGS were born in a village in Mingxi county that began sending many migrants to Europe in the 1990s.[1] Their mother was born in Fuzhou and fled to Mingxi from the Japanese during the war. Today, only she and her husband live in the family home; their eight children long ago moved either to the county town or abroad. The highly complex story of the Luo siblings, their spouses, their children, and their children's spouses encapsulates almost all of the main themes of this book: the simultaneous importance of individual entrepreneurial spirit and social networks in starting, maintaining, and directing migratory flows, the rapid growth of a migratory tradition in an area previously untouched by international migration, the many connections between urbanization, internal migration, and international migration, and perhaps most important, the resilience and proactive role of migrants, who may on occasion allow policies and external events to shape their migratory decisions, but never waver in their determination to improve their lives by moving to places that promise better opportunities for success.

Luo Jia, the eldest brother, teaches at a vocational college in the county town: according to a younger brother, he has no experience in business and does not want to go abroad. His son and daughter, however, went to Hungary and then on to Italy together with their father's younger brother Luo Bing in 1997. Both have since obtained residence papers in a regularization for illegal immigrants and visited home in 1999, where the son made arrangements to get married and take his wife back to Italy.

Luo Yi, the second brother, is approaching 50. He is a diminutive, active, and jovial man who lives in a three-story house in the county town. He built it from money earned when he was trading in electronic parts. He served in the army and afterward first joined a company that traded in crafts. Then he contracted with a company owned by the military that traded in electronic parts. Luo Yi had to pay a fixed amount to the military every year; beyond that, the profits and expenses were his. He bought electronic parts from the agent of a Japanese company in Shenzhen and sold them to both civilian and military manufacturers in all of China's major cities, but mostly Beijing, Xi'an, and Fuzhou. He continues doing this, but complains that business is bad. In 1999, Luo Yi wanted to go to Yugoslavia, reckoning that there were not many Chinese there and that business after the war should be good. He obtained his passport, but gave up the idea when his younger brother, Luo Bing, who lives in Hungary, told him that war had erupted in Yugoslavia once again.

Luo Yi's wife works at a factory. She was born in Fuzhou, and her parents went to Taiwan with the Nationalists during the civil war (1946–49). During the Cultural Revolution, she was sent down to Mingxi to do farm work. Luo Yi's mother helped her and she ended up marrying into the family. Because of the direct family connection, Luo Yi and his wife have been able to visit Taiwan several times since 1998 for periods of three to six months. On those occasions, both worked illegally, but Yi's wife was caught after a month, locked up for a day, and deported.

Luo Yi's son, born in 1979, graduated from upper secondary school in 1999 and at first worked in Fuzhou at a factory making water pipes; later he helped out in a shop in Mingxi. His parents were concerned that he would not find a real job and might end up just loitering about, as many other youngsters do.

Luo Ding, the fourth brother, was the first of the siblings to leave China, in 1992. A female acquaintance in Moscow sent him the papers necessary for the passport and visa. His family opposed his decision to go and did not give him financial support. The money came from friends and a bank loan, ostensibly to buy a car, which made sense because of his occupation: like the two brothers before him, he was a driver.

Ding and a female acquaintance went to Moscow in 1992, where they traded for half a year, but business was bad at the time, so they went to Italy "on a tourist visa." Originally, they wanted to go to

France, but when they were unable to locate their friend in France, Ding called a schoolmate in Prato, near Florence. The schoolmate agreed to help Ding and his friends if they came over.[2] In Moscow, Ding and his friend found a Cantonese-speaking, Prague-based Malaysian facilitator who got them Malaysian passports. With these passports they went by train to Italy via Poland, Germany, and Switzerland. They were part of a "tour group" of eight or nine people, accompanied by an associate of the facilitator, who spoke good English.

In Italy, Luo Ding was regularized in 1995. The following year he traveled back to China to accompany his wife to Italy, where they worked in Chinese-owned leather workshops in Prato that mainly perform contract assembly work for Italian companies. Later they provided financial help to all of Ding's brothers when they migrated, and to Luo Bing when he opened his shop in Budapest. In 1999, Ding felt that he had accumulated enough money; he got a driver's license, bought a car, and began looking into opportunities to open his own business. Luo Bing wanted him to invest in Hungary, but the Hungarian embassy refused to give Ding a multiple-entry visa, and he gave up the idea. Instead, he found a job at a small family-owned Italian factory in Treviso near Venice that made marble floor tiles. Since Ding could not read Italian, he found the job by knocking on factory gates. He started with a gross hourly wage of 10,700 lire (US$5); after a year he was making 12,000 lire an hour. With overtime, this added up to 2.2 million lire (US$1,100) a month, minus about 400,000 lire tax. Ding's wife found work at another factory.

Whereas in Prato the Luos, like other workers, had lived at their employers' workshop, in Treviso they rented a two-story suburban house that they had found with help from the factory. The Luos share the four bedrooms of the house with three other Mingxi families. In June 2000, they had their first baby, a girl. After two months, they took the baby back to China and left her in the care of Luo Yi and his wife; they plan to bring her back when she is about 2 years old. While they spend most of their leisure with other migrants from Mingxi and other parts of Sanming prefecture, the husband also regularly goes out to Italian and Chinese restaurants with his Italian boss and colleagues. When their second child, a son, was born the colleagues gave him presents. His fellow workers, Yi says, helped him get a raise. By contrast, he does not believe Chinese associations are doing anything for the migrants: their purpose, he says, is just to give their leaders "a little prestige when they go home." When Ding visited Mingxi in 1996, officials from the township government invited him to a meal; that was the only contact with Chinese authorities he has had since leaving China.

Luo Bing, the third son and our main informant in Hungary, was in the army between 1976 and 1980. Later he drove a truck and subsequently was responsible for purchasing spare parts for a fleet of cars. While in the army, he joined the Communist Party, but "automatically lost his party membership" when he left China. Later he worked at a hotel in Mingxi, where his wife was what might be called a pastry chef. She made RMB 1,000 a month, which, Bing says, was better than salaries in other state work units, and stable, but still not enough to live on.

Luo Bing first left China in 1997, when a friend of his, who was returning to China from Italy and had stopped in Rangoon on the way, invited Bing to join him there to do business. Bing flew to Rangoon, but found it too poor and went back to China. But soon afterward he went to Hungary with a business visitor visa and registered a company with his nephew and niece (the children of his eldest brother, Luo Jia); he then obtained a residential visa. Having obtained his residence permit, Bing went to Russia, where he had an acquaintance from home, to scout for business opportunities. He spent a month there but left because, he says, he found the currency unstable. He then went back to Hungary and on to Italy. He stayed with Luo Ding in Prato for a month and then returned to Hungary to extend his residence permit and has since stayed there, even though, had he stayed in Italy, he would have qualified for the 1999 regularization.

Bing explained that he preferred living in Hungary because there he had his own business, whereas in Italy he would have to do wage labor and endure poor living conditions for an income similar to the one he now has. At a restaurant in Italy, he said, wages were around US$1,000 a month, and in a leather workshop, US$2,500 a month for an eighteen-hour workday, seven days a week. Yet in Hungary, Bing and his family have to face continuous legal uncertainty. His residence permit has to be renewed every year or every other year, and the renewal process takes many months, during which he has to use a temporary residence permit that, in turn, has to be renewed every month or even more often. Although Bing applied for permanent resident status in 2000, authorities in Budapest in the 2000s practically stopped granting such status to Chinese.

At first, Luo Bing rented a stall at the Four Tigers Market, the center of Chinese trade in Hungary, where he sold Chinese clothes and shoes he bought from Chinese wholesalers. He opened his stall at 5:00 A.M. and closed at 5:00 P.M. Monday through Friday; he closed earlier on Saturdays and did not work on Sundays. Later Bing opened a shop in the middle-income XIVth district of Budapest with money from fourth brother Luo Ding. The shop consisted of two small rooms. Like all Chinese shopkeepers, he got his merchandise—Chinese-made clothes, shoes, and some toys—at the Four Tigers and bought a used Fiat minivan to transport them. By posting advertisements in the neighborhood, he hired a Hungarian saleswoman and paid her the minimum wage plus 1 percent of the profits. In what he says were the best two months of the business, May and June 1999, he sold merchandise worth about 2 million forints (Ft; nearly US$9,000) for a profit of around 30 percent. But after all expenses—rent, wages, social security, food, car—Bing said he could save only a few hundred dollars a month. Still, he was satisfied: "Even though I don't have cash, I have about quadrupled or quintupled my initial investment of US$5,000," he said in November 1999.

Later he handed the shop over to his younger brother Luo Liu and rented a stall at one of the former factories converted to markets across the road from the main Four Tigers Market. Business there was bad, so later in 1999, together with his cousin Huang, Luo opened another shop in the middle-income, semi-suburban XXIInd district. At the time his was the only Chinese shop in the neighborhood, but by November 1999, there were three, and in December 2000, five, all selling similar things, and Luo's business suffered accordingly. In addition, a general decline in profits in Chinese business had been taking place since the mid-1990s, and Luo had trouble with the Hungarian saleswomen he employed. He believed they stole from him, and he had to replace them every few months.

Luo Bing's wife said her son had wanted to go abroad all through upper secondary school as he saw his classmates leave. One had gone to Hungary after graduating from lower secondary school and was now studying English there. Another had gone to Hungary and was studying Hungarian; a third had gone to Italy and learned Italian so quickly that she was asked by an Italian boss to work as a hostess in his restaurant. Yet Bing's wife did not want him to leave China until he had graduated from upper secondary school; nor did she want to leave before that time, since she was concerned that he would not take his studies seriously. His education had cost RMB 15,000 for three years. She finally applied for a Hungarian visa in May 2000, using Bing's sponsorship letter. Her application was rejected. Bing then paid

US$2,000 to a northern Chinese in Hungary who said he would ensure that his wife's long-term visitor visa would be approved. She submitted another application and duly obtained the visa.

Bing then passed his stall at the "small factory" site near the Four Tigers on to someone else. He himself subleased a stall at the main Four Tigers Market from another Chinese. There business was better. The rent was Ft 300,000 (around US$1,000) a month. However, in December 2000, Bing told us that the shop—which he had left in the hands of the Hungarian employee—and the stall together had made less than US$3,000 that year, and he wanted to move the shop to another city where there would be less competition.

After his wife's arrival, Bing moved to a rented flat near the Four Tigers Market. The flat had two bedrooms and a living room, and for the time being it accommodates, besides Bing and his wife, Luo Liu, his wife, and her younger brother, who had come on a long-term family visit visa. In December 2000 the rent was Ft 60,000 a month (around US$200).

As for his son, Bing did not see an immediate chance of getting him over to Hungary because they had had a bad year in the business, and he was convinced that getting him over would again cost US$4,000. Many of his friends had tried to bring their children without "buying the visa" and had been rejected. But in 2001, Bing became concerned about bringing his son because he was to graduate from upper secondary school in July and "would have nothing to do, so he may easily get into gambling or fights."

The fifth son, Luo Wu, worked as a driver in a government department before he went to Hungary with a friend in 1995. He registered a company and opened a stall at Four Tigers. In 1998, though, he returned to Mingxi empty-handed, blaming the unfavorable conditions in Hungary. He had found business "very hard" and not profitable enough. He and his friend, who shared accommodations, were cheated by a Hungarian landlord, and then his friend was severely beaten by skinheads. Luo Wu emphasized that the "Bald Party" (*guangtoudang*, i.e., the skinheads) were so powerful in Hungary that they threatened to remove the prime minister if all foreigners were not kicked out of the country.

Luo Bing said that Luo Wu had gone back to China because he heard that he could make lots of money as a migration facilitator, which is what many others were already doing. Luo Wu confirmed that after returning to China he made it his business to help people go to Hungary and Italy. This consisted of getting people abroad to send documents that enabled those who wanted to migrate to get a passport and visa. Sometimes he helped a client register a company in Hungary, and then the client could apply for a business visa. The prospective migrant then had to apply for the visa himself or herself. But Luo Wu's business suffered when people learned that it had become more difficult to obtain residence papers in Hungary. Moreover, as more and more people engaged in the "people business" (*rentou shengyi*), prices were driven down. According to Luo Bing, Luo Wu helped only three persons migrate, making only about RMB 10,000. To make matters worse, at the end of 2000, Luo Wu was arrested in the anti-snakehead campaign that followed the Dover incident. He was detained for a day and fined RMB 40,000.

Luo Wu's wife spent about eight months working in Hong Kong in 1999, visiting a relative who had moved there in the 1980s and married a local woman. She plans to return to Hong Kong to work some more. Luo Wu and his wife also considered going to Australia with a tourist visa; they were also interested in going to Britain but did not want to take the risk of illegal passage.

Eventually, both Luo Wu and Luo Yi's second son made up their minds to go Italy. In March 2001, because it had become so difficult to get to Hungary, they paid US$1,500 each for a ticket and a three-month visa to Yugoslavia. After they had waited for a week in Belgrade, a migration facilitator from Zhejiang, who was a friend of a Mingxi man who had earlier worked as a facilitator with Luo Wu, arranged for them to cross into Hungary at night and be picked up by a Hungarian for US$1,000 per person. They were then delivered to the Four Tigers Market, and the facilitator on the Hungarian side called Luo Bing to pick them up. Bing said he had known they would try to go to Italy, but not that they would come via Hungary. Wu and Yi's son were concerned that it would be difficult to get to Italy; they had spoken to Luo Ding and to Luo Jia's son there over the phone, but they did not offer any help in getting there. The two stayed with Bing, not daring to leave the flat for two months, when they were called by a broker who agreed to take them to Italy. On the way, they were intercepted in Croatia. They applied for asylum but, according to Bing, agreed to give up their application and return to China in the UN High Commissioner for Refugees' Voluntary Repatriation Program, which paid for their airfare back to Beijing.

The youngest of the brothers, Luo Liu, and his wife went to Hungary in 1998, followed by his wife's brother in 1999. Luo Liu registered a company in Budapest with another man. While Liu was running the shop in the XIVth district that Luo Bing had handed over to him, his wife subleased a stall at the Four Tigers for Ft 300,000 (US$1,300). According to Bing, she was making US$300 a day in November 1999. Later, but still in 1999, Liu sublet the XIVth district shop to someone else and purchased the leasehold on a pavilion at the Four Tigers for over US$20,000. In addition, Liu and his wife opened four shops across Hungary. Luo Liu made a round of the shops once a week, which were run by Hungarian employees the rest of the time. Liu applied for permanent residence in November 1999, but by the time of this writing in 2001 had not yet received a reply.

According to Luo Yi, the money Liu sends home is put in the bank. It has been used for the next brothers to go abroad, but not for investment. As Luo Bing said, "People are unwilling to invest in Mingxi because there is no future for development." Because all of the brothers have now left the country, Luo Ding has stopped sending money home regularly.

CHAPTER 2

Old and New Transnational Villages in Fujian

MIGRATION FACILITATORS or "snakeheads" play an important role in maintaining migratory flows from Fujian, but should not be seen as the root cause of migration from this part of China. In the course of our fieldwork in two villages in central Fujian, we found that emigration is strongly embedded in local political, sociocultural and economic institutions and histories. Under the impact of sustained migration, local institutions, in turn, have been created or transformed and have come to play a critical role in mediating the scope and nature of international mobility. Migration facilitators are certainly a part, but not more than that, of these local institutions.

The local embeddedness of migration renders population mobility from each area in China highly specific, and broad generalizations on the causes, nature, and direction of the totality of Chinese or even Fujianese migration are bound to misrepresent a highly complex reality. In this chapter, we describe how international migration from our two fieldwork villages to Europe belongs to separate migration configurations, entailing different types of transnational connections and histories of previous forms of mobility. We also found that the migratory flows from our two study villages are a part of the larger phenomenon of the "new Chinese migration" that commenced after the onset of the reforms in China in 1978. Technological advances in long-distance transport and the increased professionalization of Chinese migration have greatly facilitated the international movement of Chinese labor. As one interviewee noted: "Leaving for overseas has become the same as going to Fuzhou, Xiamen, Beijing, or Shanghai."[1] This new migration thus illustrates some of the new opportunities and inequalities spawned by specific patterns of Chinese globalization that are part of the rise of the "network society" (Castells 1996) and "economic globalization" (Sassen 1996) more generally.

As explained in the introductory chapter, for the fieldwork we decided to compare two counties with contrasting patterns of migration to Europe. We selected the two counties on the basis of several informal investigations in Fujian itself and interviews with Fujianese migrants in Europe in 1998 and 1999 conducted by Thunø and Nyíri; a local researcher who wishes to remain anonymous conducted the fieldwork. One of the counties we selected was coastal Fuqing in Fuzhou prefecture, which has a long history of migration to Southeast Asia and more recent large-scale emigration to Europe. The second county was Mingxi, located in Sanming prefecture in the mountains of northwestern Fujian. Although this county has no history of overseas migration, emigration to Europe from Mingxi has been significant since the early 1990s.

In each county our local researcher began by identifying a village specializing in migration to Europe. The village selected in Mingxi (village B) had the highest rate of emigrants in Europe in all of Sanming prefecture. The authorities in Sanming immediately approved fieldwork there. Securing cooperation from the authorities was much more difficult in Fuqing, where migration brokerage is more significant and emigration is a very sensitive issue, a fact reinforced by the suffocation of fifty-eight illegal migrants in a truck in Dover in July 2000, twenty-eight of whom were from Fuqing.[2] The Fuqing authorities did not approve the first village we proposed, and they suggested an alternative that we accepted (village A). However, it proved difficult for our fieldworker to work long-term even in this village and completely impossible to conduct a systematic survey as we had done in village B. As a consequence, our information on village B is much richer than that on village A. In the two counties together, we conducted 106 interviews in 1999 and 2000 with officials at all administrative levels and with emigrant households. In June 2000 we conducted a survey in village B among a sample of eighty-one emigrant households in village B, who constituted 26 percent of all households (and 50 percent of all emigrant households) in the village.

Emigration from Fujian

At least since the Tang dynasty (618–907), Fujian province was heavily involved in international trade. Indeed, the city of Quanzhou was the greatest port of China during the southern Song dynasty (1127–1279) and remained an important port until its harbor silted up and its role was taken over by nearby Xiamen during the mid-Qing dynasty (1644–1911). In the seventeenth and particularly the eighteenth century, merchants from southern Fujian roamed far and wide, dominating much of the trade between China and Southeast Asia. Fujianese mercantile dominance was every bit a match for the growing European naval prowess in the area; in fact, the symbiosis between Spanish, Dutch, French, and British military and mercantilist expansion, the weight and sophistication of the Chinese economy, and the Fujianese trade network linking the two made this part of the world one of the main hubs of the world economy during this period. Trade also led to settlement; eventually, a permanent population of locally born Chinese (often the offspring of Chinese fathers and local mothers) became a prominent feature in cities such as Manila, Batavia (Djakarta), and Bangkok.

The Opium Wars of the mid-nineteenth century fundamentally reshaped the relationship between China and Western powers. Again Fujian was at the forefront of these developments. The provincial capital Fuzhou in central Fujian (Minzhong) and Xiamen in southern Fujian (Minnan) were among the five original treaty ports opened after the Opium War of 1840–42. Trade was no longer dominated by the Chinese themselves, but by Westerners. With it, China's role was downgraded to that of a dumping ground for Western merchandise (including, most infamously, British opium) and an inexhaustible source of cheap, docile, and expendable coolie labor that was put to work to serve the rapid expansion of territory under Western colonialist rule in the Americas, Southeast Asia, Australia, South Africa, and Siberia.[3]

Xiamen quickly became the main Fujianese harbor through which coolie labor was recruited and transported. As a result, further overseas migration took place mainly from southern Fujian, in what nowadays are the prefectures of Zhangzhou, Quanzhou, and Xiamen (see Map 2). In central Fujian, a certain amount of out-migration also took place, but remained much less prominent until 1900, when the coolie trade was started by the French from Mawei harbor near Fuzhou.[4] Yet the total number of coolies shipped from Fuzhou in the few years that the trade lasted (1900–1908) amounted to a mere 3,121 men, many fewer than from Xiamen during a comparable period at the beginning of the coolie trade, when 12,261 coolies were shipped between 1845 and 1853 (Fujian sheng difangzhi bianzuan weiyuanhui 1992: 14–16).

Fuzhounese themselves were also actively involved in migration, and it is inaccurate to think of the coolie trade solely as representing Western victimization of Chinese. The role of Chinese was by no means limited to that of lowly recruiter or "crimp." Of particular relevance to central Fujian was the agreement between Huang Naishang (Wong Nai Siong), a native of Minqing county in Fuzhou prefecture, and Charles Brooke, the second Rajah of Sibu in Serawak, to bring immigrants from central Fujian to open up and develop the area of Rejang. A first group of 1,072 settlers arrived in 1901 and 1902. After initial setbacks this Fujianese colony eventually prospered from growing rubber, attracting increasing numbers of new immigrants and spreading into adjacent areas (U. Chin 1997; Wu 1994: 148–49).

Nowadays, central Fujian has a sizable overseas population. Nevertheless, as an overseas Chinese area it remains a distant second to southern Fujian: even in 1990, only an estimated 10 percent of all overseas Chinese from Fujian traced their origins to Fuzhou prefecture (Yang and Ye 1993, cited in Hood 1998: 33). Like southern Fujian, central Fujian specialized in migration to Southeast Asia. According to data of the Fuzhou Office of the Fujian Overseas Chinese Affairs Committee (Fujiansheng qiaowu weiyuanhui Fuzhou banshichu), in 1928 more than 200,000 people from central Fujian resided overseas, among them 100,000 in the "New Fuzhou" of Sibu, Serawak; 20,000 in Singapore; 85,000 in other parts of the Malayan peninsula; and smaller numbers in Sumatra, Java, Kalimantan, Burma, and Japan. An additional 70,000 lived in the Japanese colony of Taiwan. Emigration to Southeast Asia continued apace, and after the lifting of the anti-Chinese U.S. immigration laws in 1943, a modest number of central Fujianese also migrated to the United States as students, usually from Hong Kong or Southeast Asia. According to statistics of the overseas Chinese departments in Fuzhou prefecture, overseas Chinese of central Fujianese extraction amounted to a total of 720,000, of whom 358,000 resided in Indonesia, 145,000 in Malaysia, 78,900 in Singapore, 35,600 in Burma, 35,000 in the United States, 11,200 in Japan, and smaller numbers in Thailand, Vietnam, and Canada.[5]

Linguistically and culturally, Fujianese from these central coastal areas are very different from the southern Fujianese. The latter are speakers of the Chinese Minnan (literally "southern Fujianese") language, and are known in Southeast Asia as Hokkien (literally "Fujianese," a testimony to their historical and numerical dominance in the area). Central Fujianese are divided into two separate linguistic groups. Immediately north of the Minnan area lies Putian prefecture, and further north along the coast is Fuzhou prefecture around the provincial capital of Fuzhou city. Each prefecture has its own language, speakers of which are known in Singapore respectively as Henghua (Putian) and Hokchiu (Fuzhou). To confuse matters further, among the Hokchiu (i.e., Chinese from Fuzhou prefecture), those from Fuzhou city itself are called Foochow, while those from Fuqing (the southernmost county in Fuzhou prefecture that borders on Putian to the south) are known as Hokchia in Singapore (L. Cheng 1985: 22–23, 97–99; see also Pan 1998: 24–25).

Fujian Province: The Heartland of China's Economic Reforms

Fujian is surrounded in the Northwest by high, rugged mountains, has no major rivers crossing into other provinces, scarce arable land (less than 10 percent of the province's total area), and a relatively large population of 33 million (1997). On the eve of the reforms in 1978, Fujian province ranked nationally as the twenty-third largest (of twenty-nine provinces) in per capita gross domestic product (GDP), far below other coastal provinces (Shieh 2000: 84). However, Fujian's lackluster economic performance during the collective period (1949–78) had less to do with geography than with politics. Fujian's location along the Taiwan Strait rendered the province a military frontier in the struggle between the Chinese Communist Party (CCP) on the Chinese mainland and the Guomindang (GMD) on Taiwan. As a result, sFujian received a mere 1.5 percent of the total national capital investment (the fourth lowest percentage among all the provinces) during the period from 1949 to 1978, forcing the province to focus on agricultural production and abandon its long tradition of maritime trading and coastal development. Instead, the limited national and provincial funds available for industrial development were invested in the interior parts of the province, which were deemed less vulnerable to enemy attacks. Particularly under the so-called Third Front policy of the 1960s and early 1970s, transport infrastructure and state heavy industries with iron and steel complexes, machine-building factories, and chemical plants were located in the remote Nanping-Longyan corridor in the western hills and mountains.[6]

In the 1980s and 1990s, however, economic liberalization and opening up to the outside world made the strategy of containment of Taiwan a thing of the past. Fujian's position changed rapidly from a military frontier zone to a key region of economic development. Rather than a liability, the province's proximity to Taiwan became an asset as Taiwanese and ethnic Chinese investments began to pour in, particularly in the southern parts of the province that have close historical, linguistic, and cultural links with the majority Chinese population of Taiwan. Along with Guangdong province, which has comparable overseas relations to Hong Kong, Fujian became one of the first experimental economic zones targeted for modernization. Local authorities were given substantial autonomy to open up for foreign investment and trade with the outside world. In 1980 decentralization was promoted with the establishment of Xiamen city in southern Fujian as a "special economic zone." Later the provincial capital Fuzhou was designated an "open coastal city" in 1984. In 1985 the coastal cities of Quanzhou, Zhangzhou, and Xiamen were earmarked to become a "golden triangle" of economic development (Yeung 2000: 8–9). In 1987, Taiwanese businessmen for the first time were allowed to visit and invest in the People's Republic of China (PRC). Between 1991 and 1996, 122 more economic development zones in the coastal area were approved (Hu and Hu 2000).

The geographic advantages of the coastal cities and the location of the majority of "ancestral villages" of overseas Chinese and Taiwanese in the coastal area reversed the artificial pattern of state-induced economic development of the interior during the collective period. By 1997 the economic transformation had raised Fujian's position nationally from one of the most backward provinces in China to number seven in per capita GDP. As in the Mao era, however, economic development in one region of the province was realized through the unequal distribution of investment, resources, and income (Fujiansheng jihua weiyuanhui and Fujiansheng tongjiju 1999; Lyons 1998; Yeung 2000: 8).

The two research sites of our study clearly reflect the reversal of economic development from western to eastern Fujian. Village A is situated in today's industrial and economic development zone of the east coast, whereas village B is located in the former industrial western interior. These field sites represent, as intended, two different economic and social environments; nevertheless, recent international migration has been significant from both villages.

Despite their dramatically different developmental trajectories, in both field sites the wage gap with Europe remains great. In 2000, peasants in the two villages earned on average between RMB 3,100 and 4,500 (US$300–540, not including overseas remittances) *annually;*[7] in contrast, their average *monthly* wages in Europe might reach US$1,000.[8] However, it has by now been well established that income differentials alone do not explain why people migrate. Hatton and Williamson, for instance, found that "migration rates did not ease but rather surged" from Europe to the New World, when wages in source and destination countries converged. The effects of industrialization and demographic changes are offset by chain migration that continues despite the decline in wage gaps (Hatton and Williamson 1998: 52). Similarly, Douglas Massey and his colleagues have pointed to the significance of migration producing structural changes in source societies that in turn perpetuate migratory flows (Massey 1988; Massey et al. 1998). Our research confirms these findings. Emigration in our field sites has become self-sustaining under the impact of economic changes in the villages caused by migration and the actions of individual migrants. Our research also confirms that a focus on migration or migrants alone, either as individual fortune seekers or as parts of larger family or ethnic networks, ignores the active role played by the sending and receiving states in initiating and maintaining migratory flows (Hatton and Williamson 1998; Massey et al. 1993: 12).

Village A: Migration as an Unintended Policy Outcome

Village A is located in the southeastern corner of Fuqing county. Fuqing's 1.18 million people went from being among the poorest in Fujian in 1978 to among the most prosperous in terms of GDP per capita in 1999 (Fujiansheng tongjiju 2000: 388–89). In fact, by the late 1990s, Fuqing had become one of the hundred most economically and environmentally developed prefectures in the PRC.[9]

In the previous section we outlined how Fujian under the reforms capitalized on its proximity to Taiwan and its many connections with overseas Chinese, particularly in Southeast Asia. Although both the southern and central coastal strips were eventually included in this

strategy, the timing differed. Whereas Xiamen became a special economic zone in 1978, Fuzhou became an open city in 1984, and only in
1987 was the decision made to open up and develop the economy of
Fuqing (Edmonds 1996: 89–90; Y. Zhu 2000: 424–31).

This difference in timing continues to inform the pattern of economic
development and international migration that pertains to coastal central Fujian in general and Fuqing in particular. Although it is impossible fully to explain why migration brokerage became such a prominent
feature in this part of China, American criminological research points to
at least two factors. First, in the 1970s and early 1980s agencies or individual officials of the Guomindang government on Taiwan appeared to
set up a network of migration brokers that provided the vital link with
Latin American migration facilitators who brought the first batches of
Fujianese into the United States (DeStefano 1997; Myers 1997). Second,
in the 1960s and 1970s local fishermen developed a lucrative smuggling
trade with Taiwan. This generated both the cash and the cross-strait
smuggling networks that in turn spawned the migration trade in the
1980s (K. Chin 1999: 12; Giese 1999).

Attempts in the early 1980s to use money raised from smuggling to
set up rural enterprises in central Fujian reportedly came to naught because of heavy taxation (K. Chin 1999: 12), itself part of policies that at
that time continued to deemphasize local economic development in
the area. Between the start of the reforms in 1978 and 1984, when
Fuzhou became an open city, migration facilitation networks and an
emigration orientation thus could grow, an orientation that has since
been crucial in perpetuating and intensifying migratory flows (Myers
1997: 124). Furthermore, and particularly relevant to Fuqing, once foreign investment–led economic development gained speed in the early
1990s, it happened in a very different way from in the overseas Chinese areas in southern Fujian. In the latter areas around Xiamen, the
early start of overseas Chinese investment set a pattern of relatively
modest investments in enterprises across the countryside by groups of
households using their own savings and remittances from relatives
abroad (Y. Zhu 2000: 415–22). In Fuqing, by contrast, foreign investment lagged behind at least ten years. Only in 1987 did the local government and overseas Chinese tycoons establish two investment
zones[10] that by the early 1990s began attracting large-scale foreign and
ethnic Chinese investment in often sophisticated enterprises (Edmonds
1996: 89–90; Y. Zhu 2000: 424–31).[11] By the mid-1990s, foreign investment in Fuqing enterprises thus generated much economic growth and

employment, but unskilled and often temporary work in these enterprises attracted mainly workers from outside Fuqing, who are more
pliable than local rural residents.[12] Local Fuqing residents were found
among the minority of supervisors and blue-collar workers in stable
employment, but peasants are usually not qualified for these well-paid
jobs. Domestic trading in prosperous Fuqing city itself is an alternative,
but conducting business also seems to be restricted to better-educated
or more skilled persons.[13]

Finding Europe: International Migration from Village A in the 1990s

The fact that the population in Fuqing living outside the investment
zones gains little from foreign investment is as much a consequence as
a cause of international migration. Locals turn to migration because
they lack access to employment opportunities, but equally important,
also often prefer to focus on the more lucrative opportunities for overseas migration that were already well established ten years before the
first meaningful foreign investments. In village A, only ten minutes by
car south of Fuqing city, the local economy is based primarily on fishery
and agricultural production. Yet despite the lack of economic activities,
the average income of the 2,549 villagers (756 households) in 1999 was
high by provincial standards (RMB 4,500 or US$540).[14] The local wealth
comes primarily from donations from ethnic Chinese in Southeast Asia:
80 percent of the residents in the township of village A have relatives
overseas.[15] According to local statistics, since 1978 these donations have
amounted to RMB 13 million for collective projects such as schools, a
hotel, a hospital, dikes, an ancestral hall, a theater stage, and a local
temple.[16]

　However, the population of village A did not simply live off its contacts with relatives who had migrated before 1949: migration was once
again a current issue. This is immediately visible from the appearance
of the village, which is dotted with expensive five- and six-story
houses: 80 percent of all houses in the village are newly built with remittances from recent migrants at a cost ranging from RMB 300,000 to
RMB 500,000. Emigration from Fuqing to Southeast Asia started immediately after the onset of the reforms in 1978 (Shi 2000: 27–28). Ethnic
Chinese from village A, primarily in Singapore, arranged for their relatives in the village to obtain visas for contract work and family reunifi-

cation. Those without relatives abroad or with aspirations to earn even higher wages than in Singapore started emigrating to Japan for study and work. It is unclear how the migratory route to Japan was created. During the late nineteenth and early twentieth centuries, peasants from the area had migrated to Japan, but inhabitants from village A were not among them. In the 1980s and early 1990s, new migrants from villages in southeastern Fuqing traveled to Japan for family reunification, as self-paying students, or illegally, and it seems likely that the first migrants from village A to Japan followed their example, perhaps using kinship or other connections with these villages.[17]

Migration to Japan had slowed by the mid-1990s when job opportunities dwindled and wages decreased as a consequence of the economic recession in Japan and a crackdown on illegal migrant workers. Subsequently, Europe became the preferred destination. The constraints imposed on our fieldwork in village A prevented us from inquiring into the reasons why migrants turned to Europe. However, it seems likely that the same reasons applied as for Fuqing more generally, with the vital first links provided by jumped-ship sailors and students. Pioneering migration to Europe (and the United States) must also have received a boost after 1989 when the Tian'anmen crackdown made gaining political asylum easier than it had been before.

At this writing in the early 2000s, on average more than one young person (usually male) per family in village A has migrated overseas. The remaining village inhabitants are mainly old people and young women with children.[18] According to local statistics, by 2000, 489 persons in village A—equal to 19 percent of the village population or almost all young male adults—had emigrated overseas. Half of these migrants worked as contract laborers in Singapore, 40 percent lived in Europe (primarily the United Kingdom and Italy), and the others were scattered in South American countries, Japan, and a few in the United States (see table 1).[19]

For the people living in village A, (mainly illegal) migration to Europe or migrating to Singapore to work legally in construction for two years with the possibility of staying for another year were more lucrative options than cultivating land or employment in a local factory. The wife of a migrant in Europe expressed this situation in these words:

If my husband had not emigrated, our life would have been duller. It is mostly a question of economy. Many are just peasants without skills, which makes it difficult for them to earn more money [here]. If my husband had not left, it

TABLE 1

Migrants from Village A by Destination

Destination	Number of Migrants
Singapore	230
United Kingdom	75
Italy	35
Honduras	25
Belgium	27
Japan	25
Hungary	18
Spain	16
France	12
Argentina	12
Israel	7
United States	7
Total	489

SOURCE: Interview filename Z00082111 (according to incomplete statistics).
NOTE: Migrants in Singapore are mainly contract construction workers. Only 55 of the 230 had obtained a residence permit.

would have been difficult for us to buy appliances such as electric fans, a color television, a washing machine, and so on. Not to mention building a house.[20]

Up to this point, we have explained international migration from central Fujian in general, and Fuqing in particular, from the local opportunity structure. A migratory flow, once started, is sustained by the presence of migration brokers. This in turn is a consequence of a history of smuggling across the Taiwan Strait, contacts with relatives and friends abroad, and little local economic development until the mid-1980s.

These circumstances resemble but are by no means identical to the explanations offered locally in Fuqing that highlight the history of migration of the area: the people of Fuqing migrate because it is in their nature, and they have always done so. Such explanations should be taken seriously because they help us understand why the people in rural Fuqing were so quick and unanimous in grasping the opportunity to emigrate once it arose in the late 1970s and early 1980s, and why the migratory flow continues even when, with a similar effort and much less risk and expenditure, local opportunities might be explored. In short, whereas the structural facts of opportunities and constraints go a long way in explaining the specifics of where, when, and how people migrate, a historically informed cultural explanation is required if we want to understand why these people from remote villages are prepared to move literally around the globe in search of wealth.

"History," however, can hardly be viewed as a social force in its own right, perpetuating a disposition for emigration after decades of very limited mobility during the collective period. What is important, therefore, is to gain a better understanding of how the successes brought by past migration are remembered and celebrated in Fuqing. In other words, we must understand how a history of migratory events is recast as a proud tradition of migration that highlights emigration as the best, even the only, avenue to true wealth, power, and success. Such a tradition, in turn, can only be understood if we treat villages in Fuqing, as we treated village A, not as isolated local communities, but as part of transnational communities of villagers, migrants, and former migrants.

Since 1949, Chinese government policies have been informed by, and oscillated between, the twin goals of insulating China from the corrupting bourgeois Western influence of the overseas Chinese and attracting from them remittances and investments in areas with a history of high overseas emigration. Since the early 1950s, the authorities in village A have solicited donations from former inhabitants of the village who became prosperous businessmen in Singapore and Indonesia. In Singapore, these businessmen were organized in a clan (village A is a single-surname village) and temple association that maintained direct connections to the village.[21] From 1954 onward, the association has been instrumental in raising funds for donations to projects in the village. Although former residents' contributions have also helped to pave roads, build dikes, and install running water, the lion's share has supported what could loosely be called the "cultural sphere" of the village, such as elementary and secondary schools, the ancestral hall, and the main temple.[22]

These donations have increased the educational level of the village in which, according to local officials, now 85 percent of all youth attend senior high school.[23] Despite such achievements, most youngsters do not continue in higher education or vocational training, but emigrate overseas. For the young generation, substantial donations from abroad have set the standard for gaining social status in the village: getting rich through migration, rather than through professional employment made possible by higher education.

The continuous donations from overseas define cultural life and local village identity. In the 1990s, substantial donations for the restoration of the local ancestral hall contributed to the revival of communal ancestor worship activities.[24] Traditional village identity is also strengthened by the restoration of the main village temple and the recognition of its ritual superiority by the transfer of temple ashes (*fenxiang*) to a branch temple in Singapore. Recently, Chinese local authorities also allowed local religious practices, such as parades of local gods across the village territory (*youshen*), a ceremony in which three thousand participants from Singapore and locals participated for more than a week. Such local religious practices, which in nonoverseas Chinese areas in rural China have to be negotiated much more carefully, have explicitly been allowed in village A because of its official status as a village with overseas connections.[25]

The sponsoring and sanctioning by Chinese authorities of such traditional social practices all enhance local identity constructions, but, being financed from Singapore, these identities refer to a transnationally dispersed community, rather than one that is locally based and developed. The construction of a theater stage in front of the temple in village A illustrates this particularly well. On this stage the family members of a migrant can have plays performed by professional troupes (which may cost up to RMB 2,500) or movies shown as an expression of gratitude to the gods who protected the migrant's voyage overseas.[26] These shows entertain the gods as well as the entire village, and are a visible expression of the central role of migration overseas. Hence, overseas migration brings amusement and recreation directly to the village, building the cultural capital and social status of migrant families, and celebrating the village's incorporation into a transnational social space.

Contemporary overseas migration from village A is more than simply the consequence of chain migration along existing overseas connections that enable villagers to fulfill their financial ambitions. Social practices related to former migration both celebrate the village's identity as part of a transnational community and reaffirm the importance of international migration as the avenue and marker of success, regardless of the destination and presence or absence of other villagers there. It is true that villagers emigrate because they want to be rich. However, given the lack of sufficient opportunities to emigrate to the areas in Southeast Asia and Japan where most of the earlier migrants and their descendents live, villagers were quick to explore alternative destinations.[27] In the 1980s, on the basis of few and often tenuous connections, villagers capitalized on the opportunities provided by professional migration brokers in the Fuzhou area to travel to European countries without any earlier Fujianese presence.

To safeguard the economic interests of the village, the village leadership encourages emigration in order to increase remittances;[28] it even loaned village funds to villagers for their migration expenses at a monthly interest rate until this practice was prohibited by higher authorities in 1999.[29] However, more important than the direct support for emigration from the village leadership has been the local implementation of provincial and county policies intended to stimulate economic growth by activating the links with the overseas Chinese. Village A is an example of local Chinese authorities' continued concern with wooing donations for public projects and family remittances, while ignoring the possible use of these funds for local economic development in order to create job opportunities in a village with limited cultivated land.

Our study of village A reveals that the flow of migrants from the Fuzhou area is generated, directed, and perpetuated by a migration configuration that includes a range of institutional and cultural factors in the areas of origin and destination. These factors include a lack of government investment and the prominence of migration brokerage during the collective period, the late start of overseas Chinese investment in the area, and the active promotion by the village leadership of overseas Chinese links and emigration. The current migratory flow to Europe is also closely connected with other internal and international migratory flows from the area, such as short-term labor migration to Singapore, Xiamen, Shenzhen, Macao, and Hong Kong and female labor circulation to Putian and elsewhere in southern Fujian. We also found evidence of the importance of internal migration to destinations across the length and breadth of China for traders, vendors, repairmen, contract laborers, and even entrepreneurial investors. All these flows are part of the highly elaborate migration system of the Fuzhou/ Fuqing area that enables potential internal migrants to raise the cash and accumulate the experience for the journey to Europe.

The Fuzhou migration configuration and transnationalism also includes an important cultural component, which has strong references to a tradition of emigration. Interestingly, the current celebration of the ongoing connections with former villagers in Southeast Asia and Japan is strongly informed by patrilineal ancestor worship and the desire to perpetuate patrilateral kinship ties between villagers and former villagers overseas. In village A, transnational connections are clearly gendered, and, as a result, so is international migration. Like before 1949, few women from the village emigrate; they stay home with the children and parents-in-law or work as short-distance migrants in shoe and textile factories in Putian county immediately south of Fuqing, where they can earn RMB 400–500 a month.[30]

Village B: Engineering Migration

The kind of migration history and transnational tradition found in village A are absent in village B, which was deliberately planned and built virtually from scratch since the early 1990s. Migration from village B is much more directly connected with the drying up of local employment opportunities compared with village A, where a migration orientation is one of the chief *causes* of the continued lack of self-generated local economic development. As a result, migration from village B is embedded in a distinctly different migration configuration, in which agents of the state play an even more active and open role, migration brokers are less of a factor (although by no means absent), urban and rural residents participate in equal measure, and women migrate almost as frequently as men.

The economic development in Sanming prefecture reflects the relocation of human and economic resources from the coast to the hills and mountains of western Fujian during the collective period, when Sanming prefecture, despite its remote location, became somewhat of a miniature regional cosmopolitan area. Many of the urban and rural residents of Sanming, or their parents, who spearheaded emigration to Europe in the late 1980s and early 1990s, had moved to Mingxi from elsewhere in Fujian or even farther away in the 1960s and 1970s (Mingxixian difangzhi bianzuan weiyuanhui 1997: 116–18). In this period, the Sanming area was developed into the main provincial center of heavy industry, producing iron and steel, machinery, and chemicals. As a result, by the late 1970s Sanming county (the central county of the prefecture with the same name) ranked among the richest in all of China in terms of distributed collective income (Lyons 2000: 334). Similarly, before the reforms, Mingxi county, with twenty major heavy industrial plants, had among the highest gross value of agricultural and industrial output in Fujian (Lyons 1998: 410; Lyons 2000: 388, 406; Mingxixian difangzhi bianzuan weiyuanhui 1997: 5).

This privileged status has become a thing of the past. The economic reform policies have significantly reduced the industrial output of the Sanming area relative to the formerly impoverished coastal area. In 1984, Mingxi's agricultural and industrial output and gross domestic product had already significantly declined in comparison to the coastal areas. By 1996, industrial workers in Mingxi earned annually on average half the amount (RMB 5,291) of workers in coastal Xiamen (RMB 11,133) and also significantly less than workers elsewhere in the coastal area;[31] likewise, Mingxi rural incomes were much lower than those in Xiamen (Fujiansheng tongjiju 1997: 392, 394; Fujiansheng tongjiju 2000: 388, 406).

As the economy's center of gravity shifted to the coast, many among Mingxi's small population of 115,000 returned to primarily agricultural production. Simultaneously, the agricultural reforms in the early 1980s assigned responsibility for production to individual families. The main crops are grain and fruits (Fujiansheng tongjiju 1997: 384, 408; Fujiansheng tongjiju 2000: 394–96, 422; Mingxixian difangzhi bianzuan weiyuanhui 1997: 4, 155). Attempts to diversify agricultural production have largely failed. The introduction of new crops such as tobacco has been hampered by a general lack of available arable land, which fell from 5.66 mu (0.93 acre) per capita in 1950 to 1.55 mu (0.26 acre) in 1994 (Mingxixian difangzhi bianzuan weiyuanhui 1997: 4, 141). Logging in natural forests is banned, and as a result forestry—until recently an important source of income—has almost ceased. One official from the local Forestry Department expressed the current situation in this way:

Mingxi is a poor and backward mountain region in the interior [of Fujian]. Recently, state-owned factories are not prospering and quite a few workers have been laid off. Originally timber production was the mainstay of this county, but now it is not permitted to cut down natural trees. The financial income of the county has decreased and the economic situation is difficult. . . . If we just rely on agriculture then it will be very difficult to break out of poverty.[32]

As a result, local rural enterprises have not been able to flourish. In 1996 there were 5,000 township and village enterprises (TVEs, *xiangzhen qiye*), employing a mere 15,000 people. Likewise, foreign investment has been limited. In the 1990s, foreign direct investment for twenty-five projects with a total value of US$68 million were realized (Fujiansheng tongjiju 1997: 400, 402, 404; Fujiansheng tongjiju 2000: 422; Fujiansheng renmin zhengfu bianzuan weiyuanhui 1999: 342). In fact, Mingxi is among the eighteen counties in Fujian whose local governments are designated as impoverished. Each year, the province supports the Mingxi government to the tune of more than RMB 8 million.[33]

Village B reflects the general conditions of economic decline in Mingxi. The village is located in an area covered with forests in the hilly and mountainous eastern part of Mingxi. The population is predominantly engaged in forestry (China fir and mason pine timber and pine resin) and agriculture (rice, oranges, tobacco).[34] Since the late 1990s, the prohibition of unauthorized cutting of natural trees to prevent flooding caused by erosion has significantly reduced a main source of income in the village.[35] With the decline of forestry, related sectors are dying out as well: transportation, machine and transport repair shops, and the like.[36] Since the beginning of the 1990s, the solution to these economic problems for many urbanites and peasants alike became to migrate to Europe. By the end of 1999, at least 3,700 persons from Mingxi county had emigrated, of whom 70 percent went to Europe, mainly Italy, Hungary, Spain, and Russia. In village B, 257 persons, or 22 percent of the total village population, were living overseas.[37]

Discovering Mobility: International Migration from Village B

In their study of European historical migration, Hatton and Williamson (1998) argue that structural transformations displaced peasants and as a result increased general mobility. In China in general and in Fujian in particular, economic reforms, commercialization of agriculture, diminished land holdings, and growing environmental calamities (mainly floods and pollution) all contribute to a similar displacement of the rural population. As a result, from 1985 to 1995 internal labor mobility in Fujian increased, with an estimated 1.4 million migrants seeking employment primarily in the coastal areas of eastern Fujian (Shen, Tang, and Lin 2000: 463). The inhabitants of village B, however, did not embark on internal migration. International rather than internal migration from this village only commenced in the beginning of the 1990s, when a network of contacts and information about international migration to Europe had been established.[38]

Previously, county residents had pursued neither internal nor international migration. On the contrary, the rich resources and industry of Mingxi county had attracted merchants from neighboring Jiangxi at the beginning of the twentieth century, as well as political refugees in the early 1930s from Guangdong province and the provincial capital of Fujian. After 1949, cadres, students, workers, and even peasants from elsewhere in Fujian and beyond were allocated employment or land in Mingxi county. By 1973, 486 persons who had been allocated jobs by the state had settled in the township where village B is located, in addition to an unknown number of in-migrants from poverty-stricken areas.[39]

The first migrants from Sanming prefecture (including Mingxi county) to eastern Europe and Italy in the late 1980s and early 1990s were mainly well-educated city dwellers between 20 and 30 years of age. Many were employees and cadres in state enterprises, and quite a few were teachers. These migrants used their contacts with and became part of a much larger flow of urban migrants to eastern Europe after the disintegration of the Soviet bloc. This flow had started with shuttle trade from northern and northeastern China to Moscow and the Russian Far East; soon, traders reached Hungary, Poland, and Czechoslovakia, where they looked for more permanent opportunities for investment, trade, and settlement.

The Sanming pioneers in the late 1980s and early 1990s could not depend on routes established by migration brokers and networks of relatives. Instead, they had to carve out their own space and often relied on their original, pre-Sanming regional identities to link up with migrants from other areas in China. Furthermore, these early migrants did not travel from Sanming to a preselected destination, but chose their direction and destination on the basis of information received en route from Chinese and even non-Chinese fellow migrants and local brokers, and simple curiosity. Migration for them was very much an exploration of the unknown: events, contacts, information, and decisions made during migration determined where they headed and what they ended up doing for a living.

The origins and growth of rural migration are partially connected with this history of exploration; yet, much more than urban migration, rural migration has quickly developed a chainlike pattern strikingly similar to migration from many traditional overseas Chinese areas, such as the New Territories in Hong Kong (J. Watson 1976, 1977), the Pearl River Delta in Guangdong (Woon 1997: 8–9, see esp. n. 26), southern Zhejiang (M. Li 1999), and indeed the Fuzhou area in Fujian. Migration chains channel migrants from specific places of origin to specific destinations, and often jobs, in a highly segregated ethnic enclave of the local economy.[40] The experience of village B is highly illustrative in this regard. The nature and speed of the establishment of the migratory chain from this village to Europe show that the persistence of such chains cannot simply be attributed to tradition or even plain inertia.

The pioneers of migration from village B were a certain Hu Zhiming and one of his brothers. In the early 1960s their father had migrated to Mingxi together with a group of other poverty-stricken villagers from Qingyuan county in the southernmost part of central Zhejiang and subsequently married a widow living in village B. According to one account, Hu Zhiming was employed by a state chemical factory in Mingxi county, which like many state enterprises in the 1980s was forced to make many of its employees, including Hu, redundant (*xiagang*). According to another account, Hu Zhiming and his brother were poor and dropped out of junior high school. Hu Zhiming got a temporary job with the township broadcasting station installing the cable network in the area. At this point, Hu Zhiming's Zhejiang family connections became relevant. Relatives told Hu about the riches of the Zhejiangese in Europe and the opportunities awaiting enterprising individuals, particularly in Italy. With the help of his Zhejiang relatives, Hu Zhiming and his brother duly made it to Italy, where they quickly became successful entrepreneurs, inviting first their direct kin and later friends and other kinsmen from village B, and (according to one account) former colleagues from the chemical factory to join them.[41] A local schoolteacher explained the influence of these pioneering international migrants:

Within a very short period of time they had become rich. In village B this caused a sensation and had a large effect. That such poor persons could within such a short time become rich was simply unbelievable. Hu Zhiming and his brother would return home and take their closest relatives with them overseas. As a result, a lot of people would start to imitate the brothers and emigrate like a chemical chain reaction. From this one family, it extended to friends in the village, from village B to Chengguan township in Mingxi town, and from cadres to peasants. The troops of emigrants are like a snowball that constantly is growing larger and larger.[42]

Drawing on an incidental link with the extensive and well-established networks of Zhejiangese in Europe, chain migration was initiated and flourished within just a few years.[43] By the summer of 2000, local authorities estimated that 257 people had left the village, and between 900 and 1,100 people (12 percent of the population) had left the township for overseas destinations.[44]

Since peaking in 1997 and 1998, migration to Italy has become a new way of increasing income. Migrants enter as tourists, businesspeople, or family visitors. The journey may cost between RMB 40,000 and 80,000 (US$4,800–9,600), plus interest payments at an annual rate of 3 to 5 percent. Migrants are generally able to repay their debts within two or three years. Our survey in village B, conducted in 2000, confirmed that 98 percent of the informants believed migration to be a wise decision, because, in the words of one questionnaire respondent, "You can earn money and improve the economy of the family." Admittedly, most respondents were family members of migrants rather than migrants themselves and thus often the chief beneficiaries of migration: only nine out of the fifty-eight households surveyed stated that they had to support relatives living abroad financially; the remaining forty-nine households received remittances. Official estimates of average annual remittances sent to village B are in the range of RMB 50,000 (US$6,000) for migrants who are still paying off travel debts, and RMB 20,000 (US$2,400) for migrants who have repaid their debts. This amounts to an estimated total for the whole village of RMB 8.5 to 10 million (US$100,000–120,000) annually. Since 1995, remittances in all of Mingxi county have officially been estimated to amount to US$10 million annually.[45]

Income and wage differentials undoubtedly provide immediate and primary reasons for migration. However, as in village A, migration decision-making is determined by far more than economics. During the 1990s, migration from village B and Mingxi county in general soared as the connections with emigrants in Europe multiplied.[46] Young men between 20 and 30 years of age paved the way to Italy.[47] Subsequently, they started facilitating the passage overseas of villagers with a broad range of backgrounds by providing information and the funds to cover the costs. According to our migrant household survey, 38 percent of all migrants from the township were women, and 87 percent had only primary or lower middle-school education. Furthermore, preestablished migration routes concentrated 83 percent of village B migrants in Italy in 1999.[48]

As in village A, the most striking signs of the wealth brought by international migration are the luxurious houses in modern Taiwan and Hong Kong style and the ubiquity of international telephone connections, video recorders, and color televisions. The significance of this display of wealth was formulated as follows by the head of the village's branch of the Overseas Chinese Federation:

In village B, basically all able-bodied and skillful people have vanished. Those without skills are just like always, it does not matter much. But the building of a house is the way by which people really make invidious comparisons. If you build a house with three stories, I will build four stories; if you use concrete to wash the walls, I will use tiles on my walls.[49]

In addition to building houses and buying consumer goods, families who receive remittances deposit them in savings accounts, lend money to potential migrants, and use the money for unforeseen expenses. Fewer than five families in our survey had spent their remittances to set up a business or contemplated using their savings for business purposes.

The purchase of houses, consumer goods, and clothing such as Italian leather jackets and gold necklaces are about more than just social status or the good life. Conspicuous consumption should also be read as a practice that reflects a desire for modernity that previously had been beyond reach, indeed may never have been contemplated as a possibility. Likewise, migrant families in village B have openly adopted a modern notion of leisure previously unfamiliar in agrarian society. Wives of successful migrants are seen on the streets all dressed up, demonstrating their freedom from work in the fields and their ability to spend their time as they like. Similarly, when business is slow in Italy, migrants return to the village on vacation for periods of several months. In fact, three dance halls have been established in the township to cater to the increasing demand for entertainment. Overseas migrants have also funded a dozen investment projects in hotels and entertainment centers, reinforcing the link between migration, leisure, and entertainment as aspects of the new-found modernity.[50]

Simultaneously, overseas migrants have begun donating to more traditional cultural activities such as abandoned Buddhist temples and neglected ancestral halls in the village.[51] Plaques detailing the amounts given and the names of the donors are placed in the temples. By renovating the old temples migrants have reestablished cultural practices that previously were politically impossible. Foreign currency not only makes possible a return to old traditions, but also manifests a local modernity that negates the Maoist orthodoxy.[52]

Through the discovery and funding of new and "traditional" forms of leisure and consumption, migrants from village B have developed a modernity and an identity that underline the backwardness of the remaining population in the village, thus leading the entire village population to regard migration as the best and indeed the only future. In this respect village B is constructing aspects of a migration configuration that in village A already existed. In both villages popular religion and ancestor worship are crucial in cementing transnational ties between the village and the migrant populations abroad. However, in village A, with its preexisting and affluent migrant population in Southeast Asia, the revival of popular religion and ancestor worship preserved and strengthened the villagers' migratory disposition. Existing transnational ties were thus one of the causes of the commencement of fresh migration in the late 1970s and early 1980s. In village B, by contrast, the new migration could not build on such a remembered tradition of migration. Instead, the opposite happened: the new migration, once successful, built transnational ties through the promotion of popular religion. In both villages transnationalism and migration shape and strengthen each other. Yet in village A transnationalism caused migration, and both are perceived locally as the perpetuation of a long-standing tradition. In village B, migration caused transnationalism, and the local perception of both is more explicitly shot through with notions of modernity, progress, and even Westernization.

Village B's lack of well-established transnational connections before the 1990s is more than compensated for by the attitude of the local authorities toward emigration. In village A, it was the county, township, and village authorities' encouragement of transnational connections with the well-established community of overseas Chinese in Singapore that kick-started and perpetuated the new migration of the 1980s and 1990s. Except for the village cadres, however, all other levels of government steered clear of encouraging or facilitating new migration. In Sanming and Mingxi, however, local authorities not only tacitly condone new migration, but even enable it. A provincial newspaper described the official attitude toward out-migration from Mingxi county to Europe:

The Mingxi county party committee and government attach great importance to the work on labor export and the new migrants. They express a clear-cut stand of developing the ideology and strategic aim of increasing the pace of labor export to construct a rising overseas Chinese area (*qiaoxiang*) in the interior of Fujian. Every year, the county calls several meetings of public security, foreign trade, labor, and other departments for research on special topics in order to solve existing problems in labor export, to reduce as much as possible the number of steps, to simplify the procedures, and to set up offices for labor exporting companies and the prompt translation of foreign materials, sparing no effort to support and promote in all possible ways the export of labor. To solve worries of domestic attachment among people leaving the county, the county has decided to let peasants keep their leased land.[53] [Similarly], the relations of employees to state or collective enterprises can be transferred to the administration of labor service bureaus in the county, while administrative personnel may keep their former positions for three years after leaving their jobs. The government regards people who leave the country as overseas migrants (*qiaomin*) and their relatives at home as overseas Chinese dependents (*qiaojuan*). [Upon their return, they and their dependents] are treated as returned overseas Chinese (*guiqiao*) and overseas Chinese dependents, and receive political privileges, support in production, care in life, and emotional encouragement. Every year at Chinese New Year the government intensifies the contact with migrants, promotes amiable feelings between migrants and fellow villagers, and stimulates the sentiment of migrants to love the fatherland and the local community by paying family visits, setting up seminars, holding interviews or surveys, and other methods. Simultaneously, the government vigorously adopts a range of preferential policies to accommodate, guide, and assist returned migrant investors. [The local government] plans to spend five years to multiply the number of migrants and gradually to establish an office and a Mingxi street in eastern Europe to expand the export trade of Mingxi products and Mingxi companies.[54]

Clearly, the export of labor is a top priority for the county authorities, which are actively and self-consciously engaged in building up a new overseas Chinese area on the model of the old overseas Chinese areas along the coast of Fujian. The local authorities in Mingxi county have in fact been so keen on promoting migration to eastern Europe that they have proposed to transfer the issuance of Hungarian visas to Sanming from the embassy in Beijing. In addition, the Sanming authorities have made efforts to establish sister-city relations with the XIIIth district in Budapest. Both proposals were turned down by Hungary.[55] Recently, county authorities in Mingxi started to plan for the establishment of a local "European village" with European-style houses to sell to migrants returning from Italy and Hungary.[56]

The eagerness of the local authorities in Mingxi county to accommodate migrants in Italy is similarly evident. The county government regards emigration as "a way out of poverty . . . migrating as laborers or traders has become an issue on the official agenda. Naturally, the government cannot initiate or organize migration, and it does not have the means to provide loans. As a matter of fact, the examples of others are the most persuasive. Especially in regard to finances . . . but the government can provide support and help them to migrate."[57]

In some localities, the government has taken the persuasive power of examples very literally, such as in one village where the authorities have erected a sign listing 156 emigrants from the village as examples of patriotic citizens.[58] The local government also recognizes migrants as "models" to be emulated by sending fresh flowers for Chinese New Year and setting off firecrackers at the homes of returned migrants.[59] The local political embrace of migration was experienced by fifty-three of sixty-five migrant families we surveyed in village B in 2000: local or county officials dropped by and sent flowers, and also helped migrant dependents to solve problems and even invited them to attend seminars. More concretely, an official exit service center helps peasants apply for visas and purchase airline tickets and provides information about job opportunities and legal issues. Vocational training is offered in sewing, cooking, computer skills, and trade issues. Classes also provide legal and cultural information about foreign countries and language training in Russian and English. Finally, the local government has relaxed its policies under which state-owned commercial banks and village credit cooperatives may provide mortgage loans or other types of loans to would-be migrants who lack the means to go abroad.[60]

Trends in Chinese Migration: Lessons from Fujian

The recent flow of international migration from Fujian province is a much more socially, culturally, and politically embedded phenomenon than the "snakehead" image suggests. Moreover, the contrast between village A and village B highlights that Fujianese migration should not be thought of as one phenomenon. The new Chinese migration from Fujian (and, we speculate, from elsewhere in China as well) actually consists of separate migration configurations, each with its own unique history and institutional arrangements. Each configuration, moreover, encompasses individual experiences and practices, which together render Chinese migration extraordinarily complex, resilient, and variegated. We found that the new migration often fans out to entirely new destinations before falling into the more familiar and conventional pattern of chain migration. One key feature of the new Chinese migration is its combination of pioneering exploration of unknown and even unlikely destinations with later mass migration to specific areas.

However, the connection between pioneering and chain migration should not be overdrawn. In both our fieldwork villages, we found that the new migration in the initial phase draws on networks and histories of previous migration, without which migration might very well never have started. In village A, labor exported to Singapore coupled with just a few first connections to Europe shaped the pattern of later mass migration from the village; in village B, contacts with Zhejiangese provided the link to Italy. However, networks and histories play rather different roles in the two villages. In village A, overseas Chinese connections and a "migration history" to Singapore shaped the migratory orientation, while in village B the Zhejiang network played a much more specific and concrete role in providing access to information, opportunities, and employment.

Central policies and especially local administration have been crucial in shaping the migration configurations in both villages. Before 1978, emigrants were often perceived as defectors and traitors. With economic reform the Chinese government began viewing the ethnic Chinese communities as a major resource. In 1999, President Jiang Zemin reaffirmed this policy when he officially claimed the overseas Chinese to be "our mine of resources."[61]

The national support for overseas Chinese connections gives local governments in sending areas the freedom to permit economic, political, and cultural developments according to the aspirations of the overseas Chinese (and those of new migrants) rather than orthodox Communist Party policies in order to create or sustain a flow of foreign revenues for capital investments, foreign knowledge, and remittances. The authorities in village A embraced the national reassessment of the overseas Chinese as soon as it was announced in 1978. The celebration and deepening of existing overseas connections and the history of migration quickly created a fresh appetite for migration. Village B, without prior overseas Chinese connections apart from its tentative link with the Zhejiang diaspora in Europe, demonstrates the effect of overseas Chinese connections in coastal Fujian. As we have seen, the main reason for the soaring international migration from village B is the confluence of peasants' interests and support from the local government. The latter were keen to follow the example of the established overseas Chinese areas along the coast and use migration to earn foreign revenue "to reduce the pressures of unemployment and enhance social stability."[62]

Once started, the migratory flows from the two villages became self-perpetuating. Each act of migration expands the overseas networks, strengthens the institutional arrangements that enable migration, augments the demand for labor by overseas ethnic economies, and produces safe conditions for new migrants upon arrival. At the same time, migration leads to structural changes in the sending villages, in turn triggering further migration. Remittances shift the relative distribution of income and wealth within the villages. Investment in lavish houses, consumer spending, and donations to ancestral halls and temples redefine local social and cultural institutions and identities. Having entered this advanced migration stage, the sending villages have been transformed into constituent elements of transnational communities. Emigration is a normal, indeed an almost inevitable act. An informant from village A whose husband went to England expressed this situation in these words: "My husband said, 'If they do well abroad, why not me, too?' I think that if my husband had not gone overseas, our life would not have been that much worse. Actually, our family is quite well off in the village."[63]

Structural changes in sending societies conditioned by migration have in some studies been related to the influence of transnational contacts between sending areas and overseas migrants. New communication technologies have made it easier to maintain contact between the source and destination societies. In our survey of migrant families in village B, 95 percent had contact with their closest family members several times a month over the telephone; but 64 percent of the migrants had still not returned from Europe even for a single visit. Regular communication and frequent opportunities to return home both make faraway destinations seem less distant and strengthen the incentive for migrants to invest in local cultural and social institutions. In village A, even migrants who had left their villages in the early twentieth century now return to invest in local cultural life.

Furthermore, the example of village B shows how increased mobility in general, coupled with more autonomy for local governments, extends migratory networks and enables the growth of migration configurations in places beyond the traditional overseas Chinese areas. This process brings emigration within reach of an ever-increasing number of people and areas. The emergence of *international* migration from places beyond the traditional overseas areas is part of the history, growth, and proliferation of complex local migration systems that include internal as well as international mobility. This point is demonstrated by the role of Zhejiang migrants in village B and by the importance of temporary female labor circulation to elsewhere in Fujian and contract labor migration to Singapore from village A. A further and particularly illuminating example comes from village B. To avoid penalties for allowing agricultural land to lie fallow, many families in village B have had to resort to renting out their land under short-term contracts to migrants from poorer areas elsewhere in Mingxi or in adjacent Ninghua county. Interestingly, in-migrants from Ninghua have begun using the money earned as contract farmers to emulate the locals and have begun migrating to Europe as well.[64] Clearly, we have only begun to witness the beginning of spatially cumulative migration from China. Not only will the number of migrants from China rise in the future, but equally important, migrants will be drawn from increasingly diverse social and geographic backgrounds.

FIGURE 1 (*opposite, upper*). Village lane, village A, paved with contributions from overseas Chinese

FIGURE 2 (*opposite, lower*). Migrant house, village A

FIGURE 3 (*this page*). The overseas Chinese building, village A

A Yong: A Restaurant Worker in Kent, England

"I AM NOT FROM the countryside; I am not like them," A Yong, in his thirties, says about fellow Fujianese in England. Born in Fuqing town, A Yong studied for a while at a university in Fuzhou and worked for a year as a teacher. Then he tried his hand at various trades: working at an aluminum smelter in the inland industrial city of Nanping, running a bookshop in Fuqing, and exporting Zhuyeqing liquor and watermelon seeds, bought in northwestern China, to Taiwan through smugglers who operated speedboats from Fujian. A Yong's wife also used to be a teacher.[1]

A Yong has four older brothers, all in China; he is the youngest. Two brothers are government officials—one in the finance bureau, the other in the land bureau—and a third is an engineer. Thanks to the official connections, he got away with just a RMB 5,000 fine when his second child was born.

"So many people around me had gone to Japan, America, or Singapore. If you don't go out you can't get rich; people will look down on you," A Yong explained. "It was my decision, but I was influenced by society. If I had stayed at home, my parents and brothers would have looked down on me." A cousin of A Yong's went to Taiwan illegally by boat many years ago and has made money there. A nephew of A Yong's went to Japan in the same manner, where he has been working as a construction worker. One of A Yong's older brothers, who had been a driver, went to Singapore on a labor contract as a construction worker. After returning to Fuqing he built a house and started a business. A niece of A Yong's has been in Singapore several times since 1998 on a contract as a waitress on a cruise ship. A Yong wanted to go to Singapore himself, but at that time it had become more difficult to get work contracts approved.

He decided to go to England because he had "heard that it was a bit freer than in Japan, even though you don't make as much money. In Japan, you can't go outside [if you have no residence papers]." In addition, he believed that going to Japan was even more expensive than going to the United States because wages were higher in Japan. At first he wanted to go to Germany, where he had a distant relative, but found that it was difficult to get there. Then people suggested that he go to England, because it is "free; you can go around and won't get deported." Relatives introduced him to a broker. To pay the agreed sum, he borrowed over RMB 200,000 at a monthly interest rate of 2.5 percent. After two years in England he had not yet fully paid it back.

He obtained a passport and a Hungarian visa in Beijing in October 1997, using papers provided by a broker. In January 1998 he flew from Shanghai to Moscow and on to Budapest, where he spent one week. From there, he was taken by truck to the Czech Republic and then to the Netherlands. Somewhere on the way, probably on the Czech-German border, he and his fellow migrants had to climb mountains: "It was exhausting." The group consisted of ten people from Fuzhou, Fuqing, and Changle. He spent two weeks in Holland and arrived in Britain in February, a journey A Yong considers fast. His two children go to school in Fuqing; his wife is at home, taking care of the children and A Yong's mother.

A Yong applied for asylum in Britain after a friend introduced him to a solicitor for £250 (US$375). After arriving in England, he had no work for two months. As an asylum applicant he could have applied for housing and welfare benefits, but he was afraid that doing so would expose him to the risk of deportation. His family had to send him RMB 9,000 (US$1,100) for his living expenses. They paid the sum to someone in Fuqing, and A Yong got it in pounds from someone in London. His asylum application was rejected in September 2000.

Later, for a £150 fee, a friend introduced him to a job in London. This job paid £80 for a seven-day workweek, but A Yong had to rent a place to live, which cost him £20 a week. Although after six months his wage had risen to £140, he quit this job because it paid too little. A friend, who again charged him a fee, then introduced him to a job in Coventry, which paid £200. His next job was back in London, earning £220, but he didn't like it because, being in central London, the boss did not provide accommodation as his first employer had. Once again, he had to pay a fee to the friend who introduced him to this job. Finally, for a £400 fee, a friend introduced him to the job he held during our interviews in 2000, which paid £250 a week.

A Yong is satisfied with his current job, in which he works six days a week from 1:00 P.M. to midnight. But now that his asylum application has been rejected, his boss is worried that A Yong will lose his right to work legally.

A Yong strongly wishes to distance himself from other Fujianese migrants. Fujianese, he says, "have a very low status here. According to an investigation by *Zoneast* [a local Chinese magazine] they are at the bottom after Hong Kong Chinese, Singaporeans, Malaysians, and Vietnamese." He emphasizes that his boss likes him "because I am the best, I am of a higher quality than the others." He claims to lead an isolated life. "I live very frugally. These clothes I am wearing, they are used clothes. I have a haircut once every half year, and I don't gamble." He does not have any contact with his numerous relatives around the world because phone calls are expensive and "we have nothing to say to each other." Earlier, he called home once a month and wrote letters to his children; now he can afford to call once a week. On Tuesdays, his day off, A Yong says he either stays home resting, doing the laundry, cooking, reading the newspaper *Haojue* ("Clarion Call"; see Chapter 5), a Chinese-language publication of Jehovah's Witnesses, or a bilingual Bible he got from the latter. A Yong's wife, who is in China, is a Christian who goes to services every week. A Yong himself was not a Christian in China, but once in London he had a terrible stomachache while at work. The pain was so strong it sent him tumbling to the floor of the restaurant. When a Christian friend came over to help him, the pain got better.

A Yong also listens to English-language tapes. Occasionally, he visits London Chinatown, but "very rarely, because the train is expensive." He knows about the Fuqing Association in Britain, but says he has neither time nor money to participate.

He sends money home by insured registered mail. "This way I save the train fare to London." Because he can speak a little English, he does not need to go through intermediaries in his dealings with British society. The money he sends home is to cover his family's living expenses and school fees. All his brothers pitch in with some money for his mother. He plans to build a house in Fuqing in two or three years: "If I don't, people will look down on me." He has donated some money via his wife to a church in his home village. Such donations are not organized by the government, but the government does not oppose them either.

CHAPTER 3

Getting Out, Getting In, and Moving On:
An Ethnographic View

IN DECEMBER 2001, a young Fujianese went to a London law firm with the request to represent him in his asylum application case. "What kind of persecution did you suffer in China?" the solicitor asked him. "Is it good if I suffered persecution?" the youngster asked eagerly; "let's just make up a story like the others do, shall we?" The solicitor started explaining that the client should provide the grounds for persecution; the law firm was there only to register them. After some time, the young man looked up and interrupted: "I understand. You can only help me if I lie to you, right?"[1]

The bulk of the writing on recent migration from Fujian is devoted to the issues of "getting out" and "getting in" (e.g., Myers 1997; Giese 1999; K. Chin 1999; DeStefano 1997; Liang 2001; Liang and Ye 2001; Zhang and Chin 2001). The focus has been on the minutiae of migration mechanisms and the organizers of migration. Because the popular assumption is that the migration is predominantly illegal, researchers, too, are tempted to focus on illegal avenues of migration, although it has been periodically acknowledged that a migration fundamentally illegal in its nature often avails itself of legal means.

This chapter eschews considerations of legal status and attempts to view migration avenues with an ethnographic eye, examining the options for migration in the terms used by the people in Fujian. We do not describe the functioning of snakehead networks, which has been amply done in earlier literature. But our findings do agree with the increasing recognition that migration brokers form loosely and opportunistically connected networks, more like suppliers in, for instance, the aircraft industry than in a mafia. Only a minority of the operations, such as those requiring sophisticated counterfeiting, may be contracted out to groups connected to organized crime (Medved 2001; Crisp 1999; Kyle and Dale 2001).

The diversity of migratory avenues and brokers' involvement in all of them underscores the fact that the *commodification* of migration does not necessarily entail its *criminalization*. Brokers provide a service that in some cases may be both necessary and legitimate. However, solicitors who help migrants apply for asylum in the countries of destination often knowingly support unfounded claims, for either material or humanitarian reasons (see below). Press articles often maintain that snakeheads instruct their clients what story to tell at the asylum hearing. But according to several employees of London firms specializing in asylum, it is interpreters—usually coethnics of the applicants—who scour ports and railway stations for asylum seekers and then prompt them during their sessions with the solicitor. Chinese migrants generally perceive the asylum system as a peculiar sort of immigration arrangement rather than a humanitarian instrument and therefore do not see "making up stories" as something illegal, much less as part of some underworld conspiracy. Before we return to the issue of contemporary Fujianese migration, we first briefly discuss the context of more general developments that have taken place in Chinese migration to Europe since its inception a century ago.

Main Trends in Chinese Migration to Europe

In the collective period (1949–78), the level of fresh emigration from China was extremely modest and largely restricted to the traditional overseas Chinese areas in the southeastern coastal provinces of Guangdong, Fujian, and Zhejiang.[2] Migration from these areas followed from existing connections with relatives abroad and had little to do with developments or mobility patterns within China itself.[3] China's overseas Chinese policies during the more moderate phases of the collective period (1949–58 and 1962–66) gave special privileges to overseas Chinese relatives and dependents living in China, and in doing so insulated China from the "corrupting" influences that the overseas Chinese in their home areas might have had.

These developments have also been visible in Europe.[4] Before World War II, small, clustered, and residentially segregated communities of Cantonese sailors lived in western Europe's main harbor cities (London, Liverpool, Rotterdam, Amsterdam, Hamburg, Antwerp), whose members, in the main, waited for recruitment and resided only temporarily in Europe (Eberstein 1988; Pang 1993; Parker 1998; Pieke and Benton 1998; Wubben 1986). Conversely, itinerant peddlers and traders from southern Zhejiang province, and to a much lesser extent Shandong province, found their way overland to Moscow and Berlin and across the sea to Marseilles and Paris. From there, they scattered all across the continent, although curiously enough not to Britain (Archaimbault 1987; Thunø 1999). Last, contract laborers were employed in large numbers in France and Russia by the Allied Forces in World War I (Griffin 1973; Summerskill 1982); the Russian Empire already had a long history of recruiting Chinese contract labor (mainly from Manchuria, Shandong, Shanghai, and Xinjiang) in Siberia, which was abruptly cut off by the Russian Revolution of 1917 (Larin 1998).

In western Europe, Cantonese seamen and Zhejiangese peddlers were the pioneers who formed the core of communities that grew rapidly after World War II. But the single most important development after the war was the commencement of large-scale immigration from the New Territories in Hong Kong (J. Watson 1976, 1977) and on a smaller scale from Malaysia and Singapore. As the People's Republic of China increasingly restricted emigration in the 1950s and 1960s, Hong Kong became the chief supplier of labor for the booming restaurant trade in western Europe, first in Britain and the Netherlands and subsequently in Belgium, Germany, and Scandinavia (Gütinger 1998; Pang 1993; Thunø 1997, 1998). As a consequence, Hong Kong Chinese and the Cantonese language continue to dominate the Chinese communities in Britain, the Netherlands, Belgium, and to a lesser extent Germany. More modest numbers of Hong Kong Chinese are now also found in France and southern Europe (Beltrán Antolín 1998; Live 1998; Teixeira 1998). Quite independent from the flow of Hong Kong migrants, economic uncertainty and persecution under the new regimes in Southeast Asia after decolonialization brought hundreds of thousands of ethnic Chinese to France (from Vietnam, Laos, and Cambodia), the Netherlands (from Indonesia), and Portugal (from Macao).

In the 1980s, the Chinese migration system to Europe entered a qualitatively and quantitatively different phase, whose full ramifications only became apparent in the 1990s. In the most general of terms, these changes can be attributed to the fact that, throughout the 1950s, 1960s, and 1970s, Europe's Chinese migration system had remained profoundly parochial. A handful of sending areas specialized in European migration, and the flows that they generated often had little to do with the global trends in Chinese migration. However, changes in the global Chinese migration system rapidly caught up with the continent in the 1980s and 1990s. The new migrants came from traditional overseas home areas, both those with a history of specialization in Europe in southern Zhejiang and those that did not have such a history (such as the Fujianese), and increasingly from areas with no history of overseas migration. Equally important, mass migration not only provided cheap labor for the restaurants and shops owned by the established Chinese communities in western Europe, but also inserted a dynamism and appetite for expansion that led to the exploration of new economic niches (vending, importing, garment manufacturing) and frontier areas in southern, eastern, and northern Europe.

Viewed from China, Europe is clearly a peripheral area and a frontier rather than the major center of the world system that it is from a Western point of view. It is thus quite logical that so many recent labor emigrants to Europe go to southern Europe, eastern Europe, or the Soviet Union, even when they have first touched base or even lived in a much more centrally placed European city in western Europe like London, Paris, or Amsterdam. Many Chinese migrants are less attracted by the bright lights of Western centers than by the underpopulated (in Chinese terms at least) frontier areas of eastern and southern Europe. Particularly attractive to Chinese migrants are those cities and regions that serve as nodes of migration, settlement, and commerce. Cities like Budapest and Prato have a certain concentration of settled Chinese (not necessarily from the same native areas), who provide the Chinese infrastructure and, crucially, the employment new migrants need. Yet the number of Chinese in these cities and regions has not yet reached the saturation point and, equally if not more important, such places are a convenient entryway into a large periphery full of unexplored opportunities.

Chinese international migration flows in the 1980s and 1990s are not only immeasurably larger, but also qualitatively different from the trickle of emigration and return migration in the earlier period. The current migratory flows from China cannot be treated in isolation from the economic, social, and cultural developments in the country as a whole, or as separate from the dense fabric of internal migration flows across China. This is equally true both for emigration from traditional overseas Chinese areas, and for the rapidly increasing level of emigration from many other parts of China that do not have such a tradition.

With the onset of the reforms in 1978, and particularly after the emigration law of 1985 came into force, a completely new emigration regime took shape in the overseas Chinese home areas. Being granted a passport became a right of overseas Chinese dependents; furthermore, any other person with a letter from an overseas Chinese sponsor could apply for a passport. The immediate result was the infusion of new blood into the aging and increasingly isolated communities of overseas Chinese. Soon, new migrants began to explore destinations beyond the ones their home areas traditionally specialized in. In the process, the long-established and geographically specialized diasporas were turned into truly global transnational communities and professional migration networks. Established Chinese communities have become both much larger and ethnically more diverse than in the past, while areas—or even whole continents such as Africa—that previously had only few Chinese have become home to vibrant overseas Chinese communities.[5]

As the new flows of migrants invigorated the traditional overseas Chinese communities and explored new frontiers, Chinese emigration also became more enmeshed with socioeconomic changes and migratory flows in China itself. In our fieldwork, we interviewed many informants who had spent considerable time elsewhere in China. For example, one of the fifty-eight Fujianese illegal migrants who died aboard a ferry destined for Britain in 2000 had spent more than ten years as an itinerant watch repairman in Shandong province before his wife asked him to return home. But his meager local earnings quickly led him and his wife to decide that he should follow the example of the overseas migrants.[6]

Similarly, many of our informants had worked for a few years in Singapore, Macao, or Hong Kong on fixed-term contracts before returning to Fujian and subsequently emigrating to Europe. Equally important, we found that international migration in our field site in Fuqing county near Fuzhou was often supported financially by the wife or other female family members who commuted to work in nearby Putian county factories producing shoes and other consumer items—principally for export. Areas of emigration in Fujian are also significant destinations for migrants from elsewhere in Fujian and farther asfield. Migrants in these areas do agricultural and menial work that local residents no longer find worthwhile, or simply can no longer do because they are absent.

As emigration from traditional overseas Chinese areas became more professional and global in the 1980s and 1990s, it blended with other, new migratory flows. These flows were less linked to specific areas of origin, involved migrants across a broader spectrum of social backgrounds, and often had no direct historical connection to earlier, pre-1949 types of migration. Among the new, more cosmopolitan migrants leaving China after the onset of the reforms, the most visible were students and visiting scholars. They left in rapidly increasing numbers for the United States, Australia, Canada, and Japan, adding to the already large numbers of Chinese students from Hong Kong, Taiwan, and Southeast Asia in these countries. Although they planned to leave China temporarily, only a minority ever returned.

Initially, Europe received only a trickle of this Chinese brain drain, mainly because of the limited funding available to students, restrictions on work-study, and a more strictly enforced requirement to return upon graduation. Gradually, however, Europe has become more popular among Chinese students (although European universities still find it difficult to compete for the best students, particularly with the top U.S. universities). Germany, France, and Britain are the most common destinations, and numbers are rising fast.[7] As at least some students and scholars become more involved in local Chinese life, the Chinese communities in Europe simultaneously become endowed with a Mandarin-educated elite, supplementing the economic and political elite of overseas Chinese businessmen and community leaders and the locally educated second generation.

As China gets richer, its new entrepreneurial elite can afford to pay for a university or even primary and secondary school education for themselves or their children. For students with rich parents, self-financed study abroad is an alternative if they do not score well enough on the college entrance examination to gain admission to a good Chinese university. Many Western universities actively cater to this emerging market in higher education, recruiting in China and offering remedial English courses to prepare students for the regular university education. Furthermore, in some private European high schools, students from rich mainland Chinese parents are becoming a common phenomenon, similar to the "astronaut" families and "parachute" kids from Hong Kong in North America (see Skeldon 1994; Zhou 1998). Certain British schools, such as David Game College in London, even have recruiters in China targeting children of the newly wealthy.[8]

It would be a mistake to think of Chinese students and scholars as constituting a migratory flow unrelated to other flows of new migrants from China. A student visa can be a safe and cheap way to gain entry for those with the required qualifications, which usually include a sufficiently high score on a foreign language test. For potential migrants, foreign study may simply be another way to go abroad, for reasons that include family reunification, acquiring a share in a business, temporary contract labor, quota immigration for skilled professionals, an invitation to work in a Chinese enterprise, postgraduate on-the-job training, political asylum, or illegal entry. Indeed, migrants often move from one category to another in the course of a migratory career.

International study and research are best viewed as part of a much broader phenomenon. In the late 1980s state enterprises and other state units such as schools, hospitals, and administrative organs began to shed increasing numbers of personnel. Moreover, to many Chinese, state sector employment, previously viewed as high-prestige, became a dead end, merely a meal ticket without any prospects of a career or personal challenge. A significant number of the Chinese explored employment or business opportunities elsewhere: in a large, modern city such as Beijing, Shanghai, or Guangzhou perhaps, in one of the Special Economic Zones, or indeed abroad.

In the late 1980s and early 1990s, the new internal mobility of both urban and rural Chinese quite literally began to spill over into North and Central Asia and Europe. As mentioned earlier, the most highly qualified often went directly to urban centers in North America, Australia, Japan, and Europe as students, entrepreneurs, and skilled professionals. Equally interesting, particularly from a European perspective, were cross-border traders and teams of construction and agricultural workers from Manchuria and elsewhere in northern China to the Russian Far East, where they quickly became an essential part of the local economy. In fact, in the 1990s the Chinese presence grew so much that it sparked considerable anxiety among the Russians, who suddenly remembered that the Chinese empire had involuntarily ceded these territories to an expanding Russia under unequal treaties in the nineteenth century. From the Russian Far East, Chinese shuttle traders rapidly made their way to Moscow, which, as in the period just before World War I, became a hub for further mobility into eastern and central Europe (de Tinguy 1999; Shkurkin 2000; Portyakov 1996).

In the last few years, migrants from northeastern and northern China have migrated directly to western Europe as well, either as students or illegally. Although this phenomenon still awaits research, it does seem to suggest that the increasing connections between Chinese migratory flows are part of a distinct Chinese pattern of globalization in which it is increasingly artificial to distinguish between migration from areas with and without a tradition of overseas migration, or to distinguish Chinese illegal migration from legal migration for study, work, or family reunification.

Getting In: The United Kingdom

Most Fujianese migration to the United Kingdom is illegal. Migration relies on brokers and involves an asylum application, which is as a rule rejected.[9] This is due to a number of circumstances. First, Fujianese migrants to Britain come mainly from the counties of Changle and Fuqing in Fuzhou prefecture. As was discussed in detail in the previous chapter, in the Fuzhou area emigration is more tightly controlled than in Sanming prefecture in western Fujian, whose migrants specialize in eastern and southern Europe. Second, owing to the geographical obstacles associated with getting to Britain, clandestine migration there requires more professional organization than to continental European countries. Third, until recently an asylum application in Britain carried an important practical benefit: asylum applicants obtained the right to work after six months in the country.[10]

As heirs to the world's foremost colonial power, the British state and society have been more candid about the country's multiethnic nature and the realities of immigration than other European countries. Although there has until recently been no recognition of immigration as a necessary or desirable process and no systemic approach to immigration, since the 1960s many ad hoc initiatives have resulted in large numbers of immigrants from the Caribbean, the Indian subcontinent, Africa, Southeast Asia, and Hong Kong. Many of these initiatives were connected to decolonialization. Several have also served to satisfy labor demand—for instance, for nurses, teachers, and domestic workers—albeit on a smaller scale than Germany's guest worker scheme in the same period and without a quota for employment visas such as in the United States. Finally, the United Kingdom took its share of refugees, particularly after the wars in Vietnam and more recently the former Yugoslavia.[11]

London's role as a hub of metropolitan life from finance to the arts has attracted additional migrants from all over the world, who now account for one-quarter of the city's population. Urban agglomerations outside of London are much less diverse but often have pockets of Pakistani populations and scattered Chinese residents. Smaller towns and agricultural areas still make an overwhelmingly homogeneous impression but have recently been relying on immigrant (especially eastern

European) workers in agriculture and, increasingly, the construction, packing, tourism, and contract cleaning industries (Glover et al. 2001). Education in the United Kingdom, which is more market-oriented than education in most other European countries, is an obvious destination for the burgeoning numbers who want an English-language education. Glover et al. 2001 estimate that 31 percent of Britain's doctors, 13 percent of nurses, and 70 percent of those occupied in the London restaurant and take-out food business are immigrants.

As a result, the concepts of race relations, racism, immigration, and integration of immigrants have firmly become part of Britain's public discourse, legislation, and institutional structure. There is antidiscrimination legislation, and a number of high-profile nongovernmental organizations (NGOs) help ethnic minorities and migrants. Although, according to the United Nations, the United Kingdom's foreign-born population accounted for only 6.5 percent of the total in 1990 (compared to 7.9 percent in the United States and 10.4 percent in France; see Crisp 1999; United Nations 2001: 29), the Labor government that came to power in 1997 has promoted the idea of a multicolored Britain, and members born in India and Hong Kong were appointed to the House of Lords after its reform. In the 2000s, Britain has also moved in the direction of a more proactive immigration policy, a version of which was delivered in a 2002 government white paper (Home Office 2002).

In the late 1990s, Britain experienced an increase in net immigration (Glover et al. 2001: 22), and immigration, especially "illegal" immigration, became a central theme in politics. Britain has thus come to participate in the global migration debate characterized, on the one hand, by the perception that immigration is needed to compensate for an aging population and declining economic competitiveness and, on the other hand, by calls to curb "abuses" of the asylum system by an increasing number of "illegal" immigrants.

After Germany, the United Kingdom has the largest estimated number of asylum applications in Europe. The number of applications peaked in 2000, when there were 97,200, accounting for 22 percent of the European total and exceeding the number of applications in Germany. This was a rise from 46,015 applications in 1998 and 5,900 in 1987; the number dropped to below Germany's again in the first nine months of 2001. Asylum applicants are concentrated in London. The Greater London authority estimated in 2001 that there were between 352,000 and 422,000 refugees and asylum seekers in London, constituting nearly 5 percent of the population.[12]

The tabloid press reacted with what *The Economist* described as a concerted and virulent campaign against asylum seekers.[13] The 1999 Immigration and Asylum Act (IAA), which went into effect on April 1, 2000, included the provision to disperse asylum applicants across the country and to give them vouchers instead of the previous cash subsistence support. Asylum applicants continue to be eligible for council housing support, and they can apply for a work permit if they have been in the United Kingdom for longer than six months and their asylum applications have not yet been acted on (Glover et al. 2001: 37). In practice, asylum applicants are also free to change residence, since the United Kingdom, unlike some other countries in the European Union, does not require residents to carry identification documents. In the 2000s, partly in response to the Dover case, the government has set up camps for asylum seekers it deems likely to disappear and has attempted to speed up the adjudication of applications—the average wait has been thirteen months—and step up deportations.[14] In 2000, the UK "removed" 46,635 foreigners (Glover et al. 2001). Still, most of these remain free and were in fact not deported. During the first ten months of 2000, only 7,610 of the 58,885 rejected asylum applicants were removed[15]—and several restrictive provisions of the new system have been criticized and challenged in court. As a result, the voucher system was scrapped in 2002.

In 2002 the United Kingdom launched a scheme that for the first time permitted foreigners to enter and eventually live in the UK on the basis of the skills they bring to the country. Foreign entrepreneurs are allowed to enter Britain for up to eighteen months, with six months to establish a business and twelve months to create revenue, cost, and tax data that the Home Office can examine. After four years, they are allowed to apply for permanent residency.[16] Another set of new rules aimed at easing labor shortages stipulated that foreigners who graduate from college in the UK can apply for a work permit without having to leave the country.[17] The government in 1999 also launched a campaign to attract more foreign students to the country (Glover et al. 2001: 35). In 2002, it launched a points-based Skilled Migrant Program similar to programs in Canada and Australia, which allows highly skilled foreigners to come to Britain for employment, self-employment, or entrepreneurship. Furthermore, foreigners legally residing in Britain can apply for their direct family members to join them, and after four years of working there can apply for indefinite permission to remain, a route also available in principle to asylum seekers who have not been removed. Naturalization policy is liberal: foreigners can apply for British citizenship after five years' residence and are allowed to retain their original citizenship as well.

As elsewhere, immigration has become more commercialized. A *Sunday Times* reporter posing as an asylum applicant found several London law firms that encouraged her to submit false asylum claims that they would support for a fee of £1,000. She told the law firms that she had used a fake Italian passport to enter the UK, had not suffered any political repression, and was not in danger in her homeland. She was advised to change her name to the false one in her passport and lie about the route she took to get to Britain.[18] In fact, the Law Society had already shut down several law firms in 1999 for touting their services at entry ports and abusing Legal Aid, the government-funded scheme that pays solicitors for most asylum work, taking on the costs of legal representation for asylum seekers. The British system allows law firms to employ persons without legal education as legal representatives who deal with clients. Often, they are selected for their knowledge of the language of a group of migrants, who come to depend on them because they have no direct contact with the solicitor. Solicitors, in turn, are reluctant to control such interpreters, because they bring in most—indeed, one London immigration law firm told us, *all*—clients. The government has now introduced a licensing system for immigration consultancies.

Getting In: Italy

Traditionally, Italy has been a country of emigration rather than immigration. Since 1980, however, Italy has maintained a positive net migration balance, prefiguring a similar shift ten years later in other southern European countries such as Spain and Portugal (Farina 2002). There were two causes of this shift. First, internal migration from the South, which had provided the factories in northern Italy with the manpower needed for economic development, was gradually coming to an end. Second, industrial production throughout Italy decentralized with the reemergence of small businesses.

Until the end of the 1990s, though, the need for immigrant labor was not recognized, and for about fifteen years immigration was simply accepted as a fact but not regulated. A series of amnesties was offered during the 1980s and 1990s—in 1986, 1989, 1995, and 1998. Amnesties temporarily addressed some of the problems that accompanied large numbers of illegal migrants, but at the same time indirectly attracted additional migrants who hoped to gain legal residency with the next amnesty (Ambrosini 2001).

The 1998 migration law introduced some significant new elements. First, annual quotas were adopted for the entry of foreign workers. In this, Italy is far ahead of the rest of Europe, where most countries continue to deny that they have effectively become countries of immigration, "as if trying to exorcise the symbolism that this definition implies" (Zanfrini 2002). The quota system was put into full effect for the first time in the year 2000 with 63,000 admissions. In 2001, 83,000 admissions were authorized, and a ministerial decree on migration included a modest opening in favor of qualified immigrants with special quotas reserved for professional nurses (2,000 places) and workers in advanced technologies (3,000 places).

A second new element of the 1998 law was the guarantee system, which introduced the figure of the "sponsor." Companies or individuals—not necessarily of Italian citizenship—legally resident in Italy were allowed to sponsor the entry of no more than two foreigners in Italy to facilitate their access to the labor market.[19] In the first two years (2000 and 2001) of the program, most sponsored migrants were foreigners already residing in Italy (Fasano and Zucchini 2002); thus the program has effectively become a way to regularize existing migratory flows (Zanfrini 2001). All in all, in the new management of migratory flows the regulatory procedures have actually encouraged the arrival of migrants who perform low-grade unskilled work, despite the tentative admission of a limited number of nurses and workers in advanced technology sectors.

Entry to Italy for family reunification now accounts for a quarter of the residence permits issued. Family reunification is linked to the stabilization of the immigrant population (see later discussion), and Italian legislation has been particularly liberal on this point. The 1998 migration law allowed family reunification to include parents, grandparents, brothers, and sisters, as well as more distant relatives, as long as the applicant takes responsibility for them (Marazzi 2002).

It is estimated today, approximately twenty years since the arrival of the first immigrants in Italy, that workers born abroad and in regular employment number around 650,000 (Caritas di Roma 2001) and those in irregular employment 360,000 (Reyneri 2000). Immigrant labor has been embedded in the Italian development model, and immigrant workers are found all over the country and even in the smallest Italian firms (Ambrosini 2001; Zanfrini 2001). Research has identified several ways in which immigrant labor plays a crucial role in the Italian economy (Ambrosini 2001; Ambrosini and Zucchetti 2002). First, immigrants are employed in a broad range of industrial sectors and districts, especially small businesses that specialize in a particular product. A second pattern is found in the big cities, especially Milan and Rome, where immigrants provide labor-intensive services, especially domestic help and care for the elderly. Nationally, the number of foreign domestic workers in Italy is close to 50 percent of the total number of registered regular workers; in the provinces of Rome and Milan three out of four domestic workers registered with the Italian national insurance scheme are immigrants (Ambrosini 2001). As in the other family-oriented systems of southern Europe, the demand for family and personal services is particularly strong in Italy, because the public sector cannot satisfy the growing need for domestic help. The third sector where immigrant labor has become vital to the Italian economy is agriculture and tourism, where immigrant labor is employed seasonally and temporarily, particularly during the harvest and tourist seasons.

The geographic distribution of immigrant workers reveals the importance of the North-South divide that continues to characterize the national economy. In recent years immigrant employment has been highest in the Northeast, followed by central Italy. In these areas immigrant labor is employed in a broad range of sectors, including engineering, woodworking, textiles and garments, and leather and shoe-making industries, so much so that "an incipient process of foreign worker inclusion can be observed in the fabric of wide-ranging industrialization . . . producing traditional 'made in Italy' goods" (Zanfrini 2001).

Moreover, since 1998 Italy witnessed growth in immigrant self-employment—albeit modest in comparison with that in other European countries with larger resident migrant populations. The right to be self-employed, however, was denied for almost ten years—from 1989 to 1998—to immigrants from countries with which Italy had not signed reciprocal agreements, creating a considerable obstacle to independent entrepreneurship for many immigrant groups, including Chinese. After this prohibition was lifted in 1998 the number of immigrant enterprises grew quickly. In 2001 in Milan, one of the Italian cities with the largest number of immigrants, approximately 4,000 immigrants had their own businesses, an increase of 57 percent over 1999 (Ambrosini and Zucchetti 2002). Nationally in 2000, approximately 83,000 firms had owners born outside the European Union who had a residence permit for self-employment (Caritas 2001). However, a growing number of immigrants are self-employed in a rather nominal sense by subcontracting simple manufacturing tasks from Italian employers on whom they remain fully dependent (Zanfrini 2001).

In general the immigrant presence in Italy is heading toward stability, as confirmed by data on permanent residents. The number of temporary residence permit holders (a measure of total immigration) in the four-year period 1997–2000 increased by 9 percent; during the same period the number of permanent residents recorded grew annually by 13 percent, showing the strong tendency toward stable immigrant settlement in the country (Blangiardo 2002). The large number of family reunification migrants confirms the trend toward permanent settlement: residence permits for family reasons constitute about 26 percent of all residence permits (Blangiardo 2002; Caritas 2001). The birth rate for children of immigrants in Italy is twice that of Italians, thus compensating for the natural negative growth rate of the Italian population (Farina 2002).

Nevertheless, a growing number of scholars highlight the gap between the inclusion of immigrants in the economy and their lack of integration into the social fabric, evidenced by difficulties in accessing social services, serious housing problems, and cultural marginality (Ceccagno 2001a; Cesareo 2002; Zanfrini 2001). Businesspeople, recognizing the extent to which immigrants are indispensable to the Italian economy, have pushed hardest for their admission. For several years, business associations—those of the North and Northeast in particular—have protested the small annual migrant quotas.[20] Since 1999 the Unioncamere (national association of chambers of commerce) conducted annual investigations into the need for workers from countries outside the European Union, according to which Italian businesses could have taken on 100,000 new immigrants in 2001 (Zanfrini 2002).

In July 2002 the recently elected center-right government in Italy introduced a new immigration amnesty law (law 189 / 2002), according to which one housekeeper per family and an unlimited number of care workers for the elderly or handicapped can be legalized. The sponsorship mechanism was repealed in the law. Another law in September 2002 (195 / 2002) extended the amnesty to all undocumented immigrants who already possess a work contract for employment in Italy. Under this law, those without employment at the end of the two-year duration of their residence permit are permitted to continue residing in Italy for another six months while looking for work, after which they will have to leave the country. This will at least partially meet the objections of employers, although it will not solve the shortage of highly qualified personnel that employers are also concerned about.

The amnesty was implemented in December 2002 and promises to be by far the biggest ever granted. In fact, while the last two amnesties in 1995 and 1998 allowed the regularization of 246,000 and 217,000 immigrants respectively (Carfagna 2002), migrants who have applied for regularization under the 2002 amnesty numbered almost 700,000, of whom around 340,000 work as domestic employees, household help, or assistants for dependent people such as the elderly or handicapped, and about 360,000 who work in other sectors.[21] In mid-October 2002, an additional 20,500 admissions were authorized through the quota system, of which 2,000 were reserved for highly qualified immigrants for self-employment. Finally, in the course of the year 2002 several ad hoc decrees allowed the admission of 56,000 seasonal workers.

Getting In: Hungary

In contrast to the United Kingdom, migration from Fujian to Hungary is overwhelmingly legal, based on business, employment, and family reunification visas, although Hungarian migrants too rely to a large extent on brokers to obtain their visas. As Hungary progressively restricted the issuing of visas during the 1990s—refusing most family reunification visas even to relatives of permanent residents—an increasing number of migrants resorted to clandestine passage from neighboring countries.

In Hungary, as in other more economically developed eastern European countries, the liberalization of border control that followed political democratization in 1988 marked a dramatic increase in mobility, including transit migration and immigration. Ethnic Hungarians from neighboring countries account for most of the foreign population, which was 144,000, or 1.5 percent of the population, in 1997 (Organisation for Economic Cooperation and Development 2001: 50). They are believed to make up a large part of the unreported work force in agriculture and construction. Although in the registered work force their presence is insignificant, the informal sector is estimated to account for one-third of Hungary's economy. Apart from ethnic Hungarians, visible immigrant groups include Chinese, Mongols, Vietnamese, Russian speakers, and Arabs, as well as western Europeans. Most immigrants, except for the Mongols, who are generally low-skilled wage workers, are either entrepreneurs or highly skilled workers. Most of these groups number only a few thousand.

Hungary's English-language tertiary education programs also have attracted a few thousand foreign students. A peculiar, but gradually declining, feature of Hungary's migration landscape is the presence of shuttle traders who trade in consumer goods between markets in Hungary and the neighboring eastern European countries (Wallace, Bedzir, and Chmouliar 1997).

As a neighbor of Ceausescu's Romania and Miloševic's Yugoslavia, Hungary experienced periodic influxes of refugees after it began liberalizing its border controls. Although the number of refugees peaked in 1990, the government and the media became increasingly concerned with "illegal" migration in the late 1990s and early 2000s. This was partly due to pressure from the European Union, which fears losing control over its borders after its future eastward expansion. In the late 1990s, the composition of asylum seekers also shifted to include fewer refugees from the Balkans and more from Asia, fueling arguments about "bogus asylum seekers." In a 2001 survey, 43 percent of a representative sample of Hungarians said they would let no refugees into the country, the highest proportion since the polls started in 1992.[22]

Students, holders of work permits (which can be applied for by employers only), and those with entrepreneurial and long-term family visit visas usually get temporary residence permits valid for one or two years, which can then be extended. There is no formal rule prohibiting a change in visa status, but in practice such adjustment is not allowed. After five years of uninterrupted residence with a residence permit, foreigners can apply for permanent resident status. But permanent residence can be revoked if, for example, the holder is found to evade taxes. In July 2001, 81,000 foreigners—most of them ethnic Hungarians—had permanent residence permits.[23] Temporary residents can purchase state health insurance and have to pay for their children's schooling (although the latter rule is often not enforced). Permanent residents have the same access to health care as citizens. Their children are entitled to free primary education and, until 2001, they had the right to vote in local elections. Naturalization practices are strict: only very few foreigners who are not ethnically Hungarian have obtained citizenship.

The legislation, however, contains clauses that leave so much room to the discretion of the immigration official as to deprive the process of any predictability and transparency. The application of the law has seen swings between more liberal and stricter periods, but overall, beginning in 1992 when the administration first wanted to curtail the unexpected influx of migrants, it has progressively moved toward more and more restriction. At each stage of the process, from visa to permanent residence, procedures take months, and officials arbitrarily require ever more documents, sometimes making applicants queue up for a full day every week. Applicants in the same situations obtain differing rulings from different officials in different years. The issuance of a work or entrepreneur visa does not guarantee the issuance of a residence permit—at least it did not until the reform of the visa system in 2001. Foreign residents do not have the automatic right to bring dependents, even minors, to Hungary. The Budapest City Administration Office suspended the issuance of permanent residence permits to citizens of certain countries, including China, in 2000. Information about immigration procedures is not publicly available, a circumstance that benefits a host of middlemen, many of them former immigration officials. Middle-ranking officials in charge of approving visas and permanent residence permits have been arrested on corruption charges.

Foreigners are subject to arbitrary checks by police, border guards, customs, tax and employment officials, and public land superintendents. Border guards are entitled to enter the homes of foreigners, including permanent residents, to check their documents. Foreigners whose residence title is owner or manager of an enterprise are not allowed to perform any manual work. When employment office inspectors find such managers carrying goods from a warehouse, or sometimes even typing a letter, they frequently fine them or even initiate procedures to cancel their residence permits. Foreigners unable to produce valid residence documents are placed in immigration detention, as are most asylum seekers, who thus are not free to move around the country. Nonwhite foreigners in particular are often subjected to police brutality and extortion.[24]

Discussions on the institutionalization of ethnic pluralism have been limited to so-called traditional minorities, while immigration has been discussed and regulated only in the context of security and diaspora policy toward ethnic Hungarians. Only in 2001 did the government raise the idea of immigration as a source of labor, but this was again directed toward ethnic Hungarians. The only NGO dealing with migrants focuses on care for refugees and has not engaged in public discourse, in which immigrants appear almost exclusively as criminals or shady businesspeople. With the exception of ethnic Hungarians and war refugees from Yugoslavia, statements of government officials have positioned them as criminals or a hazard to economic stability. For instance, despite the fact that foreigners committed fewer than 2 percent of the crimes in Hungary in 1997, Prime Minister Gyula Horn blamed them for most of the crimes (Nyíri 1998a).

Getting Out

Doomsday reports of unending streams of Chinese migrants invariably gloss over the fact that getting out of the People's Republic is still no simple matter. With the partial exception of group tourism to the fifteen Asian countries that have signed agreements with the PRC, any foreign travel involves a protracted fight with multiple obstacles. In the case of group tours, participants get single-use passports that are carried by the group leader and surrendered upon return. Residents of the PRC who are officially registered as dependent family members of overseas Chinese (*qiaojuan*) can get passports on demand. In all other cases, until 2002, getting a private ordinary passport (*yinsi putong huzhao*) was not a right, but required proof of the intended travel itinerary, an invitation from abroad, proof of funds, agreement of the spouse, and for those studying or working at state institutions, agreement of the employer or school. Some schools required students, even graduate students, to withdraw from school in order to obtain permission for private travel abroad. In 2001 the PRC announced that a letter of invitation would no longer be required beginning in 2002, and that the other requirements would be gradually abolished by 2005, starting in selected cities. By that year, all PRC citizens would be able to obtain a passport upon production of their birth and household registration certificates.[25]

Having secured a passport, the next obstacle is to obtain a visa, which for European, North American, and wealthier Asian countries is exceedingly difficult for an ordinary Chinese deprived of official status or connections in the destination country. The most common type of cross-border mobility is tourism. But desirable tourist destinations, for fear of immigration and out of a general distrust of the PRC, practically close the door on Chinese who declare themselves tourists.[26]

Faced with such severe barriers to mobility, disguising the real motive or destination of travel becomes commonplace. Travel for tourism, study, or business becomes increasingly indistinguishable from travel for migration, and a burgeoning industry has emerged to cater to both. An anecdotal illustration of this can be found in a Chinese guidebook on Germany, which contains information about how to obtain not only tourist but also student visas, as well as visas for official passports, and introduces this section with the sentence, "There are three kinds of visas that are relatively easy to obtain for Chinese citizens" (Jin 2000).

For Chinese who live far from the metropolitan centers, do not have overseas Chinese relatives, do not have connections with officials, and know little about the procedures involved, obtaining a passport may already seem an insurmountable obstacle, and they are likely to engage the services of middlemen. These can be travel agencies, labor export companies, or individuals, who may or may not employ fully legal methods to obtain the passport, depending on their own convenience or the client's need. The issuance of passports in Fujian is periodically more tightly controlled—and occasionally suspended in some places— as part of national measures to curb illegal emigration. This happened in Sanming in the late 1990s, overriding the local government's generally supportive attitude toward migration, and in Fuzhou after the Dover incident in 2000 for all applicants younger than 35 years of age. As a result, middlemen often had to obtain passports for their clients from Yunnan and other provinces. Another way around the restrictions is to obtain a service passport. According to Hong Ye, secretary-general of the Moscow Association of Overseas Chinese (Mosike Huaqiao Huaren lianhehui), "Most Fujianese come with service passports but don't want to go back."[27]

According to our informants in Europe, there are three kinds of service passports in the PRC, all of which are issued by the Ministry of Foreign Affairs through the "work unit" and higher public security (police) departments.[28] The first one, *waijiao huzhao* ("diplomatic passport"), is issued to officials on a diplomatic mission and is not relevant to migrants. The second one is called *gongwu huzhao* (a passport for official business, commonly referred to as *da gong huzhao*, "big service passport"), and is intended for officials on missions that are not diplomatic. The third is called *yingong putong huzhao* (a normal passport for public use, commonly referred to as *xiao gong huzhao*, "little service passport") and is issued to students, researchers, and personnel from state companies sent abroad on cultural or economic exchange programs. While little service passports do not carry the same privileges as big service passports and cannot legally be renewed abroad, they still offer greater protection from the scrutiny of immigration officials than normal passports for private use (*yinsi putong huzhao*), which are issued by the local public security office. Little service passports may be relatively easy to obtain—although more difficult in Fujian than elsewhere—for instance by joining an overseas "delegation" of a state enterprise (J. Chin 2002).

The difficulties of obtaining a passport pale in comparison with getting a visa. Most European countries will not issue a visa of any kind to a PRC citizen unless the applicant has (1) an invitation from a relative, friend, corporate sponsor, employer, or school in the destination country; (2) a financial guarantee; and (3) proof of his or her relationship with the inviting party. Invitations from direct relatives and local companies have the greatest chance to succeed.

Of course, such documents can be and are sold and forged, and it is here that migration brokers are instrumental. Indeed, in some countries they appear to be vital. In both Italy and the UK, legal foreign residents are entitled to bring spouses and dependent children to join them. Hungary, though, does not consider family reunification an automatic basis for the right to enter the country. Not a single relative, including spouses and children, of our informants from Fujian in Hungary was able to obtain a visa for family members to join them during the period of our investigation (1999–2001). By contrast, those who engaged the services of middlemen had a mix of success and failure. They paid a fee of US$2,000 to US$4,000, but only after a visa had been issued.

Shopkeeper Luo Bing from Mingxi (see Case 1) is one of many Fujianese in Hungary who consider the involvement of brokers indispensable. In 1999, after two years in Hungary and holding a long-term residence permit, Luo sent his wife the documents necessary to apply for a long-term visitor visa, but she was reluctant to apply because she was afraid of a rejection. Luo said:

It seems that now you can't get a long-term family visit visa. They used to give TM-2 family visit visas for over 300 days, but now people get only M-2 visas for three months, and then they can't extend their stay. That's useless. Do you know anyone in the police who can arrange long-term visas? I heard of a Hungarian woman who does this for US$2,000; she is acquainted with the minister of the interior. You send the invitation, the person applies for a visa at the embassy in Beijing, and when they send the application for approval to the Ministry of the Interior they already know. If you get a long-term visa you pay; if not, she returns the money. For example, a relative of my brother's has come this way.[29]

As his wife expected, the application was rejected, and in December 1999 Luo paid US$2,000 to a northern Chinese who said he would ensure that his wife's long-term visitor visa was approved. Luo told us: "My wife sent the papers to the embassy herself. Now they have already faxed the request to the Ministry of the Interior in Budapest. The snakehead is only taking care of the part here at the ministry. [If my wife doesn't get the visa] he says he will return the money."[30]

In 2001 the issuance of visas was even further restricted: except for official delegations, practically all applications were rejected. Brokers then resorted to other means, as in the following case.

A Chinese couple in Budapest turned to a broker to get their nephew a student visa to Hungary. The broker helped him apply to take an engineering course at a major university in Budapest, but his visa application was rejected twice. Because they were not immediate relatives, the couple felt that applying for a visitor visa with an invitation from them had no chance of success. Instead, the broker obtained a business visit visa at the Hungarian consulate in Hong Kong using an application from a Chinese company in Hungary and also paying a bribe: according to the rules, only Hong Kong residents can obtain visas at the Hong Kong consulate.[31]

Although migrants do not attribute much importance to the distinctions between various kinds of migration brokers, and may call any of them a "snakehead," brokers can be individuals, travel agencies, labor export agencies, or migration service consultancies. The way migrants get in touch with each type of broker is different, as may be the latter's degree of involvement in the execution of the migration project (cf. Schloenhardt 1999). It must be borne in mind that different types of brokers are parts of the same phenomenon rather than either/or options. Brokers of different types can be linked to each other or can act on one another's behalf. We discuss each type of brokerage in some detail in the following section.

Individual Migration Brokerage

The institutionalization of migration brokerage has been a gradual process. Individual brokers probably have the largest share of the migration business and have been most frequently described (K. Chin 1999; Liang 2001; Liang and Ye 2001; Zhang and Chin 2001). In the Wenzhou area, migration brokerage in the mid-1980s was conducted by relatives, and those who did not have relatives abroad sought to invent them through adoption or fake marriages (M. Li 2001). At first, people assisted with such transactions out of friendship; only later did they start involving money.

Initially, migration brokerage focused on destination countries that already had migrants from a particular area. For Europe this was mainly southern Zhejiang; for central Fujian the destination was chiefly the United States and to a much lesser extent Britain and the Netherlands, which had a small number of (former) students and sailors from Fujian, the latter of whom had jumped ship between the 1940s and the 1960s. These resident Fujianese, though few in number, played an important role in shaping the Fujianese elites in these countries. Yang King Far, executive vice-president of the Fujianese association in the Netherlands, estimates that former Fujianese sailors in the Netherlands brought over 500 or 600 families in the 1970s. Most of the children of these families married men and women from China and in turn brought their families to the Netherlands in the 1980s. In this way, a few thousand Fujianese families established themselves in the Netherlands.[32]

The sense of duty to the family no doubt motivated people to assist with the migration of relatives. The inviting parties were also of course motivated by economic benefit. By this time, most operated Chinese restaurants and were interested in attracting cheap coethnic labor, which they had trouble finding locally. Yang King Far said that, in the 1980s, there were already 200 Fujianese-owned restaurants in the Netherlands, and each sponsored one or two workers from China.

In urban areas lacking the kin-based tradition of chain migration, such networks were also formed by students and other highly skilled migrants. In Britain, as in the United States or Australia, a number of students, or migrants who claimed to be students, were granted indefinite leave to remain after the Tian'anmen Square crackdown in 1989, making it possible for them to sponsor relatives to join them.

A vice-president of the Fu Tsing American Association, for instance, taught at a middle school in Fuqing. He went to the United States illegally in 1990, at about the same time that his sister went to the Netherlands and his brother to France. After two years he obtained political asylum based on persecution after the 1989 crackdown, and then sponsored his wife, children, and other relatives to join him in the United States. After washing dishes at a restaurant for a few months, he realized he could, as he put it, "use my English and my brains to do migration work [*gao yimin*]" and has been doing that ever since. In fact, he started "doing migration" even though he did not yet have papers himself. "Do you think the bosses around this table all have papers?" he exclaimed. "Not necessarily! In America, even millionaires can be without papers!"[33]

In the early 1990s, migration brokerage became particularly common among entrepreneurial migrants and students in eastern Europe. They were able to communicate in the local language and, having started by issuing invitations to their relatives and friends, realized that this new line of business could supplement their incomes. Many told clients what merchandise to bring with them, then bought it from them and resold it, thus combining the "people business" (*rentou shengyi, zuo ren*) with trade (*zuo huo*). In other words, for most migrants, migration brokerage was one of several profitable businesses that complemented one another. Most migration brokers subsequently expanded their services to helping new migrants apply for residence permits. Having accumulated considerable capital, many of the early migration brokers subsequently opened restaurants or moved to North America as investor immigrants, or both.

The early brokers in eastern Europe arranged for the documents needed to get a passport in China and go to an eastern European country, and some also helped migrants cross clandestinely into western Europe. The latter was a much higher-risk activity, requiring a higher degree of familiarity with the terrain and more dedication because it involved getting in touch with local human smugglers or even recruiting them from among local drivers (Nyíri 1998b: 355). The majority, who engaged in migration brokerage only as a way to make extra cash in addition to their main businesses, limited themselves to eastern Europe.

In his book on the Chinese in eastern Europe, Mao Chun reports on a former student in Austria turned shuttle trader in Hungary, who first issued invitation letters to Hungary for US$1,000. His acquaintances resold the letters for US$2,500 to US$3,000. By June 1989, the student was issuing 100 invitations a month, with a pricing system based on the customer's place of residence. Clients from Fujian, Zhejiang, and Guangdong provinces, traditional migrant homelands where going abroad was most strictly controlled, paid US$6,000 to US$10,000, those from Shanghai and Manchuria US$3,000 to US$6,000, and those from Beijing and inland provinces US$2,000 to US$3,000 (Mao 1992: 4–5). Ten thousand dollars might seem like a high sum for an invitation that, in the absence of a visa requirement, was at the time needed only to get a passport, but it was still several times cheaper than what brokers in China were charging for passage to western Europe, North America, or Japan (Smith 1997).

In comparison with the kin-based networks that spawned early Fujianese migration to western Europe, in eastern Europe both a sense of family duty and economic need for cheap labor were less important for these higher-educated, more mobile brokers, who conceived of this activity as a more purely commercial enterprise. They still recruited clients mainly via acquaintanceship ties, but some also took out newspaper advertisements, particularly in Chinese-language papers in their countries of residence, and sometimes also in China. The latter practice was possible outside the main southern provinces seen as the hotbed of illegal emigration, where the authorities closely monitored such activities.

Even in areas with highly developed migration brokerage such as Fujian, fees charged by individual migration brokers differed greatly, depending not only on the demand and difficulty of obtaining a passport in the client's place of residence, but also on the client's relationship to the broker and the extent of services offered. As in classical migration chains, close relatives were very often invited free of charge and then sponsored until they could stand on their own feet. Services included in the price could range from a simple invitation to a full package of documents needed to apply for a visa to obtaining a passport; applying for a visa on the client's behalf; and arranging clandestine passage to western Europe. The degree of irregularity of methods employed varied accordingly.

Clients evaluate brokers based on their reliability, quality of service, and price. As in any unregulated and semilegal business, breach of trust by either the broker or the client sometimes occurs. Not only are clients vulnerable to the broker, but the broker is also vulnerable to his clients: a bad reputation can seriously damage a broker's business. A man from Tianjin city in northern China came to Hungary in 1998 after noticing a broker's advertisement in a Tianjin newspaper. The broker worked with his relatives in Hungary and charged RMB 100,000 (US$8,300), of which the client had to pay US$2,000 (RMB 17,000) up front as a deposit. But because the client had no money, he paid only another US$2,000 upon arrival, and when he found out that "it actually cost only RMB 10,000 to get here" refused to pay any more. In the event, the broker was unable to collect the agreed amount. According to a friend of the client, "The snakehead won't dare to touch us. Now that we know people and the situation here, he has more to fear than we do."[34]

Many individual migration brokers in China are people who have returned from abroad and now use their local knowledge and connections there. One man who returned to Mingxi after spending some time in Hungary and Italy has been helping people go to those two countries. His job, he said, was limited to getting people in Europe to send the necessary documents. His clients in China had to go to their local public security bureau to obtain the passport and then to the Hungarian embassy in Beijing to get the visa. At the time of the interview, he complained that it was getting more and more difficult to obtain the documents. Also, more and more people were engaged in this business, depressing his profits.[35]

Like this informant, many other Chinese in eastern Europe pulled out of migration brokerage after it became more difficult and risky in the early 1990s, and invested the money they had earned in other businesses. A few became full-time migration brokers and developed contacts with brokers transporting people from China to western Europe, as well as with local drivers who could smuggle people across the border into western Europe.

In the second half of the 1990s and the early 2000s it became increasingly difficult to get people from China to Europe, legally or illegally, because of tighter immigration policies and border controls as well as the crackdown on brokers in China. Risks rose, and so did prices, while the number of customers willing to suffer the hardship and risks of illegal border crossings appeared to drop. To lure clients back, brokers increasingly took on the risks of failure. According to James Chin, in the Fuzhou area,

> they abolished the practice of asking for a 5 percent deposit before departure. Migrants thus did not have to pay a cent until they reached their destination. Furthermore, the fine of RMB 5,000 [levied by Chinese authorities for illegally leaving China] could be claimed back from the snakehead, provided the client did not inform the authorities of the snakehead's name. Needless to say, such new practices greatly reduced the financial risk carried by migrants and once again encouraged a new flow of migration. (J. Chin 2002: 249)

With such arrangements, brokers exposed themselves to even greater chances of bankruptcy and needed ever more capital to ensure liquidity. According to an informant, a major broker from Qingtian in southern Zhejiang told her in 1999 or 2000 that he had lost approximately US$100,000 when ten of his clients were apprehended at Beijing Airport; their accents had aroused the border guard's suspicion that they were not from the places indicated on their passports.[36] Smaller brokers are in even more dire straits. One of them complained to one of our informants that he had to pay monthly electricity and water bills and haul large sacks of rice every day for the sixty people he was currently housing because they could not move on to western Europe. Normally, he complained to our informant, a "guest" (*keren*) paid him US$2,000 to US$3,000, from which he still had to pay local drivers and other personnel, and he counted himself lucky if he earned US$1,000 to US$2,000 on a client. At the top of his business he had had 100 to 200 clients a year. Now he had to pay an additional US$1,500 in bribes alone to bail out clients who had been apprehended and taken to immigration community shelters, leaving him without any profit at all or even with a net loss.[37]

Because of such bottlenecks and the risk of clients in the end not paying up, groups of Fujianese have appeared in Hungary who buy shipments of clients from brokers, much like financial companies buy bad debts, and then attempt to collect the money from them. At other times, informants say, groups from Fuqing buy clients from poorly paid local helpers of the Chinese brokers, such as drivers, who are offered US$1,000 a head instead of the US$100 they would have received from the broker. Others help clients escape from community shelters, or simply snoop around "safe houses" and kidnap migrants.[38] If the client is kidnapped and someone pays ransom for him or her, the original broker not only loses his money, but will also be asked to compensate family members in China for the loss. The only way out for a broker is to hire a rival gang to free his clients, but they are often unable to do so. We would like to emphasize that these kidnappers do not engage in migration brokerage, but merely prey on it.

Labor Export Agencies, Travel Agencies, and Migration Service Companies

Labor export agencies and other fully or partly state-owned enterprises in China licensed to recruit for overseas employers receive special prerogatives in obtaining passports. Migration agencies and migration consultancies, by contrast, are usually small and private and receive no such prerogatives, although they may want to make their clients believe they do.

Mao relates the story of Pu, a deputy department head for eastern Europe of an influential state enterprise in China involved in labor and construction projects (Mao 1992: 137–43). The enterprise had the right to trade in foreign currency and handle private passports. But since the mother company's overseas investment proposals had not been approved, the company ordered Pu to apply for a private passport to eastern Europe himself and invest there in his own name.[39] He chose to set himself up in Leningrad. Pu held an MBA degree and spoke English and Russian.

The first contract Pu signed was for setting up a farm jointly with a certain Russian province. Pu's company provided sixty Chinese peasants on two-year work contracts. Pu attracted the attention of Zhejiang, Fujian, and Cantonese migration brokers operating in eastern Europe, whose biggest bottleneck was obtaining passports. At that time, they earned US$10,000 to US$20,000 per customer. Pu's mother company could obtain a passport in as little as three and no more than thirty days as long as there was a letter guaranteeing employment accompanied by a registration document from a company abroad. Pu and the brokers provided the necessary paperwork from abroad, while Pu's mother company took care of the passport application process. Because it was difficult to obtain passports in coastal provinces, Pu's company applied for them elsewhere. Within half a year, Pu procured over 1,000 passports. For each passport, Pu received US$1,000 on top of the official "labor management fee." At the same time, the party committee of his company called on employees to learn from him.[40]

The role of labor export companies is not limited to Fujian, Zhejiang, or other traditional sending areas. According to Marc Paul, some migrants from Northeast China in Paris reported that their superiors put them in touch with "semi-official" labor export agencies and encouraged them to go abroad when their state enterprise had to lay off employees (Paul 2002). One informant of Paul's paid RMB 53,000 to such an agency for a passport, visa, and ticket to Paris.

There has been a minor boom in Chinese *travel agencies* in several European countries, particularly Germany and Hungary, since the late 1990s. Chinese-language newspapers in these countries are full of advertisements of travel agencies. Some primarily sell air tickets to local Chinese, but many also deal with incoming travel and offer visas. Chinese tour guides we met in Berlin say that these agencies also often act as intermediaries in obtaining invitations necessary to get a business visa. Furthermore, at least one company openly advertises that service.

Travel agencies have had a large share of the Chinese migration business in Russia, in part because overland group tourism between the bordering provinces of China and Russia was exempt from a visa requirement between 1993 and 2000. On the Chinese side, this business appears to be controlled by travel agencies in the Northeast (consisting of the three provinces of Heilongjiang, Jilin, and Liaoning, which are also known as Manchuria). Travel agents in Moscow and Chinese tour guides in Vladivostok, on the Russian side of the border, told us that although the number of travelers from the south of China has been increasing, they are forced to go through travel agencies in the Northeast to arrange the tours and for passports.[41]

According to the manager of a Russian travel agency in Moscow, there are two ways in which Fujianese travel to the West through Russia. One is to use tourist invitations for two to three weeks on a single-use regular passport for private use, first to Blagoveshchensk across the border in the Russian Far East and then on to Russia on domestic flights. Another is to use business invitations that entitle the applicant to visas valid for three months and longer. However, in his experience, travelers on such visas spend their three months in Russia and then go back. Some, though, obtain one-year residence permits from the Russian immigration authority (UVIR, the Visa and Registration Directorate), although it is technically not allowed to change one's visa status once in the country.

Many business invitees come with service passports. The business partner of one of our informants was a travel agency in China based in Fujian with branches all over the country. The Beijing and Harbin branches handled tourism to Russia. The Harbin branch, according to our informant, was known to arrange for service passports for people wanting to travel abroad: "I saw a[n ethnic] Korean woman at the [Russian] embassy [in Beijing] with a service passport; they asked her who issued her passport, and she told them the travel agency." The Russian travel agency of our informant was responsible for getting the visas. In 1999 the agency processed approximately 150 tourist visa and fifty business visa applications, approximately half of which were from Fujian. This share, the manager emphasized, was probably so high because their Chinese partner agency was based in Fujian.[42]

Migration service companies, which have various names (*yimin guwen gongsi, yimin shiwusuo*, and so on), advertise their services both inside and outside China, and more recently on the Internet and through mass-distributed e-mail messages. In immigration countries where there are Chinese-born lawyers, such as in the United States and the United Kingdom, these are sometimes law firms, but most of the time they are simple middleman agencies, often with ties to non-Chinese legal firms or immigration companies.

In the destination countries, these firms perform paralegal work, translations, accounting, and other services for their clients, but they also offer assistance in leaving China. To take an example from an advertisement in the fifty-seventh anniversary booklet of the Fukien American Association, published in New York in 1999, the Huamei Yimin Ruji Gongsi (Chinese American Immigration and Naturalization Company) offers the following services:

Chinese and American passports and validity extensions, letters of sponsorship for invitations to the U.S.; fast and complete procedures for sending children back to China for their upbringing; complete services for going back to China for marriage and spousal immigration procedures; all kinds of authorizations and fiancée letters; application and complete procedures for naturalization; travel documents; documents for return to America (for asylum applicants who have not yet received green cards); all visas and extensions; extension or replacement of green cards and declarations; marriages and divorces in China and the U.S.; home and business loans . . .

Such companies are also active in China itself. In a 1997 investigation, Guangzhou city authorities found hundreds of them, most of which were not licensed for the emigration business. Some of these companies were state-owned; others were offices of companies registered abroad, and others were private. One Hong Kong–based investment company was licensed for car parts exports, but called itself the "XX Immigration Counseling Company." Some companies tried to look respectable by posing as state organs or multinational corporations, renting luxury offices or government guesthouses, organizing seminars on study abroad and immigration, printing glossy booklets, and inviting former foreign immigration officials or famous lawyers as immigration advisers. Some had offices in Canada or the United States, or had their headquarters registered there. But most had only one room or not even that, and many absconded with their customers' money, while the latter were waiting for their visas. The companies charged high "consultation fees" and "information fees" for each step of a visa application. The fee for a fake invitation letter or sponsor's guarantee was RMB 2,000 to RMB 3,000, and for a passport from some small country, more than US$30,000. Some companies passed business, employment, or two-year Canadian visas off as immigrant visas. They also offered fraudulent documents about relatives abroad, forged invitation letters, and even forged passports and visas.[43]

Although the Guangzhou survey can reasonably be expected to highlight the negative aspects of the business, the level of detail provided by the report presents a credible picture. Other sources, moreover, provide similar descriptions. After Dover, British authorities no-

ticed that some brokers provided clients with forged university diplo-
mas and language exam certificates to apply for student visas.[44] Advertisements have appeared in Chinese newspapers of companies that offer bank letters certifying the presence of HK$500,000 (US$42,000) in
the bearer's account; the cost of this service is HK$500 (US$42).[45]

Young, a restaurant worker in London Chinatown from Changle in
Fuzhou prefecture, says: "My business partner chatted with a person
who worked at a state-owned company—but not a labor export company; he doesn't know what its profile was—in Fuzhou city." This
man told Young's partner that he could help Young get into a school in
England. "Because he worked at a government company, with official
stamps on papers, I believed him." The price he asked was the same as
the usual broker's price to England, but said it included tuition fees.
The man gave Young a service passport in Young's name. Young flew
to the Netherlands and then took a train to England in 1997. The broker met him at the railway station and sent him to Birmingham, where
the school was supposed to be, but "I realized there was no school.
The snakehead had cheated me. We were angry and tried to look for
him, but in vain."[46]

It may appear that the unequal but mutual vulnerability of migration broker and customer to each other's breaches of trust is created by
the fact that the migration business, while not necessarily illegal in itself, is not recognized as a fully bona fide business either. From the
standpoint of the migrant, however, the role of trust and the risk of the
other side's reneging on an agreement do not necessarily appear
greater than in other transactions: workshop owners in Italy may with-
hold their workers' wages; clients may refuse payment for goods received from importers; debtors may refuse the repayment of loans.
Such experiences are part of everyday business for Chinese, at least in
eastern and southern Europe. Only in a very few cases do they attempt
to seek legal redress: in most cases they wait and negotiate; in others
they may enforce their claim through threats or complaints with the
Chinese embassy or authorities in China. Thus, in this respect too, the
relationship with a migration broker may not be that different from any
other business transaction. This does not apply, however, to the steps of
migration where clients risk exposure to physical danger or violence—
including rape, which many women know is one hazard of illegal migration. Migrants are keenly aware of the dangers of traveling in trucks
or holds of ships. Many refuse such means of transportation and turn to
brokers who promise that the whole trip will be made by air.

Flexibility of Routes, Choices of Destination, and Alternatives

In the early 1990s, commercial migration brokerage spread and became increasingly disconnected from kin networks, sometimes even clashing with them. It became common for people to migrate without notifying in advance the—sometimes very remote—relative in the destination country, hoping that the latter would pay the fee for passage when confronted with a fait accompli (M. Li 2001). Despite more numerous commercial migration brokerages and less kin-based assistance, however, many migrants to Europe use the resources of their own family and acquaintance networks as well as commercial brokers for particular tasks or parts of the journey as needed, rather than getting the "package deals" typical for many Chinese migrants to North America. One reason is that the journey to Europe is often in part overland via eastern and southeastern Europe. Migrants can more easily stop along the way, perhaps even find temporary employment, and wait for an opportunity to move on. The trip to America, by contrast, is either a direct one or through Latin American or Caribbean countries where new migrants are less well established. Migration routes to and across Europe depend more on circumstances encountered along the way: economic opportunities, immigration policies, availability of contacts in particular countries, or simply chance.

Xu, an informant in Prato, recounted his own rather complicated story that illustrates this point well. In 1995, he said,

I got out of China with an official passport. A fake one. I mean it had my details, but a snakehead got it for me. We only learned later that he got it in Ningde prefecture [north of Fuzhou]. . . . I spent a week in Hong Kong, in Clear Water Bay. Hong Kong is beautiful. Then I went to the Ukraine. I spent three months in Kiev, then I took a boat from Odessa to . . . let's see . . . Romania.
Question: A big or small boat?
Xu: A small boat. At that time I still had the official Chinese passport, and you didn't need a visa to Romania with that.
Question: So why did you have to cross the border illegally?
Xu: There are safety considerations for the snakehead. . . . From Romania I went to Greece, and from Greece with a large boat to Italy. That was dangerous because [by then] I had a Japanese passport. The Italians caught me at the border and returned me to Greece. Then they put me in prison for four months. I was there together with two Englishmen, Mark and Michael. There were very good, really very good. To this day, it is them that I thank most. Even from Prato, I have called them. I learned some colloquial English from them. So my boss [in Prato] asked me whether I used to teach English. He noticed that I

could talk a bit in English when I was dealing with Italian customers. He thought I had taught English. . . . Michael and Mark were drug smugglers. They told me that they had traveled between Hong Kong, Greece, and Britain smuggling drugs. But in Greece they were caught and sentenced to six years. At that time they were going to be released. The father of one of them had already come to Greece to take him home. . . . Eventually the Greek police took me to the Turkish border at night and told me to go to the other side. I didn't know what was happening; they were pointing their guns at me. Then it turned out they were helping me cross into Turkey!

Question: Why do you think they did that?

Xu: We didn't know! We still don't know! The Greeks had some conflict with the Turks, maybe that's why. On the Turkish side I got caught, returned to Greece, then the Greeks returned me to Turkey again. For three days I was there wandering in the mountains without eating. Finally I ran into an Iraqi who was in the human smuggling business. He told me how to take a bus to Ankara. In Ankara, we felt very ragged and were very hungry. Finally we found a run-down hotel. We explained to the owner that we were tourists, and all our money and tickets had been stolen, and the owner let us stay. Then we started asking around where there was a Chinese restaurant, because usually Chinese restaurants are in touch with snakeheads. Eventually we found one, but in that restaurant they didn't know any snakeheads.

Question: Who ran that restaurant?

Xu: Someone from Harbin. He had been living there for fifteen years or so. He told us to go to a restaurant in Istanbul; there we would find snakeheads. With that new group of "human snakes" (*renshe*, smuggled migrants) we went to Egypt. When we left Turkey we used a Chinese passport, but when we arrived in Egypt we used a Korean one, because with that one you didn't need a visa.

Question: So you had two passports with you?

Xu: Yes. But in Egypt there was some trouble. We didn't get caught, but there was some trouble with the snakehead, it became dangerous, and we had to go back to Turkey. For the second time it was OK, and we flew from Egypt to Austria, and then from there to Italy. My older sister's husband came to Venice to fetch me. It took me eleven months to arrive here.[47]

Conclusion

Hungary and Italy in the early 1990s were relatively easy to get into: Italy because of its regular amnesties and Hungary because it exempted Chinese from the visa requirement. The UK generally was and remains the most popular destination country in Europe, probably for a mixture of reasons that include its association with the imagery of Anglo-Saxon modernity familiar to the migrants from the media and the greater freedom of movement and employment that asylum applicants and other undocumented foreigners enjoy. This translates into a perception of "better human rights" and appears to override the scarcity of jobs, low chances of regularization, and lower living standards Fujianese currently face in Britain than in other European countries.[48] Many Chinese apply for asylum in the UK, but few do so in Italy. In the UK, an asylum application is for many Fujianese the most convenient way of legalizing their status (albeit possibly only temporarily) and getting a work permit. By contrast, in Italy, an asylum application is not necessary for employment and eventual legalization. This suggests that migrants see the asylum process as an avenue for immigration rather than a remedy for injustice in the home country.

Fujian migrants choose their preferred destination on the likelihood of actually getting there, expected income, and the presence of relatives or friends. At the receiving end, visa requirements, perceived ease of obtaining refugee status, and amnesties for illegal migrants all play an important role in directing Fujianese (and other Chinese) migrants to particular countries at particular times, either directly from China or from other countries in Europe. The inability to migrate to the first-choice country, or new opportunities to migrate somewhere else, can easily change migrants' minds. Under these circumstances, brokers, eager to expand their market, play an important role in maintaining the flow of migrants by searching for new client populations, destinations, and routes. However, brokers are merely service providers to migrants already determined to go. In the final analysis, developments and circumstances in sending and receiving areas are the crucial factors explaining the nature, volume, and direction of flows.

The Wu Siblings: Workshop Owners in Italy

WU SI, NUMBER FOUR of five siblings, was a teacher at a big kindergarten in Mingxi town. Her husband, Bing, is from Youxi, a county that borders Mingxi, where he was a high-school physics teacher at Mingxi First Upper Secondary School. Wu Si's eldest brother, Wu Yi, the second-oldest sibling, was an English teacher at the same school between 1986 and 1990. The father of the Wu siblings was a watch repairman. Bing and Yi graduated from the same vocational college, Sanming Teachers' College.[1]

The first one of the family to migrate was Wu Yi. He left China in 1990 and arrived in Italy in September, just missing the deadline for the 1990 regularization. Wu Yi explains the "genealogy" of his migration like this. There was once a bamboo mat weaver called Hu who had come from Zhejiang to a village in Mingxi a long time ago.[2] He went to Italy, where he may have had some relatives. His son went to Italy around 1987, along with a certain Hu Zhiming. Hu Zhiming "received" (*jie*) his friend Luo; Luo "received" Xiao and Liu Jia; Liu "received" his brother Liu Yi.[3]

A third Liu brother, Liu Bing, was a colleague of Wu Yi's at Mingxi First Upper Secondary School. Wu Yi had originally applied to study in Japan in 1988 and received his passport, but his visa application was rejected because his guarantor in Japan turned out to be "fake." Because his colleague Liu Bing already had a passport, he was looking for a place to go. After he heard that Liu Yi had reached Italy, Wu Yi inquired with Liu Yi's brother Liu Bing and then called Liu Yi, who "basically" agreed to "receive" Wu Yi.

There was the problem of getting an exit permit. "You don't have to go to the same country as your visa," Wu Yi heard from Liu Bing, who also told him that it was easy to get a Ugandan visa; many others were getting Tanzanian visas. So he got a Ugandan visa. At the Ugandan embassy, he met a man who asked him where he wanted to go. He said to Italy. The man told him how to do that. "At that time illegal migration was a really scary crime," said Wu Yi, "so we didn't want that." So he went to Hungary, which required no visa, via Mongolia and the Soviet Union, changing trains in Kiev. He stayed in Budapest for only half a day and went on to Yugoslavia, and from there to Italy. In Hungary he met a man from Zhejiang, and they went to Italy together. The man helped Wu Yi get a job at a leather workshop in Florence, which was owned by a Zhejiangese.

Wu Si and her younger brother Wu Xiao followed in 1991. All of them went legally to Russia and Hungary, and illegally crossed into Italy from there. Wu Si stayed in Hungary for twenty days. In retrospect, he said: "Now I think perhaps I should have stayed in Hungary; then perhaps I could have gotten rich. Here I tire myself to death. But at that time we thought Italy was, after all, Italy, and it must be better than Hungary." Wu Yi introduced Wu Si and Wu Xiao to jobs in Florence.

Soon Wu Yi met an Italian man who had a jewelery shop in Turin; he had come to the workshop where Yi worked to order pouches for his jewelery. This Italian hired Yi, who spoke English and by then Italian, to do domestic work and occasionally to help out in his shop.

In 1993, Wu Yi said, "Many Mingxi people went back" from Italy "because they found the work too hard and many 'black' workers were being caught here." Wu Yi also went back via Moscow. "Because we had all left China with visas, we had no problems when we went back." On the way, he stayed long enough in Moscow to get a residence permit, which he used while there to issue an invitation to his sister Wu Lao, the oldest of the five siblings, and some other relatives. In 1994, Wu Lao went to Hungary via Russia. She was planning to go to Italy, but saw that business in Hungary was good and that "she could be her own boss, while in western Europe you have to work for others" and stayed there. The same year, Wu Xiao, who was still in Italy, decided that work in Italy was too hard for him and went to Hungary to join his sister Wu Lao. Together they now rent a pavilion at Four Tigers Market.

Soon after Wu Yi's return to China, his Italian employer visited Mingxi and Fuzhou wanting to do business there, and Yi helped him as an interpreter. Yi also got married when he returned: "No one had wanted me before, but overseas Chinese are rich, so it was easy to find a wife," he explained. In 1995, Yi left China again and went to Bulgaria, where he had some friends, "because it was easy to get a visa. Whenever it is easy to get a visa somewhere, lots of Chinese go there, and then it stops being easy. At that time Hungary wasn't so easy anymore; besides, business wasn't as good as it had been there. A new place may be better for business."

In 1995, Wu Yi's former Italian employer invited him to Italy on a business visitor visa, and he returned there. Both Wu Si and Wu Yi were regularized in the 1995 amnesty in Italy. Once this had been done, Yi's Italian employer issued an invitation for Yi's wife to come to Italy on a business visitor visa. Yi's son Marco was born soon afterward. Both Si and Yi visited China in 1997 and 1998. Their visits were separate and limited to Mingxi: "eating with friends, drinking with schoolmates." The local overseas Chinese affairs bureau looked Yi up both times, expressing their wish that the Wu siblings would invest in China. But they only sent money to their parents. In 1998, Si sponsored her older brother Wu Er to come, and in 1999, she went back to fetch her parents, who now live with her in Italy. Wu Lao's child and Wu Er's wife and child are still in Mingxi, but Wu Si and Wu Yi no longer send any money to China.

In 1997, Yi left his employer and opened a garment workshop in Bologna, but the business did not take off, and he closed it. The same year, Si and Bing opened a workshop in Empoli with their own savings and money from friends. In 1998, both Si and Bing got married. In the first year, the workshop relied on the work of the two of them, plus two hired workers. Business improved the following year. In 2000, the workshop had five or six Italian customers, most of them long-term clients who had been placing orders for over a year. Usually, there are no contracts; the client can take his business away at any time. Business contacts with customers are established mainly on the initiative of Si and Bing. They look for advertisements by Italian leather companies and visit them, introducing themselves and offering their services.

The workshop is on the ground floor of a house in the center of town, which they rent together with a flat on the first floor for 3 million lire (US$1,500); altogether, they have a floor space of about 200 square meters. Most of the money the workshop makes goes to pay the rent, monthly payments on the two cars (a pickup truck and a van), and other expenses, so they do not save much.

In 2000, there were eight seamsters, one cutter, and two unskilled workers, all with legal residence papers. A seamster makes around 3 million lire (US$1,500) a month. All employees were from either Mingxi or Youxi, another county in Sanming prefecture, except the cutter, who was from Zhejiang. Three of the seamsters were relatives of Si and Bing's: a younger brother, a brother-in-law, and a cousin twice removed. The brother-in-law had come to Italy in 1998, sponsored by Bing. The brother-in-law obtained his passport as a participant in a business delegation at the invitation of an Italian company, but then applied for a Hungarian visa instead and went to Italy via Hungary. Some migrants from northeastern China also showed up looking for jobs, but "they couldn't take the hard work." In 1999, Er worked at Jia's workshop as a leather cutter, but in 2000 there was little demand for that work because Italian customers began to cut the pieces themselves. Jia already had one cutter and "wasn't too satisfied" with Er, who was inexperienced. Therefore, Er left to work in the same job at another workshop. Si and her father, who is also in Italy, explained that, whether relative or not, Er had been paid by the piece like anyone else, and this was how it should be.

There is no set work schedule; work is allocated according to the customer's needs, but the workday is at least fourteen hours long. Workers are free to go elsewhere and the bosses are free to lay them off. Somebody might get a phone call tomorrow, saying, "Over here the pay is such-and-such, and they need workers," and take their leave. If there is no work in this workshop, it is normal for workers to look for work elsewhere, and then either come back or not. But Si and Bing try to arrange for orders to be back to back, so that there is continuity among the employees. It is not acceptable for a worker just to go off to another workshop and then come back again the next day. Most of the workers are recruited by telephone; some employers also post advertisements in Chinese shops or take out advertisements in Chinese newspapers. Si and Bing have not yet done the latter.

The Wu siblings talk to relatives in China and Hungary over the phone once every fortnight, or whenever there is something to discuss. Lao visited them from Hungary in 1997; this was the first time the siblings had seen each other in seven years. Si, Yi, and Er have never gone back to Hungary: Si wanted to several times, but was too busy. Her parents, however, have visited their children in Hungary. Yi has considered doing business with Hungary, such as exporting Italian Chinese-made leather goods there, but decided that clearing the goods through customs would be difficult because Hungary was not a member of the European Union.

Si and Bing, Yi and his wife and son, and their parents live together in a three-bedroom flat. They spend their leisure time mainly with friends from Mingxi, visiting them in other cities such as Rome, going to restaurants or to the beach for a day or two in the summer and to casinos in Venice or Salerno. They have not joined Chinese associations because, according to Yi: "To do that, people have got to know you to some degree, and you've got to have some economic strength to pay the association fees." A vice-president of the Tuscany branch of the Fujianese Association has repeatedly invited Yi to join, but he refused: "Our work is hard enough as it is; we wouldn't like to get involved in politics." According to Yi, "The newspapers say that they hope organizations can promote understanding toward the Chinese," but "they don't do this work well."

CHAPTER 4

Work and Life in Europe

THE AREA AROUND the provincial capital Fuzhou has dominated recent migration from Fujian province across the globe. The rural counties in the immediate vicinity of Fuzhou city (chiefly Changle, Lianjiang, Minhou, and Mawei; see Map 2) account for the bulk of Fujianese migrants in the United States, where they are often collectively referred to as "Fuzhounese" rather than "Fujianese" both in English and Chinese. In Manhattan's Chinatown it is in fact more common to see restaurants and shops that have "Fuzhou" than "Fujian" in their English names. The county of Fuqing, which constitutes the southernmost tip of the Fuzhou area, has not been very heavily involved in the latest wave of immigration to the United States,[1] although English-language publications occasionally talk about the notorious "Fuk Ching Gang."[2] Chinese generally consider the small Fuqing community relatively affluent, associating them with immigrants from the 1960s and 1970s.

In Europe, by contrast, migrants from Fuqing are probably more numerous than those from any other county of Fuzhou prefecture, though Britain has a large population from other counties as well, particularly Changle. Most migrants in Europe from Fuqing county are from Jiangyin (this group is dominant in Hungary), Jiangjing (dominant in Britain), Yuxi, Sanshan, and Gaoshan townships, and Fuqing town itself. In southern and eastern Europe they share the stage with migrants from inland Sanming prefecture, whose social and demographic profile and dialect are quite different; migrants from other parts of Fuzhou are very few. In some places, there are almost purely Fuqing communities. In Szeged, a Hungarian city of about 250,000 on the Yugoslav border, all but a few of the several hundred Chinese who trade at the market are from Fuqing, and most are from Jiangyin township; as a result, some Chinese from outside Fuqing are reluctant to move to Szeged for fear of harassment.

In the mid-1990s in particular, the Fujianese of Szeged had a bad reputation among the Chinese in Budapest and were sometimes hired as debt enforcers. Across Europe, "Fuqing people" are often blamed by other Fujianese for crime, a stigma that has contributed to the formation of a distinct identity. The stereotype of Fuqingese as hotheaded, violent, daredevil, and even criminal is widespread and also found in Southeast Asia and China. To an extent, it is even cultivated by Fuqingese themselves.

Fujianese in Europe, from both Fuzhou and Sanming prefecture, have a wide range of profiles. At one extreme are farmers and fishermen recruited by brokers, mainly in Fuqing, Fuzhou, and Changle. As in any voluntary migration, these people need contacts and money to make migration possible, so they are not drawn from the ranks of the poor. At the other extreme are educated businesspeople and cadres aiming for entrepreneurship abroad, with all sorts of backgrounds between the two extremes, such as small-town factory workers, drivers, and traders who had a mind to go abroad and were given a push by a relative or migration broker. Transitions from entrepreneurship to wage labor and back occur, just as migration between eastern and western Europe and back happens. Our interviews covered a cross-section of migrants from different origins and social backgrounds and with different current status and occupations. They included inmates of immigration detention camps, restaurant and garment workshop workers who had entered their current countries of residence illegally, market traders, shop and restaurant owners, owners of import-export businesses, and professionals who had earned higher degrees in Europe.

This chapter maps the social spaces that Fujianese in Europe inhabit. These spaces, we find, are to a considerable degree transnationalized. Contacts with family, friends, customers, suppliers, employers, and officials in the country of residence, China, and other countries in and outside Europe are part of migrants' daily lives and affect their migratory and other decisions. Yet Fujianese migrants are also in daily contact with local Chinese populations and the broader receiving societies they live in. In which circumstances, then, do particular local or transnational connections come to the fore? In what ways does transnationalism impede or aid successful local incorporation? In this chapter, we approach these questions by looking at the way Fujianese in Britain, Italy, and Hungary adapt to the local economy and articulate their place in local society, including the Chinese population from other areas in China. In Chapter 5, we investigate more specifically the transnational dimensions of Fujianese lives in Europe and China, such as the politics of Chinese organizations.

Immigrants in Britain

Britain has one of the largest Chinese populations in western Europe, although Chinese still account for only a small share of the total number of immigrants in the country. The 1991 British census reported nearly 160,000 ethnic Chinese residents, almost 40 percent of whom lived in greater London (Parker 1998: 77–78). Chinese organizations in Britain estimated 250,000 for the year 1997 (European Federation of Chinese Organisations 1999: 19). Apart from the small Chinatowns of London and Manchester, which are more business than residential enclaves, it is hard to define areas of compact Chinese settlement. Nonetheless, Westminster City Council in London has a Chinese community liaison officer (who is a Malaysian Chinese); Britain has Chinese justices of the peace, and more recently also a Chinese member in the House of Lords (a Hong Kong–born medical doctor).

Most ethnic Chinese in Britain are post-1940s immigrants from the rural New Territories of Hong Kong and their descendants. The first generation mostly operates restaurants and take-outs, while the second generation has entered the professions. Urban migrants from Hong Kong, Malaysia, and Singapore, who generally are highly skilled, and their descendants constitute a second group, most of whom are in the professions. A third group are the ethnic Chinese refugees from Vietnam, who like the first group rely mainly on the catering trade, and their descendants. First-generation members of the first and third groups are still numerically the largest. The Chinese ethnic economy therefore continues to be dominated by catering.

Yet this situation is rapidly changing as a British-born generation comes of age. According to the 1991 census, 26 percent of Chinese had a higher education, but only 13 percent of whites (Parker 1998: 81). The upward mobility of the second generation means that the Chinese restaurant business has to look for new sources of labor. Whether the employment of non-Chinese as waiters and cooks is culturally unacceptable, impractical, or simply too expensive, the fact is that Chinese restaurant owners have long looked to the poorer among Chinese migrants—mainly Malaysian students and "tourists" and mainland Chinese—to supplement the work force, a situation that gradually began to change in about the year 2000. This situation has raised the risks of business, since the employer faces a fine if illegal workers are discovered.

As a consequence of the dominance of Chinese from Hong Kong and Southeast Asia, Cantonese is the lingua franca among the Chinese in Britain. The dominance of the Cantonese culture and language is reinforced by popular Chinese-language newspapers, magazines, satellite television, and videos, which carry mainly Hong Kong "Cantopop" fare. But some new periodicals—such as *Worldwide Chinese* (*Tianxia Huaren*)—have sprung up that are managed by new, Mandarin-speaking migrants who position themselves within a broader network of Chinese migrants in Europe and globally.

The Established and the Outsiders

Migrants from mainland China have been arriving in Britain in increasing numbers since the 1980s, mainly as students at universities and pre-university and language schools. In the late 1990s, Chinese authorities believed that there were around 10,000 Chinese students in the United Kingdom (X. Cheng 2002). Data from the British Home Office on student visas issued to PRC nationals reveal that this number continues to rise very fast: in 2000 no fewer than 18,900 such visas were issued.[3] While these migrants come from all of China's major cities, anecdotal evidence gathered during our fieldwork suggests that there is a preponderance of students from northern and northeastern China. Most students work while (or instead of) studying and have, as a cheap and legal source of labor, largely displaced Malaysians from London's Chinatown restaurants. The other major stream of migration from mainland China consists of asylum seekers, who arrive largely (but not only) illegally, mainly (but not exclusively) from Fujian.

Although the sights, sounds, and flavors of Britain's Chinese population are still dominated by the Cantonese culture tied to Hong Kong, the hold of this culture becomes increasingly tenuous. If migration from mainland China continues at the current pace, what happened in Manhattan—where part of the old Cantonese-speaking Chinatown was, after a period of tense standoff, taken over and expanded by a Fujianese population in the latter half of the 1990s—may be repeated in Britain.

Consequently, while Cantonese restaurant owners welcome cheap labor, they are wary of Fujianese opening businesses or establishing organizations. Any attempt to do so elicits powerful reactions, since they are seen as making inroads in the established order of Chinatown. Business owners in Chinatown have lodged repeated complaints against Fujianese hawkers selling telephone cards and smuggled cigarettes or just milling about outside their businesses, and have occasionally attacked them. While the general argument is that Fujianese are a threat to public safety and turn away clients, they obviously also undercut the business of established shops.

Periodically, the conflict escalates. One issue the Hong Kong Chinese were particularly furious about was the proliferation of street massage in 1999. Middle-aged northeastern women started this line of business, but some Fujianese joined in, and it was the Fujianese that the Hong Kong Chinese blamed for what they saw as an indecency. In another incident, seven Fujianese beat up a Hong Kong martial arts master who had pushed a Fujianese hawker away from his doorway. In reporting this incident, *Zoneast*, a London Chinese magazine, said that the attackers were from the "Fuzhou gang" (which the magazine said included the phone card hawkers and masseurs). It also claimed that Scotland Yard had increased patrols of Chinatown and was paying "close attention" to the "Fuzhou gang."[4]

In the context of this rivalry, migration history and individual background matter more than abstract geographic-dialectal identities. For instance, some of the British Chinese from Southeast Asia and Hong Kong are not Cantonese but Hokkien (southern Fujianese). They should, according to the logic of contemporary identity politics of the People's Republic of China (but not traditional overseas Chinese identity labels), share an identification with Fujianese newcomers, who are from the same province, albeit another part of it. Yet Hokkien emphasize cultural differences rather than commonalities, in the process equating all mainlanders with Fujianese and using the label "Fujianese" for all mainlanders. David Tan, head of the Westminster City Council's Chinese Community Liaison Office and a Malaysian Hokkien, led two delegations to the Home Office even before the Dover incident in July 2000, asking the Home Office to get tough on illegal immigrants from Fujian. He emphasized the difference between Malaysian Hokkien and the newcomers: "Foochows [Fuzhounese] . . . are totally different from us. We don't understand their language." Tan demanded "stronger checks at the point of entry, including the employment of Chinese to filter them out, heavier fines and regular checks on restaurants, and immediate deportation."[5] In 1999 a Hong Kong–born restaurant and real estate owner in London Chinatown, whose parents were born in southern Fujian, said:

> My parents are from Amoy [Xiamen]. But these people here [the Fuzhounese] are completely different. . . . We don't understand each other. They understand me, but I don't understand them. Hokkiens are ancient seafarers, but Fook-chows [Fuzhounese] have never been outside. There is a long way until they will be like Hokkiens. . . . They are good for the economy—many of my friends had difficulties finding people to work in their restaurants [before]—but they disrupt the social fabric.[6]

In 1999 he predicted: "These people will never dominate the economy . . . they won't find premises. . . . We don't think they are ready. . . . They won't be able to make money from other communities. They will not get a foothold in Chinatown."[7] Yet within two years, events proved him wrong. Some members of the old elite have found the new migrants too useful to be excluded. In 2001, David Tan told us: "Initially, the local Chinese resented them, but over time it changed. They proved themselves. . . . I came in contact with two excellent carpenters! So now, if you propose [to issue] work permits [to them], you have our full support!"[8] It remains to be seen if the acrimony between the established elite of Chinatown and the newcomers from Fujian really is a thing of the past. What does seem clear is that the Chinatown elite is coming round to the fact that they need the Fujianese and that the latter are there to stay.

Fujianese Work and Careers

Fujianese overwhelmingly work in established restaurants owned by Hong Kong or Vietnamese Chinese, where they are now an indispensable part of the work force. Very few of the workers have any previous experience with restaurant work in China. They start with the most menial jobs—cutting vegetables, cleaning the kitchen—and in a few years hope to work their way up to chef. In 1999 a London Chinatown real estate agent and restaurant owner, when talking about Fujianese, said: "75–80 percent of the restaurants already employ them. In Chinatown, 50 percent of the kitchen staff are Foochows [Fuzhounese], which [amounts to] 300 to 400 people. We estimate that there are altogether 15,000 jobs in Chinese restaurants in greater London."[9] The availability of Fujianese labor, as in the United States, has also permitted a renaissance of restaurants and take-outs outside London and other large cities, which had been struggling with insufficient manpower.

Unlike in America, where informants told us that wages have actually risen since the arrival of the Fujianese,[10] wages in the United Kingdom were driven down after 1999 when the job market in places like London Chinatown became saturated. The first Fujianese-run employment agency in London registered 300 job seekers, 90 percent of them from Fujian, during its first two months in business (May–June 1999), but only thirty of them found jobs during that period. According to the agency's owner, whereas a skilled kitchen worker may have made £300–400 (US$450–600) a week in the past, he may now be willing to pay £600 to be introduced to a £200-a-week job. Chefs' wages used to be £400 to £600 a week, but new Fujianese kitchen hands who have already learned cooks' skills are breathing down their necks, willing to work for up to £300 less.[11] Beginning wages are down to £140–150 per week, but we encountered one restaurant owner who offered only £80 or £100 per week, and on top of that only hired women under 30.[12] Generally, though, starting wages are still higher than in Italy, where a new worker at a garment workshop makes the equivalent of £65–85 a week,[13] but much lower than in New York, where a starting wage of more than US$400 a week is not unusual.[14] Although living costs in London are closer to those in New York than in Prato (where, in addition, food and lodging are taken care of by the employer), Britain may still sound like a better proposition—if the migrant can find a job. The main reason for this is that Fujianese migrants consider the purchasing power of their wages in China to be more important than their local value, and the high exchange rate of the pound compared to the euro and other currencies in continental Europe therefore makes Britain an attractive destination. In other words, the relative overvaluation of the British pound not only attracts capital and imported goods, but also leads to an inflow of foreign migrant labor to the British economy, both legally and illegally.

Yet work is not that easy to find, particularly for recent arrivals. Every Monday and Tuesday scores of Fujianese hang around the Chinese pavilion in Chinatown's Gerrard Street waiting for jobs. Many of our interviewees reported being jobless for half or more of their stay in Britain. Many in Chinatown had only part-time jobs, working only on the two busiest days of the week (Friday and Saturday). Restaurant owners often engage workers on a flexible schedule, demanding that they come to work only when business is good and sending them home when business is slow. It is also common for workers to fill in for friends who are unable to work. For many newcomers, such odd jobs are often all that is available.

Another option is hawking cigarettes and phone cards in the street, an activity that has aroused protests from Hong Kong business owners to the police and to Westminster City Council. Migrants can sell both items more cheaply than the local shops do, phone cards because the hawkers get them directly them from companies, cigarettes (both Chinese and Western brands) because (according to the police) they are sent by post from China or smuggled in the backs of trucks. Police say that, in fact, only five or six Fujianese women work as permanent cigarette hawkers. Police distribute Chinese-language sheets explaining that unlicensed cigarette hawking is a punishable offense.[15] According to the London-based Chinese magazine *Zoneast*, police estimate monthly sales to be a mere 3,000 packs, but profit is high: a carton of cigarettes costs only the equivalent of £4–5 in China, but sells for £22 in London.[16]

In addition to being hard to come by, jobs are also highly unstable. Workers are constantly displaced by newcomers willing to accept even lower wages. Most of our interviewees had worked less than a year in any given job, and many had changed jobs after just a few months at least once. While workers value employers who are willing to keep them, they are also on constant watch for a better chance:

You have to change jobs to improve your kitchen skills. If you stay in the same job you cannot make much more money, so you won't stay unless your boss is particularly good to you, unless he treats you as a family member. With my first boss, it was OK, but with the new one it wasn't good. There were all sorts of regulations about eating, you can't eat this and you can't eat that. Also, there were a lot of people, mostly Malaysians, and they made fun of me. So I wanted to change jobs. (Man around 30 from Jiangjing Township, Fuqing)[17]

Unemployment has a seasonal character: it is highest during the summer and in January, and lowest during the pre-Christmas season. Fujianese also increasingly have to compete for restaurant jobs with migrants from northern and northeastern China, who usually come to Britain as students. But while those often get waiters' jobs, Fujianese are practically confined to kitchens because of their lack of English language skills.

Life at the Margin

The advantage of working for Chinese employers away from China-town is that they offer both food and accommodation. This allows single male workers to make do with minimal expenses and save practically all their earnings. In Chinatown, employees usually must find lodging themselves and must spend what they consider a significant amount of money on a room (or just a bed in a shared room) and transportation. One man from Jiangjing, who worked at a London restaurant outside Chinatown, made £250 a week in 2000. He spent twenty pounds a week on rent, sharing a flat with three other Fujianese near his place of work. Together with transportation and "going out for tea with friends" he estimated spending about £200 a month.[18] Because of dropping wages and unemployment, most of our interviewees had not yet paid back the debts they had incurred coming to Britain. The time it takes to repay is now longer than for their predecessors.

Given their bad economic situation, our interviewees who were expecting or recently had babies applied for benefits from the local council, both housing and cash assistance, available to asylum seekers. Others had avoided doing so, fearing that this would make them more vulnerable to being tracked down and eventually expelled from Britain. Those that did apply were reluctant to accept housing outside London because they wanted to be close to work and sources of information. Flats received from the council were often shared with other Fujianese.

Falling Wages and Upward Mobility

Several of our interviewees considered themselves lucky to have a job just during the two busiest days of the week. Lin, a man from Changle, came to London in 1994 or 1995; his wife joined him in 1997. They are in their mid-30s and have four children in China. In 2000 she was washing dishes at a Chinatown restaurant on Fridays and Saturdays. Her husband also had a two-day-a-week job at another restaurant in Chinatown. Each of them made just over £100 a week and were sharing a rented flat with friends. Half of the money Lin had borrowed to come to Britain still had to be repaid.[19]

While Fujianese labor in the British Chinese catering industry has played a very similar role to that in the United States, there are several important differences. First, in America, Fujianese labor has reinvigorated the catering sector without driving wages down. According to a man from Changle who lives in North Carolina and has relatives in London, starting wages in New York rose from around US$1,000 a month when he arrived there in 1994 to around US$1,700 in 2001. There is little unemployment in the United States because the vast Chinese restaurant sector across the country continues to be able to absorb new-comers.[20]

Second, in London there is widespread resentment toward employment agencies, which charge £200, or more than one week's wages, for introducing jobs and refund the fee only if the client loses the job within two weeks. Workers have little protection against possible connivance between agents and restaurant bosses, and end up seeking jobs mainly through word of mouth. In New York, agencies' fees are just US$30 per introduction—less than half a day's wage—creating a better-functioning job market. Third, Fujianese in the United States are not on the lowest rung of the wage scale because those in the lowest-paid jobs are either middle-aged or older women, and they are as a rule Cantonese or Mexicans. Indeed, there are Mexican dishwashers working in Chinese restaurants.[21]

Obviously, decreasing wages in Britain benefit restaurant owners and other Chinese employers. Yet as noted earlier, the established Chinese community still resents the Fujianese presence for the perceived threat they pose not only to the safety and reputation of the Chinese, but also to the established social and economic order of Chinatown. One source of this wariness is the perceived business ethic of the Fujianese, that they want to get rich too quickly and engage in too many things all at once: for example, they are said to try to be traders and middlemen while working at a restaurant.

Some Fujianese have started their own restaurants and take-outs, but they have so far been limited to cheaper areas. The initial advantage Fujianese-run restaurants enjoy is that, thanks to greater reliance on labor of family members and fellow townsmen, they are able to operate at lower costs. Yet this development has been slower than in the United States, where many Chinese restaurants and take-outs outside China-towns are now run by Fujianese, because of the relatively small number of Fujianese in the country and the very small number of Fujianese with residence permits.[22] Some Fujianese rent take-out restaurants from Hong Kong Chinese or Vietnamese. Several of our interviewees hoped to do that in the future. But acquiring the lease on a take-out restaurant in a low-cost city like Newcastle still requires around £25,000, and asylum seekers and illegal migrants have no access to bank loans. Therefore, Futsing Finance in London lends money to migrants from Fuqing who wish to open take-outs.[23] Premium areas like London Chinatown are, of course, too expensive for Fujianese; moreover there they have to face the resistance of established business owners. As in the United States, where some of the most successful Fujianese restaurants are in the Bronx and the black areas of Brooklyn,[24] Fujianese attempt to find a niche in low-income neighborhoods other Chinese have shunned. But most asylum seekers are reluctant to invest as long as they do not have the security of legal residence. According to the owner of the Fujianese employment agency, there were only around ten Fujianese-run take-out restaurants in London in 2000.[25] The head of Futsing Finance estimated there were 100 to 200 Fujianese-run restaurants and take-outs outside London.[26]

Immigrants in Italy

Only in the past few decades has Italy changed from an emigration to a net immigration country. The number of immigrants has steadily in-creased since the early 1980s. In December 2000 there were at least 1.6 million foreigners legally present in the country, accounting for about 3 percent of the population. Of these, the Chinese are the fifth-largest cat-egory. A reliable estimate of the number of legally resident Chinese na-tionals for the year 2000 is 60,075, equal to 4.3 percent of all immi-grants,[27] making the country the principal destination for Chinese immigrants in southern Europe.

Despite frequent amnesties, not all the Chinese have legalized their position in the country. Estimates suggest that the number of illegal im-migrants corresponds to 15–20 percent of the total number of Chinese (Blangiardo and Farina 2001). This figure was confirmed by research on Chinese businesses in Prato (Ceccagno 2003b). The entrepreneurs inter-viewed stated unanimously that in many small firms run by Chinese, often one or two out of eight to ten workers are irregular.[28] This situa-tion would seem to be the opposite of that of the early 1990s, when of-ten only the employer had a residence permit and almost all the work-ers were irregular.

The actual number of Chinese in Italy is therefore higher than 60,000: the Chinese embassy in Italy has been speaking informally since about 1999 of 100,000 Chinese in Italy, and the same number is given by the European Federation of Chinese Organisations (1999: 19). Data col-lected at the local level also seem to put the reliability of national data in doubt: the number of Chinese in two significant settlement areas, Milan and Prato (12,150 and 8,086 respectively, not including their districts), together would appear to account for more than a third of the Chinese in Italy.[29]

Although small numbers of Zhejiangese have lived in Italy ever since the commencement of Zhejiang migration to Europe a century ago, Italy became a major destination only around 1980 (Campani and Maddii 1992). In the early twenty-first century, the Chinese in Italy are no longer the pioneers of the 1980s, who entered an ethnic economy that seemed to promise everyone overnight economic success. Since then, the Chinese population has become stratified, diversified, and firmly established. Owing to frequent amnesties and ample employment opportunities for unskilled people, the number of immigrants of Chinese origin (and from other countries) in Italy has undergone exponential growth. In addition, Chinese arrive from an increasing number of areas—no longer just the southern province of Zhejiang, the traditional source of chain migration to mainland Europe since before World War I (Thunø 1999), but also Fujian and the northeastern provinces.

Work and Enterprises

According to Confartigianato, a federation of small businesses, of the 31,500 small businesses run by immigrants originating from non-European countries that are registered with the Italian Chambers of Commerce, the largest number, around 4,000, are owned by Chinese.[30] Unlike in most other European countries, the majority of Chinese in Italy operate or work in garment or leather workshops, doing contract work for Italian customers. The workshops perform single manufacturing steps, mainly sewing and hemming, and mostly cater to the low-budget segment of the fashion market; their products are sold in small shops all over Italy, although some of the Italian clients in turn supply major labels such as Armani, Ferrè, Gucci, Valentino, Versace, and Max Mara (Ceccagno 2003b). A few Chinese workshops, especially in leather, have set up their own distribution inside Italy and for export. In addition, they appear to have begun expanding into related trades, such as supplying reels of thread produced in China and dyed in Italy.

Reliance on Chinese labor among manufacturers of low- to medium-priced seasonal fashions (*pronto moda* in Italian) is widespread. According to CGIL, the largest Italian trade union, Chinese produce 75 percent of the fashion output in the area of Prato at some step of the manufacturing process.[31] Having experienced explosive growth in parallel with Chinese immigration in the 1990s, Prato now accounts for 15 to 20 percent of Italy's fashion exports, and the areas of Florence, Prato, and nearby Empoli are the largest producers of leather goods in Italy. Some manufacturers contract all steps out to Chinese workshops, leaving only the packing and distribution to themselves. There were nearly 1,300 registered Chinese workshops in Prato in 2000.[32]

The workshops are family businesses that usually employ up to ten or twelve workers in total, some of them family members, others connected to the owners through native-place ties, and others total strangers. Since the skills required in leather workshops differ from those needed in sewing workshops, most workers stick to just one of the two trades. In addition, because the employer has to provide lodging as well as meals for all employees, he or she also employs a full-time maid. Some workshops have shifts, while at others everybody works through the night because the client delivers the garments in late afternoon to be ready the next morning. The length of the workday ranges from fourteen hours to, in extreme cases, twenty hours, with sixteen to eighteen hours being the norm. "Bosses" and their wives also do manual work and work the same hours, though their schedules are more flexible.

Workers start with odd jobs (*zagong*), which include cleaning, cutting loose threads from clothes, folding the finished garments, and so on. They earn between 800,000 and 1,000,000 lire (US$400–500) a month. Within a few months, a worker who learns quickly can become a more specialized manual worker (*shougong*), which requires basic ironing and sewing skills, and can earn about 1,200,000 lire (US$600), either at piece rates or as a fixed wage. When he or she becomes a tailor (*chegong*, literally "lathe worker"), the pay is by the piece and roughly equal to an average monthly wage of US$600–800, which is unevenly distributed over the year. These wages are substantially lower than those of a waiter (US$1,000) in a Chinese restaurant in Italy. We found no evidence that Fujianese receive different wages from Zhejiangese.

There are no living expenses because the worker lives with the employer and his family, who provide board and lodging; but with these wages, several years (up to seven or eight) may pass before a migrant has raised the necessary capital to start up a small family business. In the first few years after arrival, migrants must spend their money to pay off their travel debts; then there are the costs of the legalization process; later they spend their money on returning to China and pay for family members to come join them. Only then, or perhaps before the arrival of family members, is the money used to open a workshop.

Because the main assets of Chinese workshops are speed and flexibility—they routinely undertake to complete orders within a few days, or even upon just one day's or a few hours' notice—work times are long and workplace safety low. When there are no orders, the machines are idle and the workers sleep or go to another workshop where there is work. When there is no business at any of the workshops they know, the workers hope to get news of job opportunities, perhaps in other towns, from acquaintances or one of the bosses to report for work, or through advertisements posted on bulletin boards in Chinese shops and restaurants. Because of the lack of employment security, workers are also free to quit without notice, and they rarely hesitate to do so if they are offered higher pay, shorter working hours, or just better food and a more caring boss. Seasonal fluctuations are also strong. Indeed, during the slow season after Christmas and in the summer, a migratory wave arises as Chinese workers travel across Italy to visit relatives and friends, moonlight as peddlers on the seaside (or just spend a holiday there), or, if they have legal residence papers, go back to China.

Because employing workers legally means higher costs for the workshops that would make them uncompetitive, the customary arrangement is for the legal workers themselves instead of their employers to pay all or part of the tax and social insurance.[33] Every month, the workers are supposed to hand over to their employers the sums payable to the state for health insurance and the pension fund, which if fully paid often would account for a considerable part of their earnings. In practice, time worked is underreported, reducing the income tax. Some business owners say that their Italian accountants determine the taxes they pay; others say that they pay nothing and leave it to the employees to pay their own taxes (Ceccagno 2001).[34] Whatever the percentage paid by employers and by workers, it is common for contributions to be paid only when this is required for some other important reason, such as the renewal of a residence permit, the request for a family member to come to Italy, and so on.[35] In 1999–2000, the Department of Social Security in Prato inspected 216 Chinese businesses and discovered seventy businesses *in nero* (literally "black," meaning that these businesses are operated irregularly),[36] and 1,053 workers *in nero*. "Black" workers usually are fully legal residents of Italy and should not be confused with clandestine (illegal) workers, of whom the same survey uncovered a mere 238 (Department of Social Security 2000: 8).

Until the mid-1990s, ignorance of labor laws on the workers' and also often the employers' part resulted in cases of pregnant women working until giving birth, workers not daring to change workshops because they assumed that this required permission from the employer, or workers being told that they had to work without pay for a year and a half as compensation for being sponsored for regularization. Some workers realized that they were being exploited and turned to labor unions or lawyers. But such cases remained isolated (Ceccagno 1998: 59–67). In recent years the situation has changed. Although pregnant women and sick workers often still continue to work, fewer workers are illegal. They are much more aware of their rights and no longer view their boss as the person who has absolute power over their destiny in Italy. However, workers also have discovered that fighting for union rights is unrealistic in an ethnic economy dominated by small, informally organized family businesses.

Immigration, Immigration Policies, and the Ethnic Sector

Until the end of the 1990s, almost all the Chinese who arrived in Italy were integrated into the ethnic economy. Normally, the exploitation and self-exploitation that is one of the main features of the Chinese ethnic enclaves allowed upward mobility in a relatively short time and a release from dependent work to arrive at self-employment, in contrast to work for local employers. But this type of social mobility and access to self-employment was denied to the Chinese in Italy for nearly ten years: from 1990 to 1998, Italy prohibited access to self-employment to new immigrants from countries with which Italy had not signed reciprocal agreements, including China. In a community that has a strong aptitude for entrepreneurship, such as the Chinese one, this created great inequality between the small number of immigrants who had arrived before 1990 and were able to enter into self-employment, and the others who were able to work only as employees.

The 1998 Immigration Act changed this situation, again allowing immigrants to be self-employed. Many Chinese have taken advantage of the new regulations and have opened new firms or legalized those that previously operated on the borderlines of legality. The recent mushrooming of Chinese-operated businesses in Italy is particularly evident in Prato, where the 375 firms active in 1996 increased to 479 in 1997, to 862 in 1998, and to 1,288 in 2000 (Centro Ricerche e Servizi per L'Immigrazione 2001). The exponential growth in the number of new enterprises has far outpaced the growth in business, resulting in a strong fragmentation of productive capacity that is also visible in the progressive reduction in the number of workers employed in the firms. There are no official figures on the number of employees in Chinese firms, but information gathered from Chinese businessmen suggests that in the Prato area Chinese firms with thirteen to fifteen workers have become rare and are considered to be medium-sized to large businesses (Ceccagno 2003a). Clearly, the continuous arrival of Chinese immigrants has progressively saturated the market, particularly in those areas such as Prato, where the concentration of Chinese workshops is high. In the first place this means that the Chinese (who are mainly paid by the piece) now earn less per piece than they used to: according to informants, in the past few years the earnings have been reduced by almost half. Second, many immigrant businesses have closed down: in the year 2000 almost one-third of the Chinese firms started in Prato were no longer active.

The prohibition of self-employment between 1990 and 1998 gave the relatively small group of early arrivals—nearly all of whom were from Zhejiang—a head start before internal competition among Chinese started to erode profit margins. Those early entrepreneurs have best exploited the ethnic market and managed to obtain loans and financial support from fellow Zhejiangese. They were then able to broaden the scope of their activities. Many, for instance, started import-export businesses. The most striking change took place in garment manufacturing.

Rather than work on specific tasks and consignments for Italian firms, Chinese entrepreneurs have expanded their activities to include design, cutting, manufacture, and sales. The new pronto moda garment and knitwear firms run by Chinese compete both with each other and with the older firms run by Italians. Now there are at least fifty Chinese-owned firms producing ready-to-wear garments in Prato's industrial area. Some have a workshop to produce their own garments and also occasionally work for other suppliers; others do not have production facilities but turn to workshops run by Chinese, just as the Italian suppliers do (Ceccagno 2003a). Chinese "*prontisti*" have not yet reached sophisticated levels of distribution; they sell directly to shops, but their network of buyers is already impressive: they have clients—including Chinese wholesale shops—arriving from many Italian cities and European countries.

The move into the pronto moda business is significant because it involves a range of skills and contacts that, until a short time ago, Chinese small businessmen did not have: knowledge of fabrics, accessories, and the fashion market and the ability to attract clients by competing with Italians on quality, variety, and price. Access to the pronto moda business is only possible for those with sufficient capital, connections, and knowledge of the Italian language and market. These are in the main Zhejiangese who arrived in Italy early and have significant experience as owners of a workshop.

The establishment of pronto moda has been a driving force behind the Chinese shops all over Italy. In addition, some Chinese send patterns for clothes and bags provided by Italian clients to China to be made, and then import those finished goods. They do this outside the pronto moda system because the time needed is much longer. A woman's summer dress made in China of an Italian design sells in a Chinese store in central Florence for as little as US$7.50. Several shops sell suitcases and travel bags made in China along with clothes and leather bags made in local Chinese workshops. By 2000, shops engaged in the wholesale and retail trade in such goods had come to dominate the area of Piazza Vittorio in Rome: representatives of local residents' organizations complained to the city's police chief that all the shops around the square belonged to Chinese.[37] Apart from Italian retailers, immigrant peddlers who sell their goods in public places—urban squares and beaches—are major clients of these shops; they include both Africans and Chinese.[38] Chinese who engage in this business include recent migrants who as a rule do not have legal status, acquaintances, or capital, but also workers who view peddling as a "summer job" during the slow season in the garment and leather trade. Some of our interviewees said that peddling and workshop employment pay a comparable amount of money.[39]

Work beyond the Ethnic Sector

As the traditional ethnic sector, under pressure from continued immigration and decreasing profit margins, diversifies and stratifies, Chinese migrants are for the first time in Italian history seeking employment in Italian factories in the industrial belt of northeastern Italy. For example, a number of Chinese men and women work in small factories in Treviso, a town near Venice with a population of 90,000, whose production ranges from marble tiles to wine barrels. In the 1990s the province of Treviso developed a booming light industry that includes brands like Diesel, a popular jeans label. This industry employs many foreign workers. Chinese workers in Italian factories earn a comparable or even higher wage than in a Chinese workshop, but get no housing or food, which is problematic for many Chinese workers.[40]

Various factors mitigate this inconvenience and may lead to a decision to work for an Italian employer. The most important motivation is undoubtedly the progressive reduction of the opportunities for upward mobility within the ethnic sector. The need for job security is another, which becomes most acute when children are born. Other reasons are the chance to learn the language, fully legalized employment, fewer working hours than in Chinese-run businesses, and the chance to request a family reunification visa for family members still in China. All this contrasts sharply with the instability, isolation, uncertainty, and irregularity that workers encounter within firms run by Chinese.

Employment by Italians should not, though, be viewed as the opposite of work within the ethnic community. Research at the Center for Immigration Research and Services in Prato has revealed that Chinese are working for Italians on contracts that only partially cover the actual number of hours worked: workdays are frequently longer than the contractual eight hours, and often entire months of work go unpaid (Ceccagno 2003a).

For the Chinese, the choice to work for Italian employers does not seem to be a definitive and irreversible departure from the ethnic sector and community: some see it as a transitional phase and hope to be able to open their own business at a later date. For others it amounts to a short-term employment opportunity to be taken and then left again. It is not uncommon for Chinese to switch several times between working in the ethnic economy and working for Italians, showing again the great flexibility of migrants, who are capable of constant adjustment to their new environment.

The spillover of Chinese wage labor from the ethnic economy is as yet modest, and may be only a temporary phenomenon caused by reduced employment in the ethnic sector. On the other hand, it could also be the first sign of a new trend in the Chinese presence in Europe with potentially profound implications for the nature and volume of future migration flows between the continent and China; at this point it is simply too early to tell. That non-Chinese employment took place in Italy first (and only later in London) probably has to do with three key factors. First, Italy's industry more than that of any other European country apart from Spain relies on immigrants to compensate for a domestic labor shortage. Second, Italy's policy of legalizations has enabled even very recent nonelite Chinese immigrants to enter the legal labor force. Third, the substantial small-business sector of the Italian economy has generated considerable demand for cheap immigrant labor.

Life, Education, and Social Services

The amnesties of 1995 and 1998 made it possible for most migrants to legalize their status and have their spouses join them in Italy. As a result, the sex ratio of the Chinese in Italy is relatively balanced for a group of recent labor migrants. In 1992, of all Chinese in Italy holding residence permits, 35 percent were women (Carchedi and Ferri 1998: 265). In 2001 in the region of Lombardy this percentage stood at 47 (Regione Lombardia and Fondazione I.S.M.U. 2002: 117). In the same year, in the city of Prato, 46 percent of Chinese were women (Centro Ricerche e Servizi per L'Immigrazione 2001).

In view of the fact that the first generation of mostly rural labor migrants still dominates, it is unsurprising that levels of education are modest (Carchedi and Ferri 1998: 266). It is less obvious why the second generation so far seems less upwardly mobile than in Britain. Although not many Italian-born Chinese have entered the labor force yet, those that have seem to remain in the family business rather than enter the professions. This may have to do with their late entry into the Italian education system and the unpreparedness of the education system to absorb nonnative speakers, resulting in below-average school performance and low rates of university admission (Omodeo 1997).

In Italy, some social services are available to all migrants, whatever legal status they have. All children have the right to attend primary and lower secondary school, regardless of the legal status of their parents. Recent changes require that neither adults nor children may be out of the country for more than six months at a time, making it much more difficult for Chinese to have their children partially educated by the grandparents in China. Hospitals accept migrants with no papers for emergency medical help and childbirth. Immigration service centers set up by municipal governments, as well as trade unions, churches, and NGOs, provide advice and legal consultation to anyone. Local governments can grant financial aid and housing to legal foreign residents in need. Some years back, temporary housing was provided to pregnant women without residency papers for the months immediately before and after delivery of the child. At the municipal Immigration Research and Service Center in Prato, Chinese migrants regardless of legal status may request information and legal assistance. This may be due to the fact that in Italy there is a clear distinction between offices that deal with immigration control and those in charge of social services, and migrants are quick to catch on to this. The use of social services by the Chinese in Prato has been considerable; once someone has found out that a service is available, more and more Chinese try to use it. Such services in Prato have included subsidized language courses and interpreting and translation services. Chinese migrants in Prato may also send their children to state nursery schools.

For the Chinese in Italy, the past decade has been a period of significant changes. Because there are more sending areas than in the past, different dialects signal the boundaries between subgroups in the community; the second generation is actively contributing to the expansion of Chinese businesses, and the community's entrepreneurial success has become more and more visible. The Chinese ethnic sector has witnessed a growing polarization between successful businessmen—those who arrived first—and small businessmen, or those who run what we call subsistence microbusinesses (Ceccagno 2001). The precarious condition of these very small businesses is undoubtedly linked to the characteristics of production for third parties: in third-party operations the workshop has little bargaining power when dealing with the supplier and client. On the other hand, the new Chinese-managed *pronto moda* businesses, which have the potential to grow much larger than the workshops, no longer have to rely on Italian suppliers.

The Fujianese in Italy

The social makeup of the Fujianese immigrants in Italy is varied. Some are of humble origins, but many had satisfying work in China, in both the public and private sectors. The first years abroad entail great hardship, and some of the recent Fujianese migrants we interviewed, unhappy with their present living and working circumstances, said that their friends and families in Fujian often enjoyed better working conditions and pay. Some even borrowed from relatives and friends in China in order to make the changeover from worker to microentrepreneur in Italy. One explanation for the need for loans from China could be that Fujianese lack family networks in Italy. Chinese from Zhejiang who opened businesses in the 1990s could count on loans from parents and friends already well established in Italy or elsewhere in Europe. By contrast, Fujianese who open a family business find themselves in an environment surrounded by equally poor fellow Fujianese who are not able to offer loans or other forms of support.

In Italy, Fujianese have a limited presence in the more expensive restaurant trade, the crowning achievement for many Chinese migrants. Following the general growth trend of Chinese enterprises, most Fujianese workshops were established after the amnesties of 1995 and 1998, when many Fujianese gained legal residence, and after the ban on entrepreneurship for new immigrants was lifted in 1998. Since then, the growth of Fujianese companies has been exponential. In June 2000, a vice-president of the Prato branch of the Fujianese association spoke of only a dozen or so Fujianese-run workshops in Empoli, a town near Florence with a high concentration of Fujianese.[41] A year later, according to the same informant, there were at least sixty to seventy in Prato, about one hundred in Empoli, and some three hundred in the whole of Tuscany.[42] This would mean that Fujianese own about 17 percent of the firms run by Chinese nationals in Prato. Among these are the workshops owned by two executive vice-presidents of the Fujian Association branch in Prato from Lianjiang and Changle. They came in 1991 and opened their workshops in 1997.[43] The president of the Prato / Tuscany branch of the Fujian Association in Italy opened his own leather garments workshop in 1989, after only two years in Italy.[44] In Rome the president of the local Fujianese Association opened his first garment workshop in 1993. Since then, several of his relatives have also started their own workshops. Both of the latter two workshop owners grew up in Zhejiang.[45] The profile of the workshops does not differ from those run by migrants from Zhejiang, but proportionately more Fujianese are in the leather business, which is what most Chinese workshops in Empoli specialize in.

San Giuseppe Vesuviano and Terzigno, centers of Chinese workshops in the Naples area in southern Italy, saw an influx of Fujianese in 2000–2001, mainly from the Prato area. Their migration was probably triggered by lower costs and access to southern Italian clients, which made it possible for Fujianese with less capital to open workshops earlier than in Prato. The workshops in the two villages near Naples cater mostly to local Italian companies. The growth of Chinese workshops in the area started in 1993–94. A dozen Fujianese opened their own workshops there in 1995, triggering an inflow of Fujianese workers and the subsequent opening of new workshops. The bulk of them make textile garments.[46]

Fujianese request loans from relatives in China in emergencies, such as when there is a need to pay for legalization or when someone has been cheated or robbed or has lost money gambling. Unlike Chinese from Zhejiang, who can borrow from relatives and friends already in Italy, Fujianese opening their first business do not yet have family or friends there who can offer substantial financial support. Fujianese-run workshops are at an early stage of development. So far they rely nearly exclusively on Fujianese labor, and the small workshops that constitute the majority recruit labor mainly from among relatives and acquaintances.

Immigrants in Hungary

In mid-2000, nearly 12,000 Chinese held permanent or long-term residence permits or had applied for temporary residence permits in Hungary; approximately 2,600 were permanent residents. While police officials sometimes state publicly that the "real" number of Chinese in Hungary is as high as 100,000, Chinese themselves generally believe a figure of between 15,000 and 20,000 to be correct. An estimate based on the number of Chinese shops, market stalls, and restaurants yields a figure between 10,000 and 15,000.[47]

Hungary, along with Russia, has been one of the early hubs of entrepreneurial migration from China to eastern Europe. The origins of that migration lie in the border trade between China and the Soviet Union that began in the late 1980s. Informal "shuttle trade" had always been a feature of the economies of eastern Europe, but Chinese traders raised it to an unprecedented level, stepping in to fill the vacuum created by nonexistent or broken-down retail networks of low-price clothing and shoes. Venturing farther and farther by train and spending more time at their destinations, they first reached European Russia and subsequently discovered Hungary as a destination that required no visa. Later, the reimposition of the visa requirement in early 1992 and administrative harassment resulted in a secondary migration from Hungary to Poland, Czechoslovakia, Romania, and to a lesser extent other countries of the region, as well as western Europe.

Even more than in Italy, then, Chinese migrants to Hungary come almost exclusively from the People's Republic of China, but unlike in Italy, no one region dominates. Migrants come largely from the wealthier urban-coastal zones of China, and many come from places that have no tradition of migration. Nevertheless, among the Chinese who have applied for long-term or permanent residence permits, the largest groups are the same as those that make up the Italian community: the largest group (18 percent) comes from Fujian, followed by Zhejiang. This is a result of newly established migration chains that have increased the share of these provinces over the past decade. But other major groups come from areas barely represented in Italy, such as Beijing, Tianjin, Shanghai, and the provinces of Hebei (around Beijing) and Liaoning, Jilin, and Heilongjiang in the Northeast.

These migrants, including some from Fujian and Zhejiang, are upwardly mobile, have above-average educations, and are individually motivated. This is different from migrants in Italy, who come predominantly from rural areas that specialize in emigration. In a database of the Ministry of the Interior that by early 2000 contained some 11,200 entries of Chinese who had applied for long-term or permanent residence permits, 10 percent were recorded as having stated that they had been professionals, intellectuals, or students in China, and 27 percent said they were businesspeople.[48] Another indication of the relatively high level of education among Chinese in Hungary is that in a sample of 135 market traders, 45 percent claimed to have secondary education and 39 percent higher education (City of Budapest 1997).

Ways of Entry and Patterns of Settlement

As we have seen in Chapter 3, while reports on "illegal" migration indicate that Hungary is a major transit point, it appears that Chinese generally enter Hungary legally and manage, by some means, to maintain legal status or to purchase forged documents. Because of continuous scrutiny by police, border guards, tax and customs agents, and public land inspectors, it is impossible for Chinese to conduct business without having a residence title and paying customs duty (if they are importers) and corporate taxes and making social security contributions for their local workers. But, as in Italy, the amount of taxes paid is determined not by actual business conducted, but by the accountant, who advises the business owner how much he or she should report in order to pass an inspection or have a residence permit extended. The Chinese see these expenses not as tax due, but as a fixed expense for residence, called *yang lanka* ("to feed one's blue card," or residence permit).

The overwhelming majority of Chinese in Hungary have a residence status as "manager." According to the Hungarian Ministry of the Economy, around 10,000 Chinese-owned businesses, mainly limited companies, are registered in the country. This means that nearly every Chinese in Hungary is registered as owning his or her own company. The total investment capital of these businesses, according to the ministry, is US$120 million, or approximately US$1,200 each. While the number of active businesses is probably only a fraction of 10,000, almost all Chinese are indeed owners or co-owners of a business, although some of them may at the same time be employed by another.

Most Chinese reside in Budapest (82 percent of those with long-term stay permits and applicants for immigrant residence). Other large groups live in centers of cross-border trade (Nyíregyháza near the Ukrainian and Romanian borders and Szeged near the Yugoslav and Romanian borders), as well as in affluent northwestern Hungary (Sopron, Gyor) and other larger towns. In Budapest, the area near the Four Tigers Market has assumed some semblance of a Chinatown, but it serves only as a business area. Chinese residents are more numerous in the two districts around the market (districts VIII and X) and in some other relatively central, middle-rent districts (XIV, XI); many others live scattered around the city.

Entrepreneurship and Employment

Most Chinese in Hungary deal with the import, wholesale, or retail of low-price clothes and shoes from China, although an increasing number are active in other foreign trade sectors. The Chinese fill a supply gap in eastern Europe's postsocialist economies by offering affordable but popular clothes of the kind made in China for low-price Western retail chains. The business chain consists of several tiers, from imports to retail, and is centered on open-air markets where most merchants are foreigners. In the early 1990s, Hungary became the first center of such business in central and eastern Europe and attracted "shuttle traders" from neighboring countries who generated brisk business and high incomes for the Chinese. The Four Tigers Market in Budapest, with around one thousand Chinese-owned stalls and a few hundred more owned by Vietnamese, Turks, Ukrainians, Hungarians, Romanians, Afghans, and others, became the center of the business. Later on, Hungarian entrepreneurs rented former factory buildings across the road from the market and converted them to additional space for market stalls.

According to a 1997 survey, 47 percent of the traders at consumer goods markets in Hungarian cities with populations over 10,000 were Chinese (Nyíri 1999: 50). According to a 2002 survey by the market research agency GFK, markets and street vendors account for 21 and 22 percent respectively of shoe and clothes retail sales, and goods sold there come overwhelmingly from Chinese importers.[49] According to a 2001 estimate by the Chinese embassy in Budapest, there are 2,000 Chinese retail shops in Hungary, including even in remote villages. Chinese consumer goods are popular mainly because they are cheap, owing not only to low manufacturing costs but also to the underpayment of customs duties. Another advantage is the flexibility of the entire business chain. If a customer in a rural area asks a local Chinese shopkeeper for a particular item not currently available, the shopkeeper will try to obtain it on his next trip to the market in Budapest. Owners of large import businesses visit international trade fairs and have their suppliers in China speedily produce sneakers or tracksuits according to the latest fashion. Some of the largest businesses have been able to develop brand recognition and have advertised on billboards, in newspapers, and through sponsorship of sports events. But the overwhelming majority have kept overhead costs to a minimum by doing no advertising.

Contrary to the more traditional overseas Chinese communities in western Europe, Chinese migrants in Hungary come from backgrounds that often endow them with the cultural capital, mobility, and means of communication to develop close ties with enterprises in China, which supply them with goods, capital, and business information. Of these, state-owned enterprises were able to offer the "softest" money, although money transfers became more difficult after 1995 as the Chinese government applied increasing pressure on the unprofitable and mismanaged state sector. Nonetheless, such arrangements persist, especially in northeastern China, where many state enterprises are insolvent and desperately need the profits from foreign business ventures and contacts.

Some state-owned foreign trade and shipping companies asked their employees leaving for Hungary to represent their companies in scouting for business opportunities. Most such employees stopped drawing salaries and received commission on the sales instead. Although most registered the local companies as private enterprises rather than branches of the company in China, many nonetheless carried official passports. Usually, they continued to be counted as employees of their mother companies for about two years, after which they were "freed" and the relationship gradually became looser. Most people never returned to their mother companies, but continued to enjoy its backing and help as well as some benefits during visits to China.[50]

Only a minority of Chinese businesspeople in Hungary benefited from such arrangements, however, or had enough capital to engage in imports from the start. Most make their way up, starting as market peddlers buying small consignments of goods from bigger Chinese wholesalers. ("Shuttle trading," where traders brought the merchandise with them and went back to China for more, yielded to much more sophisticated forms of business in the early 1990s.) Market peddlers, working from around 5:00 A.M. until 4:00 P.M. on weekdays and until 1:00 P.M. on Saturdays, engage in both retail and wholesale trade. Their profits rely primarily on establishing long-term business relationships with shopkeepers and distributors from Hungary, Yugoslavia, and Romania, who come to the market once a week to stock up. The market thus functions as a commodities exchange, at which not only goods but also information changes hands. The market is also the destination of whole containers from China whose contents are sold only to distributors.

Successful peddlers gradually buy larger quantities of imported goods for resale, and a minority do well enough to begin importing goods themselves. Local Chinese folklore considers the pre-1995 period a golden age when one could sell anything and turn a profit. Later, profits declined as the market became increasingly competitive, shopping tourism from neighboring countries tapered off with the appearance of local Chinese businesses, customs tariffs were raised, and the exchange rate of the Hungarian forint fell against the dollar. In other words, traders incurred higher costs while simultaneously being forced to reduce their prices. This setback affected the entire business chain, from importers to peddlers, but elicited different reactions. Businesses with substantial capital can afford to look for customers outside the traditional realm of the "Chinese market." Some have introduced new brands for exclusive sale in their own chain of shops; others have targeted multinational discount stores and supermarket chains with clothes, hardware, furniture, and other durable goods, and a few have succeeded in getting contracts for a chain of stores across Europe and even North America.

Less well capitalized but educated businesspeople intensified their efforts to broker business between large Chinese manufacturers,[51] or vice versa, between Chinese local governments and companies seeking foreign know-how and Hungarian manufacturers, especially in the food industry. Others again have accelerated expanding their businesses into other countries of central and eastern Europe, often keeping their businesses and also their residence in Hungary, like an investor balancing his portfolio. The most conspicuous project in this vein is the Asia Center, which has been heralded as Europe's largest wholesale center for Asian companies. The investment, reported at US$200 million, appears to be a combination of "soft" state-sector money from China and an Austrian bank loan.[52]

Smaller businesspeople have tended to open retail shops or fast-food outlets, which spread rapidly across the country in the late 1990s and early 2000s. Both forms of business are associated with lower risk and lower profit than market trading, although early and well-located fast-food outlets were reputed to be highly profitable. Prices at Chinese shops, while still half those in Hungarian shopping centers and discount supermarkets, are almost double the wholesale prices at the Four Tigers Market, but sales volume at these shops is low. The profitability of such shops varies widely. A good shop could net a profit of US$2,000 to US$3,000 a month; a bad shop could lose money.

Chinese shops invariably display a sign identifying them as such, although Chinese are not always seen around. Especially in the countryside, Hungarian employees often run the shops, while the owners, who may have more than one shop, usually in villages or towns close to each other, visit once a week. Having a Hungarian employee is necessary because Chinese business owners are not legally allowed to perform work; also, Chinese demand higher wages than locals and prefer to own their own businesses anyway. Hungarian employees—or sometimes Romanians, who are willing to work for even lower wages—often get the minimum wage or are reported as working part-time on paper, thus reducing the social security payments required from the employer.[53] Employees are most often paid a combination of a fixed wage and a sales commission.

A more limited, but also rapidly growing, option for businesses is the ethnic Chinese service sector, which includes groceries, video rental shops, beauty parlors, phone card dealers, travel agencies, agencies providing translations and immigration help, newspapers, and companies dealing with shipping, customs clearance, and warehousing.

Onward Mobility

Chinese in eastern Europe display both an extraordinary geographic mobility and a readiness to change social roles. We have interviewed people who started trading in Hungary, were unsuccessful or lost their money gambling, and went to Italy or Germany to work in leather workshops or restaurants for three or five years; now they consider investing the money earned in Hungary or Romania once again because they want to develop their own businesses.[54] Others, whose applications for political asylum in Germany were turned down, chose to reenter Hungary illegally, because they thought it was easier to obtain legal status there. Several more who started trading in Russia in the early 1990s went on to Hungary, but returned to Russia when residence permit policies in Hungary were tightened in 1992.[55] In other words, migration, even illegal migration, is happening not just from East to West, but also in the opposite direction. Many Chinese, especially those from Zhejiang and Fujian, have family members working in garment or leather workshops in Italy or in restaurants in Spain, Germany, or England, most of whom made their way there from Hungary. A number of entrepreneurs have expanded their import or restaurant businesses to neighboring eastern European countries and now move between them.

Life, Education, and Welfare

Because of the more individualistic nature of entrepreneurial migration and the higher share of urban and educated migrants, the sex ratio among Chinese migrants in Hungary is relatively balanced for such a recent migratory flow. In May 2000, 35 percent of Chinese citizens who had requested permanent or long-term residence permits were women. But there are still relatively few Chinese children in Hungary because many parents prefer to leave them in China or send them back there for schooling. As in Britain, the second generation that grows up in Hungary is generally upwardly mobile and lost to the family business, and this corresponds to the wishes of the parents. Most Chinese parents wish to send their children to college in the United States or the United Kingdom, and so, if they can afford it, take them out of Hungarian schools at some stage and send them to schools where instruction is in English. A number of children have actually gone on to college in the West, where some have obtained degrees and corporate jobs. Those parents who cannot afford the considerable expense of an international education often send their children back to China, hoping they will eventually be admitted to college there.

The Fujianese in Hungary

In Hungary, migration from Fujian started at the same time as from the rest of China, and with no structural difference except that among migrants from southern China—both Fujian and Zhejiang—there appear to be fewer well-educated and well-connected individuals who can secure the support of state enterprises, and more former small business-people who have to fight their way up the ladder of trading. The path of a typical Fujianese migrant within the ethnic economy is no different from that of other Chinese; generally, the migrant starts as a market peddler. There is no particular Fujianese specialization; Fujianese sell garments from Zhejiang just as Zhejiangese sell shoes from Fujian. These provinces have come to supply the bulk of the merchandise because of a boom in small manufacturing, lower costs than in Guang-dong province, and ties to migrants who keep manufacturers informed about changes in the market. Businesses typically source their goods from a variety of places, depending on supply, in Fujian (the shoe paradise of Shishi/Jinjiang near Xiamen in southern Fujian) and elsewhere. The largest businesses have either exclusive contracts with plants in China or, in one case, own their own plants. Family members often handle sourcing for the smaller businesses.

Most Fujianese traders have been affected by the downturn in the low-price shoe and garment business since around 1995. Many of those who had not managed to establish well-running shops or find an import niche, but remained general market traders into the late 1990s, are losing money or making little profit. The story of Ding, a penniless former cook from Mingxi, is fairly typical.

Ding rented a stall at one of the former factories opposite the main Four Tigers Market in Budapest in October 1999.[56] By the time Ding rented his stall, profits at the Chinese markets had declined substantially, and leaseholders of stalls at the "little factories," where business was slower than at the main market, were having difficulty renting out their stalls. Therefore some were subletting their stalls to others for just the monthly "sanitation fee," DM200 (US$100), to the market.

A fellow townsman lent Ding several thousand forint to pay the first month's rent and get some merchandise. Ding paid Ft 60,000 (US$2,400) a month to the Chinese leaseholder, who in turn paid the sanitation fee. A similar arrangement at the main Four Tigers cost Ft 300,000 or more in 1999, more than Ft 400,000 in 2000, and Ft 250,000 in 2001. Ding opened his stall around 6:00 A.M. "because the Yugoslavs come very early" and closed between 2:00 and 3:00 P.M., including Saturdays.[57]

In December 1999, Ding earned US$1,000 before expenses (taxes, accountant's fee, rent, transportation, and food). Business and living expenses were US$700–800, so he could save US$200–300 a month. For the pre-Christmas season, this profit was seen as very low in comparison with earlier years and with what was usually considered worthwhile to run a business. Yet Ding was satisfied with the profit he made: "When they helped me rent this stall, I had 3,000 forint (US$14). Now there is merchandise worth several thousand dollars here."[58] Ding has been sharing flats with fellow villagers near the market, some without a bathroom. When he was faring worst, he rented a room in such a flat from an unemployed Hungarian family and shared the bed with another man from Mingxi. He never paid more than Ft 15,000 (US$60) a month for lodging. He asked if we could find a Hungarian company where he could work as a guard or warehouse worker, or even as a nanny and maid.[59]

After one year, Ding had his fixed suppliers (*fahuoshang, baohuoshang*), based at the Four Tigers, from whom he purchased his merchandise. These distributors were from all over China, not just Fujian. In December 2000 Ding said that his monthly gross income was around Ft 200,000 (around US$650), half of which went to cover expenses.[60] Ding saved the other half, or US$200–300 a month. Even this was thanks to his connections and luck. At the Chinese Christian church, Ding had met Hong, the owner of a big Chinese warehouse. Hong had been looking for someone to take his old stock of shoes, which were no longer selling well in Hungary. Because he knew that Ding, who was in his church group, had no money, he gave him a few samples. Ding was able to sell them, and then several cases of the shoes, to a Yugoslav customer, and because Hong let him have the merchandise cheaply, he made a profit of Ft 400 to 500 on a pair instead of the usual Ft 50.

At the other extreme of the income scale are Fujianese who have been in Hungary since the early 1990s and have built up major import, wholesale, and warehousing businesses. Most, like the Hong Kong businessmen in North America, move back and forth between countries in which they have business interests, a residence permit, and family (see Mitchell 1995, 1998, 2001; Ong 1999; Skeldon 1994). They operate transnational businesses consisting of companies that are loosely anchored in the local markets and connected to each other by formal and informal ties. These businesses can be described as transnational rather than multinational because, while operating across borders, they register as local companies in each country rather than as branches, and rely on kinship and personal connections to find local managers.

Of course, such people in eastern Europe are found not only among Fujianese: generally, they arise from among better-educated migrants with good connections in China, often northerners. Among Fujianese and Zhejiangese, the kind of arrangements with state enterprises that we described earlier have been less common than among northerners, probably because by the early 1990s the role of private enterprise in the South already was much greater than in the North. Most of the southerners who went abroad had been private entrepreneurs of some sort or family members of earlier migrants; only a few had been employed in state work units. An important exception were urban migrants from Sanming, which with its strong tradition of state industry was more similar to the North in its employment structure. Among our interviewees from Sanming, there were former police, judiciary, and other government employees, as well as foreign trade and factory managers. One of the two best-known Fujianese businessmen in Hungary had worked in trade companies and departments in several cities in Fujian; the other had a relative in the Sanming City Foreign Economic and Trade Commission.

These men own two of the three or four Chinese brands that enjoy a certain name recognition in Hungary thanks to advertising and the creation of a network of low-price Hungarian retail shops that display the brand logo on the shop front. The creation of a brand image has lifted them from the melee of brand names sold at markets. These are Wink, owned by Wei Xiang from Xianyou and a former arts teacher in Sanming, and Sandic, owned by Guo Jiadi, who was born in Putian, the county south of Fuqing. We will discuss the case of Guo to illustrate the patterns of corporate growth and transnationalism in more detail.

In 1980–81, Guo was trained in township enterprise management, and from 1982 to 1986 he worked as a manager in state trading companies in Shunchang and Shaowu counties in Nanping prefecture north of Sanming. Between 1986 and 1988 he was vice-director of the Taiwan trade department of a district in Putian. In 1989 he went to Thailand on a tourist visa. In 1990, when he read in the Chinese papers there about economic reforms and privatization in Hungary, he left Hungary for Thailand "to look around." Returning to China, he founded Guoshi (HK) Ltd. in Hong Kong with a local (not a Fujianese) partner and returned to Hungary again in 1991.

Guo opened the Guoshi shoe factory in Putian, directly on the Fuzhou-Xiamen road that is Fujian's main thoroughfare, in 1995. According to the company's English website in Hungary, the factory "is the biggest and best facilitated joint-venture company among the non–state owned industries in Putian city. The company fixed assets has reached over six billion yuan."[61] Guo is also engaged in real estate development nearby, on an area of 200 mu,[62] where he intends to build hillside mansions with an investment of US$6 million.

Subsequently, Guo expanded his import business across eastern Europe and beyond, and within ten years had companies in the Czech Republic, Poland, Slovakia, Romania, Yugoslavia, the United States, and Brazil, dealing with the import and wholesale of shoes and some other goods. In 1999 the company entered the Spanish market by establishing a wholesale distribution company there. This was done through a man from Zhejiang who had moved to Spain from Hungary. The company also attempted to enter Italy in 2000 with its Moon brand but failed.[63]

Nevertheless, the Sandic brand has become associated with the "Chinese market," and as such with low quality.[64] By 2000–2001, Guo himself admitted that its profitability had declined because of the problems characterizing Chinese imports in Hungary: saturation of the market, Yugoslav shuttle traders staying away, and the unwillingness of consumers to absorb the price raises resulting from the continuing decline of the forint against the dollar.[65] In 2000, Guo introduced a new brand, Moon (Moonarch), to be sold strictly to department stores and not at the Four Tigers in order to create a brand unblemished by the "Chinese-market" image of Sandic. In China, Guoshi has some sales in Dalian in the Northeast and Qingdao in the North and is planning to enter Beijing. Guo spends about half his time in Hungary and divides the rest among China, the other countries where he does business, trade fairs, and Vancouver, Canada, where his wife and children have lived since 1997 for the education of the children.

The main markets are Hungary and Brazil, but sales volume in Hungary has been declining. According to the deputy general manager of the factory in Putian, since 1997 sales have been about 1 million pairs per year in eastern Europe, and the total sales volume has not declined. Before that, sales had been limited by the manufacturing capacity. According to another manager at the factory, the company offset declining sales by expanding to Lebanon, Jordan, and in the third quarter of 1999, to South Korea.[66]

Guo's Hong Kong company functions as a service company that

supplies capital from Hong Kong banks for overseas projects; it also handles the transshipping of Taiwanese and South Korean raw materials to China and of customer goods from China. The group has bought factories from state enterprises in China. According to the head of the Putian County Foreign Trade Bureau, Guo is the largest Chinese investor from Europe in Putian and the only individual manufacturer who exports directly to Europe, rather than via trade companies. He estimated the county's exports to Europe to be about US$70 million in 1999, out of a total of US$200 million. The exports started in 1986 and picked up in 1992.[67]

The Guo network operates largely as a family business. Close relatives head the factory and the branches in different countries. The general manager of the factory is Guo's older brother; his two deputies are the husbands of Guo's two sisters. The factory employs around 1,000 workers. According to one of the company's drivers, 80 to 90 percent of them are local, from Putian. In Hungary, Guo directs several companies, although he formally owns only two. The companies import from Guo's own factory as well as from others in China. Formally, each company conducts its business independently; there is no holding company.

Guo's rise as a businessman has been accompanied by the cultivation of connections with officials. Displayed on the walls of the factory's lobby, photos show Guo applauding Jiang Zemin and meeting the vice-chairman of the standing committee of the National People's Congress and the chairman of the National Federation of Overseas Chinese. Guo has donated tens of thousands of dollars to Project Hope, an official charity for the development of poor rural areas in China. Xi Jinping, the governor of Fujian who used to be in charge of overseas Chinese affairs in the province, is, according to Guo's employees, a "good friend" of Guo's. We noted that when Chen Ernan, a vice-director of the Foreign and Overseas Chinese Affairs Committee of the Fujian People's Congress, received a call from Guo on his mobile phone he called Guo by his first name.[68] In 1998, Guo was appointed the first Europe-based overseas member of the Fujian People's Political Consultative Conference. His company has received several provincial awards, which, according to the company's website, include "Advanced Enterprise of Fujian Province," "Advanced Site Management Enterprise of Fujian Province," and "Major Tax Payer of Fujian Province," and was named a provincial technology center for sports footwear. The provincial government designated Sandic a "Fujian Quality Product" in 2000 and a "Fujian Famous Brand" in 1999.

Between the two extremes represented by Ding and Guo are Fujianese who own small and midsized import and wholesale businesses and those who have moved out of the market and opened shops around the country. Gao, a former mathematics teacher in Sanming, came to Hungary in 1994 or 1995. He opened a shop in a village about fifty kilometers from Budapest in 2001. According to his family members, the main reason for the move was that it had been exhausting to work at the Four Tigers Market, hauling big boxes of merchandise all day. In addition, Gao said that the shop made "enough money to cover the expenses" and that the income was stable, unlike at the market.[69] For Lin and Chen, a couple from Fuqing, it took two years to move from trading at the market to taking over two shops in a rural town. Expecting that the shops would earn more than trading at the market, where, they said, they had only just been breaking even, Chen and Lin raised US$43,000 from China to take over the shops and their inventory.[70] In Hungary, loans and investment from China for business expansion are, because of the nature of the business (mainly the import trade from China), more common than in Italy.

Faced with declining profits from the "traditional" ethnic sector of clothes and shoe imports, Fujianese, like other Chinese migrants, have also entered new lines of business. A couple from southern Fujian runs one of the largest Chinese warehouses in Budapest. Originally importers, they bought an abandoned factory building near the Four Tigers Market in 1996 from the district government and converted it into a warehouse. In 2000, a new story was added, increasing the building's floor space to 16,000 square meters.[71]

Two of the major Chinese weekly newspapers in Hungary have been run by Fujianese: the oldest, *Ouzhou Daobao*, by Ji Dongtian between 1994 and 2001, and *Ouzhou Luntan* (formerly *Ou-Hua Luntan*) by Liu Wenjian since 1999. Ji, a native of Xiamen, a former journalist and official of the Mingxi County CCP Propaganda Department, became a member of the Chinese Christian church in Budapest and left Hungary for Chicago in 2001, when a Chinese-American missionary at the church helped his teenage daughter go there to study. Liu, born in Putian and formerly director of a tea-packing factory in Sanming, began writing for *Ouzhou Daobao* in 1997, while peddling at the Four Tigers Market in Budapest. Since newspapers serve as information brokers for businesses in Hungary and in China, they often are instrumental to their owners in their other business. Liu, for example, acts as distributor for some Chinese importers, buying merchandise and reselling it to other Chinese wholesalers, and also brings together Hungarian and Chinese business partners.[72]

Additional businesses Fujianese have established include casinos, game parlors, and the related business of money lending. According to estimates by Budapest casinos, Chinese make up 40 percent or more of their clientele.[73] With the decline of business at the Four Tigers Market, down-market game parlors with slot machines and electronic roulette spread. In 2000 a group of Fuqing men opened a gambling club called Sunjoy opposite the market, but it closed the following year. Apart from stationing men at casinos who offer usurious loans at rates as high as 10 percent a day, this group openly advertises its loans with daily, weekly, and monthly interest rates in Chinese-language newspapers. Money-lending businesses operate as shareholding companies, with partners putting up the initial capital that is lent out. Usurious loans taken at casinos are usually not disputed, but if they are not paid back, the usurers may send enforcers who threaten the client with violence and sometimes even kidnap him. Businessmen too sometimes hire these enforcers to collect debts, and disputes arise when they add usurious interest to the debt, even though that was not agreed to at the time of the loan.[74]

In 2001 a poker club called Qianxilong, catering exclusively to Chinese, opened at one of the Chinese restaurants, with the joint investment of two Austrians, a Chinese living in Austria, and a group of people from Fuqing associated with a usury business, also known as the Huaxin Fund. This group was seen as a rival to Sunjoy's owners. According to a croupier at the club, the Austrians decided to invest in a Chinese-only gambling parlor because they believed that limiting the clientele would reduce the risks; they asked the Fujianese to join in as shareholders and help keep troublemakers from the club. The clientele is mainly Fujianese, but the croupiers are not. Later the same year, another Fujianese opened another casino opposite the Four Tigers Market.

Employment and Entrepreneurship in Europe

Relatively unregulated markets and unfilled market niches have allowed entrepreneurial Chinese migrants in eastern Europe to gain a significant market share for certain kinds of imports. Some have developed midsized regional businesses, in some cases expanding into western Europe and beyond through ties of acquaintanceship or kinship, or through western European business partners encountered on business in eastern Europe. To an extent, such entrepreneurship may serve as a model for Chinese in western Europe, who in varying degrees are constrained by the limits of the traditional ethnic economy, a lack of connections in today's China, higher costs, and more mature markets. Chinese migrants in southern and western Europe have pioneered new businesses outside catering and leather/garment assembly, but these are smaller than in eastern Europe. The most conspicuous development has been the spread of travel and other service agencies, in which Fujianese have also participated. One of the vice-presidents of the Fujian Association in Germany originally went to Germany to represent a Fujian state enterprise and now has his own travel agency. The president of the Fujian Association in the Netherlands has agreed to start up a travel agency with the backing of the Fujian Province Travel Agency. In London Chinatown, several Fujianese have also opened small hairdressers' shops, beauty parlors, video rental shops, and service agencies selling telephone cards and providing translations. A group of Fujianese imported spirits and uniforms from Fujian, but attempted to sell them only on the ethnic market: the uniforms were intended for Fujianese restaurant workers. In Italy and Spain, some longer-term Chinese residents have managed to accumulate start-up capital to open shops and import companies similar to those in eastern Europe, focusing on low-price garments and shoes. In Italy some of the wholesale garment shops at the Piazza Vittorio Veneto in Rome are owned by Fujianese.

The economic activities of the Fujianese in Europe are very similar to those of recent Chinese migrants in a similar situation (recent influx, little capital, high incidence of irregularity), predominantly those from Zhejiang, but they suffer the disadvantages of more recent arrival and a lack of a network of local kin and friends. Most are still employed as wage laborers, but some have started opening their own businesses. These lower-cost and more family-based Chinese businesses increase competition and reduce profits in the already crowded restaurant and garment/leather manufacturing sectors. Consequently, both in Britain and Italy, where these sectors are most prominent, earnings in the Chinese ethnic economies have declined.

The greater subethnic homogeneity of Fujianese-owned businesses (i.e., businesses that are purely Fujianese, without other employees) is due to the availability of manpower within the family or among acquaintances and the smaller scale of these enterprises, and it does not mean that Fujianese operate in a segregated economy. In fact, there are instances of non-Fujianese working in larger and older Fujianese-owned businesses in Italy.

Beyond making money, getting a residence permit, and opening a business of one's own, brokering large international business transactions is seen as a sign of upward mobility and success. In the words of the chairman of the Fujian Association in the Czech Republic, whom we interviewed at the World Fujianese Fellowship Conference in Quanzhou, Fujian, in 1999:

We are not interested in trading at the market anymore. We want to establish liaisons with many other organizations. We introduce Chinese products and investment [opportunities] to Czech businesses and vice versa. We introduce Hong Kong entrepreneurs to Europe, or entrepreneurs from the North, not limited to Fujian. What matters is that they are from China. Chinese investors are interested in building roads and electronics plants in the Czech Republic. Rich business visitors from Hong Kong go to Europe thanks to my introduction. Now we will use the contacts we made at this congress to spread information about investment in the Czech Republic to Singapore, Japan, the United States, and so on.[75]

There is a general sense of urgency to achieve more faster. Zhang, a garment workshop owner in the Naples area who had been in Italy for six years and had just opened a workshop, is typical in this respect. Zhang stressed that "development" was too slow and that he was not satisfied with what he had achieved. He wanted to expand the workshop and then improve his Italian so that he could find new areas of business. He had a brochure from a company in China in his car and was interested in trading opportunities, but was not yet able to start a company himself.[76]

One characteristic of Fujianese business—and more generally, of new Chinese migrants—in Europe is that capital, like people and goods, is highly mobile in both directions between China and Europe. Unlike a few decades ago, migrants, at least in the early stages of migration, often have more access to capital and goods in China than in Europe. Furthermore, migrants' families who depend on remittances are less numerous than previously, and even they rarely depend fully on remittances for a living. Instead, remittances are used to build a house, start a business, migrate, or finance the emigration and education of other family members.

Living among Chinese and Locals

A Hong Kong–born London solicitor, who founded the Fujian Chamber of Commerce in 1996 and is an adviser to the UK Futsing Association, emphasized that he spoke no Fujianese dialect and did not even know in which part of Fujian his father was born:

> Our objective is to promote trade, and we have very limited contact with the Fujian people in Britain. We are not interested in the social development of Fujian people in this country. . . . Most members of the Chamber are like me, but some have nothing to do with Fujian, and are only interested in business . . . investment in Fujian, imports to Europe. . . . Asylum seekers don't even try [to find the Chamber of Commerce.] They know I can't help them. I do immigration work, but not for free. I have to get paid for my time.[77]

Their irregular status and illegal employment in the ethnic economy isolates Fujianese migrants in western Europe from local society. At the same time, many of them display an eagerness to overcome these constraints much faster than previous generations of Chinese migrants. They want to study, make money, and enjoy the material and lifestyle benefits of the West. Having grown up exposed to globalized media, young Fujianese migrants often display a great deal of curiosity, individualism, and resistance to traditional systems of power. One young migrant from Fuqing in London said:

> My friends are mostly foreigners [i.e., non-Chinese]. I meet a lot of people at the markets when I do business. After six months here, I could already communicate in English at a basic level, although the better you want to learn a language the harder it gets. There are some words the English themselves don't know. Sometimes I say words they don't know. Anyway, I have made a lot of acquaintances because, I know, it is very easy here, there is no such thing as obligations arising from personal relations (*renqing*); people can talk to each other without any consequences, but they won't help each other if in need unless they get something for it. Some of us have married Hong Kong or Vietnamese girls, but none of those marriages are especially successful. I can't get along with those girls because they look too much at your money. They rank you according to your social position and the place you come from, whereas the English don't care, they don't know much about the Chinese or what their motives are in coming here. And because there simply are more English people around, there are bound to be at least some that like Chinese. Indians . . . are more similar to Chinese; Indian girls are not so open-minded. Blacks are very bad, they steal things and bully people. As for the Fujianese, I can't get along with them either. They just work in their kitchens and sleep. What do they know? Some of them have been here for ten years and they don't speak Eng-

lish. They don't know where the British Museum is. They don't even know where Chinatown is.[78]

Despite their subaltern position, such young Fujianese look down on the stereotypical overseas Chinese who, despite coming from more privileged backgrounds and enjoying legal residence, are content to toil in a kitchen and never leave Chinatown or learn proper English. Three young self-styled migration brokers and gang members from Fuqing we met in Prato—two of them were, despite their exciting stories, employed in a workshop—told us contemptuously that they, unlike "inland people" (presumably those from Zhejiang and inland Fujian), were not here to make a living but to make a fortune.

We found that migrants from Fujian have very little to do with Fujianese in Europe who come from Southeast Asia, such as the large communities of Chinese from Indonesia in the Netherlands or from Vietnam, Cambodia, and Laos in France, many of whom speak a Fujianese dialect as a first or second mother tongue.[79] A number of the ethnic Chinese migrants from Malaysia and Singapore in Great Britain and on the continent likewise speak dialects originating from Fujian Province and identify themselves as Hokkien (southern Fujian), Hokchiu / Foochow / Fook Chow (Fuzhou), or Hokchia (Fuqing). Typically, these groups emphasize their differences from the recent Fujianese migrants, although they acknowledge common roots and in some cases, for specific purposes, may even stress them. Unlike Fujianese sailors who have migrated to western Europe via Hong Kong, this group has not acted as a "seed community" or migration brokers for migration from Fujian. In this respect, dialect-based identities clearly are unimportant.

For these communities of Southeast Asian Chinese in Europe, the lack of a sense of belonging with migrants from Fujian comes from a strong identification with their countries of former residence (and usually birth) and current residence, as well as very different experiences of migration, class, and lifestyle and different economic interests. They maintain their dialectal identities, but localize them within Southeast Asian societies rather than in Fujian province. Within their European countries of residence, they generally identify with the long-standing overseas Chinese elites or local society more strongly than with the newcomers. The emphasis on the cultural difference between Hokkien and Hokchiu and the mutual unintelligibility of the dialects can be read as a euphemism for distancing established elites from newcomers and upstarts. These differences do not, for instance, prevent Southeast Asian and Hong Kong Chinese migrants from emphasizing their Fujianese identity when they need to establish relations with the PRC for purposes of investment or trade.

The same dynamic is at work at the other side. Migrants from Fujian do not consider migrants from Southeast Asia or Hong Kong to be Fujianese except in a historical sense. For migrants from Fujian, the operationalization of territorial identities—emphasizing belonging to Fujian, a more narrowly defined homeland, or to China as a whole—is as context-dependent as it is for Southeast Asian Hokkien. In Europe, apart from "Fujianese," other frequently heard identifications of or by migrants from Fujian are "Fuzhounese" (which is less strongly expressed than in the United States) and "Fuqingese" (which is more strongly expressed), corresponding to the Hokchiu and Hokchia labels in Southeast Asia. These identities fit together like Russian dolls, Fuqing being one of the historical "ten counties" of Fuzhou prefecture (Fuzhou, Changle, Lianjiang, Minhou, Minqing, Fuqing, Pingtan, Tong'an, Gutian, Ningde). These in turn, along with the southeastern corner of Nanping and the eastern corner of Sanming prefectures, make up the Fuzhou (eastern Min, or eastern Fujianese) speaking area of Fujian. The minority of migrants from other parts of Fuzhou prefecture (mostly Changle) typically refer to themselves as Fuzhounese and only identify the specific county when pressed. As one interviewee in the Netherlands said, "When I am outside I am from Fuzhou; when I am in Fujian I am from Changle."

Fuzhou and Fuqing identities continue to carry a special significance, as they did earlier in Southeast Asia, because they are very large groups united by a shared dialect spoken in a metropolitan area. In eastern Europe and Italy, people from inland Sanming and, to a much lesser extent, Nanping prefectures are about as numerous as migrants from Fuqing. Yet Sanming and Nanping have a great variety of dialects; moreover, many migrants are from urban centers, where they or their parents migrated from other areas. As a consequence, they do not identify strongly with any local dialect or place.

Migrants from Fujian, as newcomers associated with illegal migration and crime, are often stigmatized by other Chinese as a cohesive, closed, and crime-prone group, an image often summarized with the phrase "Fuqing gang" (*Fuqing bang*).[80] A young woman from Zhejiang who worked at a Budapest gambling club open only to Chinese related the following:

Before I came to this club I didn't know what the difference between Fuqing people and other Fujianese was. After I came here I talked to a lot of them. These people are very entertaining. They always steal, go to prison, come out, kidnap someone, go to prison again, are sent back to China, come back illegally, get fake documents, are sent back, come out illegally again.[81]

Some Fujianese, perhaps to counter their marginalization, themselves foster an image that links cohesiveness, martial valor, and cosmopolitanism. A Xing, a worker and self-styled migration broker in Italy, said:

If we trust someone, we will help, no matter what it takes. We are also equally vengeful, without regard to anything. America, England, Southeast Asia, all of that is our world. The Fuqing gang is very strong there. Hungary is our world too. Only in Italy it's no good. Our history here is only ten years, we don't have enough money [yet]. We wanted to organize a Fuqing gang here last year, but we didn't because we didn't trust the man in charge. He was saying all sorts of things, but we were not sure that if it were necessary he would really be able to kill someone. . . . No matter how much you beat us, you can't beat us to death; you can't mock us.[82]

The myth of violence is cultivated by both Fuqingese themselves (as machismo) and non-Fuqingese (as condemnation). The reputation of Fuqingese as criminals and particularly their level of organization are almost certainly exaggerated, although historical tradition and the imaginary of the tough Fuqingese may play a role. Their reputation probably also has to do with the demographic and social particularities of migration from Fuqing. Most of them are young, single, uneducated men with poor prospects of upward mobility in China for whom the administrative obstacles to going abroad were exceptionally great. Its price and risk were therefore very high, and the pressure to strike it rich correspondingly strong. On the other hand, Fuqing is a relatively prosperous area where, as discussed in Chapter 2, foreign investment is among the highest in the province, returning overseas Chinese from Southeast Asia are numerous, and consumption is much more conspicuous than in Mingxi. In the absence of other opportunities with a high payoff, then, Fuqing men may be more inclined to turn to criminality.

Fujianese are divided not only by ethnic differences but also by the same differences of class, education, and migratory experience as other Chinese in Europe. In eastern Europe, it is more accurate to speak of a divide between less-educated market peddlers (mostly from Fujian, Zhejiang, and northeastern China) and the better-educated northern wholesalers. In western Europe, the distance between the Fujianese and Zhejiang, Hong Kong, and Southeast Asian restaurant owners is an important feature of the social landscape but should not be exaggerated. On an aggregate level the Fujianese are more of an underclass than the Zhejiangese or Hong Kong Chinese, and, as we have seen in this chapter, are treated as such by members of the established communities.

In Italy and Britain their lower economic position is readily explained by their recent arrival and consequent lack of richer and well-established coethnics. In Hungary, the relatively modest position of many Fujianese can be traced back to their limited contacts with state enterprises and organizations back in China. In all three countries the difference can be expected gradually to even out, and the Fujianese are in fact already showing significant signs of upward mobility, with Fujianese purchasing lower-end take-outs, restaurants, stores, and workshops, particularly outside the metropolitan areas of western Europe.

Wariness of the "Fuqing gang" does not, in any case, deter fellow traders from Zhejiang and other places from doing business or engaging in social interaction with Fujianese. In all of continental Europe, Fujianese men, especially the more pioneering and enterprising ones among them, often have girlfriends from Zhejiang or elsewhere in China. Weng, who pioneered the Fuqing colony in Szeged, has had a relationship with a woman from Liaoning, who lived in Budapest. They also did business together. Weng also has friends and business partners from Shandong. Weng's older brother lived with a woman from Zhejiang and, before that, with one from Beijing.

Zhejiangese, like Chinese from Hong Kong and Indochina, are also employers of most Fujianese, and this leads to occasional antagonisms. Early Fujianese migrants to Italy recall with resentment the poor treatment they endured in the early 1990s at the hand of workshop bosses from Zhejiang. "We Fujianese feel like third-class citizens here. The first-class citizens are Italians, and the second-class are Zhejiangese," says the president of the Naples area branch of the Fujian Association and a vice-president of the Chinese commercial association of Campania.[83] His daughter, whose husband is from Fuqing, speaks angrily about the hard time her father had in northern Italy when he first arrived in 1992: they were staying ten to a room, and no Zhejiangese were willing to hire them. But her father acknowledges that intermarriage between Fujianese and Zhejiangese occurs and that "now we can say we are getting to the same level as the Zhejiangese."[84]

FIGURE 4. A Chinese peddler in front of the Florence cathe-
dral

FIGURE 5. A Fujianese workshop in the Naples area

FIGURE 6. Four Tigers Market, Budapest, Hungary

FIGURE 7. Fujianese looking for work at the "pavilion,"
London Chinatown

He: A Businessman in London

HE, BORN IN THE early 1960s in a village in Fuqing county, owns food-processing and export businesses in London. Today he is a British citizen. He married twice, and both of his wives were from Fuqing; he met his second wife in London. At our meetings, whether in his office or in restaurants, he always wore a suit and tie. He uses a Sony notebook computer and drives a large Mercedes with a vanity license plate.[1]

Like many in Fuqing, his family has a history of emigration that goes back generations. As He says: "My ancestors were all in Singapore; each generation in the family relied on their remittances to feed themselves. Seventy or 80 percent of families in my village were like that. As soon as they grow up, everyone wants to leave. It won't do to stay in China; everyone wants to ensure a good life."

He has relatives in Singapore, and relatives of his second wife live in Washington, D.C., and in France. He also has relatives elsewhere in Southeast Asia, but does not like to do business with them: "I have tried, but I don't like it. Then it is based on feelings rather than on business principles." Nonetheless, He has helped these relatives invest in real estate in Fuqing, because "I had the connections" and they the capital. He had a house built in Fuqing in 1988 for his mother and siblings. He himself has "[not] stayed there a single night." In the 1980s and early 1990s, He sent home "a lot of money," but since then He has set up a company in China that "pays all people I need to support: my mother, sisters, and brothers, altogether eight people."

He's father was born in Singapore but went to China in 1958 "to contribute to socialist construction." He himself came to England as a student in 1981 after graduating from upper secondary school. A paternal uncle who lived in England financed his college education, but He also worked at a restaurant while studying. After college, He studied for an MBA degree and started his first business in 1986. Later he set up food-packing and cold-storage companies in London. Their main business is the distribution of foods to corporate clients in Britain, but He also imports foods from China, runs an import-export and real estate business in Abu Dhabi, and exports British mutton to Greece with a Greek partner, whom He met in England. Another aspect of He's business is what He describes as training and providing personnel to hotels. He also owns real estate in Abu Dhabi and Britain.

He travels frequently both inside and outside England. Scheduling appointments with him was difficult because he was always on his way somewhere. When we first contacted him in 1999, He was in Abu Dhabi on business. A week later he had to go to Egypt to visit a friend who had made him a business proposition; He had met that friend in Abu Dhabi. He says the best business is in the Gulf states. He has also explored eastern Europe—friends from Fuqing who live in Budapest and Kiev invited him for visits—but He did not like Chinese business there: "Everyone there has an interpreter. This is no good. How can you do business through interpreters?" Despite his misgivings, He wanted to open a foodstuffs wholesale company in Timisoara, a Romanian city on the Hungarian border, "because it has good road connections to Hungary and Yugoslavia." But corruption and the wars in the former Yugoslavia made him reconsider.

In all of these businesses, He does not deal with Chinese, except for, according to other Fujianese businessmen, supplying Chinese kitchen workers (dishwashers and other unskilled workers) to Indian restaurants. Most of his employees in Britain are not Chinese, and most of those who are Chinese are not his relatives. In Abu Dhabi, He has a local partner. The foods He deals with do not come from China, although He does import some consumer goods such as slippers from China into Dubai.

Seeing the increasing number of migrants from Fuqing, however, He decided in late 1999 that it was time to tap into the business opportunities offered by his established position among his coethnics. Most of them, He reasoned, would want to open their own businesses, but would be unable to get bank loans because of their uncertain status as asylum seekers. Therefore, in May 2000, He opened Futsing Finance

Pte. Ltd. in Chinatown with starting capital of £250,000, 75 percent of which was put up by He and the rest by his friends.

He says that Futsing Finance is registered as a building society, the British term for a credit co-operative. The building society, as a "community banking" agent of National Westminster, a major British bank, is authorized to handle savings accounts, loans, money transfers, insurance, letters of credit, credit cards, and pension schemes. National Westminster's name does not appear in Chinese on any company information.

He says that Futsing Finance's services are open to all Fujianese whom the staff deems to be creditworthy, including asylum applicants with work permits—that is, those who have been in England for more than six months and have not had their applications refused within that time. Apart from migrants from Fuqing, several Changle people have already borrowed from the society to buy take-out restaurants. But He prefers members of the UK Futsing Association, which He heads and which operates from the company's premises, as members of the building society. In early 2001, He said the building society had over 300 members. The members were divided into groups based on place of origin within Fuqing. The head of each group was responsible for handling the deposits of the members of his group and handing them collectively to the building society. All deposits, He stated, came from wages: "We don't accept black money."

The most popular service of Futsing Finance appears to be interest-free loans for the purchase or lease of take-out restaurants. The loan constitutes half of the sum and is offered for one year, when members can again obtain a loan, but at an interest rate similar to that from a bank. Financial and property arrangements for these restaurant purchases are flexible and seem to be aimed at increasing Futsing Finance's real estate holdings, while facilitating the spread of Fujianese businesses. A Hong Kong–born solicitor whose parents were from Fujian advises Futsing Finance on real estate purchases, and the company also has a real estate agent who looks for properties. By November 2000, Futsing Finance had purchased two take-out restaurants, for which it then sold the lease to members, and took two further leases, all in London, in its own name. Most of the property is purchased from non-Chinese owners, because, He says, "the Chinese tend to cheat you and overprice." One of the properties Futsing Finance has purchased is a building with a grocery store on the ground floor and residential flats on the upper floors. The Futsing Finance member who leases the property from Futsing Finance has rented the grocery out to an Indian and the flats to Chinese.

Another popular service is money transfer. Here, He explains, there are two advantages over a bank. First, the company pools the sums to be transferred, thereby reducing the bank fee. Second, it keeps a certain amount of money in an account in China so that it can be disbursed immediately if the member cannot wait until the transfer is completed. In addition, like many other Fujianese businesses, Futsing Finance also sells international telephone cards.

The company targets not only Fujianese in Britain but also Fujianese around the world with migration and investment-related services. It advertises in *Shijie Rongyin*, the magazine of the World Futsing Association (Shijie Fuqing Tongxiang Lianyihui), a Hong Kong–based body that comprises organizations all over the world.[2] The advertisement offers the following services: information for and about overseas Chinese, the organization of trade fairs, the registration of companies in Britain, investment immigration, visas, and letters of financial guarantee for student visas. At the meeting of the World Futsing Association in Fuqing in 2000, He approached ethnic Fuqingese from Hong Kong and Singapore with suggestions to invest their money in real estate in Britain. He would also like to open a branch of the company in Manchester, and possibly in France, the Netherlands, and the United States.

The turnover target for the first year of Futsing Finance's operation was 15 million pounds. Half of the profit went to support the UK Futsing Association and the other half was divided among He and the other owners.

He's recruitment strategy for Futsing Finance is different from that used in his other businesses. All employees of Futsing Finance are recent migrants from Fuqing, and most are personal acquaintances. One used to be He's friend in China and is now in England as a student; another is an ex-sister-in-law. The distinction between Futsing Finance employees and those of the UK Futsing Association is unclear; He says that two employees are on the association's payroll and two on that of Futsing Finance.

He's days belong to his "non-Chinese" businesses, the evenings to his Fujianese activities. He comes to the Futsing Finance office between 6:00 and 8:00 P.M. to look at the balance book and to meet men—either customers or leaders of the native-place groupings in the building society—who come to report or ask for something. Sometimes He stays as

late as 9:30. In addition, He often attends Fujianese functions in Chinatown or those of the mainstream Chinatown elite.

He portrays Futsing Finance as not just a business, but a service that
aims to advance the interests of migrants from Fuqing and the rest of
Fujian. His exposition of his business activities is often couched in
moral terms: "We encourage people to set up savings accounts. We
don't give them credit cards because they would gamble and not be
able to pay back." But He also intends the Futsing Association to have
a business function. He wants the association to open a representative
office in Fuqing, using a building he owns. The office would provide
communication with relatives in Britain via videoconferencing facilities
and offer investment opportunities in businesses owned by Fuqingese
in Britain.

Indeed, He's recent inroads into Fujianese ethnic business have been
inseparable from his ambitions as organization leader. He founded the
UK Futsing Association (Yingguo Fuqing tongxianghui) in 1996. The
organization's statutes define it as a nonprofit nongovernmental organization that does not participate in political, religious, or party activities; encourages the unification of Fuqingese and Chinese in general
across the United Kingdom; promotes legal businesses of Fuqingese
and supports "homeland construction"; represents Fuqingese in their
dealings with Chinese and British authorities, protecting their legal
rights and interests; and organizes health and entertainment activities.
On paper, the services of the organization are clearly geared toward
asylum seekers. It offers to members translations (such as help reading
an official letter); a correspondence address; help finding employment,
medical care, legal aid, and accommodations; and basic English training free of charge.

According to the statutes, the association's general assembly, held
once a year, elects the president, three vice-presidents, and other officials. Members are divided into groups according to native place, each
with its head and deputy head.

Various remarks by He and by Chang, the leader of the rival UK Fujian Association (Yingguo Fujian tongxianghui), who is from Changle,
suggest that, originally, He intended the association to encompass all
Fujianese, but animosity toward Chang and Wong, an influential ethnic
Fuzhounese from Hong Kong, who founded the Chamber of Commerce, caused a split. Indeed, during our first interview with He, we
believed we were speaking to the president of the UK Fujian Association, and He did not correct us. He's own account of the association's

founding stresses the manipulation of official connections in China by his rivals Chang and Wong in order to pull the rug out from under the association's feet:

The [PRC] embassy [in Britain] didn't want us to have a Fujian or Fuqing association. [But] I know Song, the city party secretary of Fuqing. He is a very talented young official. His superior had introduced me to him once when I visited home. He called me and told me that he and the governor of Fujian were visiting Europe, and I asked him to open the association. He agreed. I had everything arranged, even sent out the invitations. But, I think, Chang gave one to Wong, and Wong gave it to someone he had a good relationship with: the second secretary at the Chinese embassy, Li. Li immediately forwarded it to the State Council [in China], and they forbade the governor to participate. I only found out about this when they were supposed to be in England and didn't contact me. So I called the embassy to ask where they are, how come I cannot find them? They were scared to meet us. Then the governor allowed Song to meet me in secret. The embassy didn't say why the delegation couldn't meet me in public, but I think the reasons were just personal ones. Frankly, I think Wong was a bit jealous.

He's secretary, herself from Changle, confirmed the existence of the rivalry among the three men, but portrayed it as an ethnic rather than a personal issue: "There are two kinds of Fujianese in Britain, those from Fuqing and those from Changle. Those from Changle have a bit of an exclusive attitude toward those from Fuqing; like, if you Fuqingese found this association, then we don't want to be in it. So they founded the Fujian Association, because some Changle people have been quite good in business."

In parallel to his efforts to build himself up as a Fujianese leader, He has also been trying to gain acceptance into the Cantonese-speaking Chinatown elite, traditionally the domain of wealthier Hong Kong business owners. In November 2000, He said that he was invited to join the prestigious Chinatown Chinese Association. To achieve that, He had to overcome considerable resistance. Back in 1999, before Futsing Finance's office opened, a well-known Chinatown restaurant and real estate owner from Hong Kong had still dismissed any prospects that He or his association would ever gain a foothold in Chinatown on their own: "We will provide them space if we know that they don't just use the name [of the association to do business]. If it's a charity, it really has to be a charity. He may have a genuine intention, but it won't work."

He's roles as leader of new Fujianese migrants, member of the Chinatown elite, upwardly mobile member of the British middle class, and transnational Chinese businessman are further complicated by the Fuqing-Fujian organizational split. This is reflected in the ambivalent ways He relates to his identity as Fujianese and Chinese. In some situations, He portrays himself as one of "the Fujianese"; in others, He distances himself from them, stressing their "backward" and rural nature and "low quality": "The Fujianese are of poorer quality than Malaysians, they are loud, don't speak English, and so on." He said that he had had to sell a hair salon he had briefly operated for Fujianese because they were just sitting there, smoking and talking loudly, and scaring away other customers.

In part, He admits that the distance he seeks to create between himself and other Fujianese migrants is because of the bad reputation Fujianese have in the established Chinese community: "As soon as you help Fujianese, other people will say you are mafia." Despite the fact that almost all recent Fuqing migrants in Britain are asylum seekers, He once said that asylum applicants could not join the Futsing Association, "not because I want to exclude anyone but because I dare not. We [our reputation] would be affected. Refugees come to us, but we can't help them and dare not help them." Yet in reality, at least recently, asylum applicants with any valid temporary residence title have been admitted, and He, while still stressing caution, turned his justification around: "If we keep it very strict, then no one will be able to help these people. If they are legal enough for the British government to allow them to work, they should be legal enough for us."

Another reason He gives for keeping his distance from Fujianese is the suspicion of Chinese authorities, who are concerned about China's image:

The [PRC] embassy dislikes any new association. There are already too many, and . . . they cause problems to society, recruit bad people, fight, like the triads. Particularly with the Fujianese, everyone talks about them, the media, and this affects the reputation of the Chinese government. Li called me over to the embassy on a Saturday and said: "I heard that you set up an association. You are providing illegal migration an opportunity." He suggested I don't spend much time and money on this. But I said, "Their parents knew my parents; I can't reject them. Think about the day I return to China. How can I face them?"

A further source of ambiguity in He's identification as a Fuqingese is his relationship with ethnic Fuqingese (Hokchias) from Hong Kong and Southeast Asia. While he wishes to exclude such ethnic Fuqingese from the UK Futsing Association, he is keen on networking with leaders of

Hokchia / Fuqing organizations around the world that are members of the World Futsing Federation. Most of those organizations, and the wealthiest ones, are in Indonesia, where the founder of the world federation, Liem Sioe Liong, lives. He pointed out that "Liem Sioe Liong's oldest son's secondary wife in China is my wife's sister-in-law's younger sister. When I go back I stay in her house. Liem Sioe Liong's oldest son comes to visit her once every one or two months." Yet here, too, He's attitude is cautious and ambivalent: "The Fuqing association in Macao was just established last year, but there are some gangs involved. So we keep in touch only with the Fuqing association in Singapore and Indonesia. We have to be careful. We can't keep contacts with just any association," particularly those in the United States and eastern Europe, which, He says, are criminal or at least suspect. Yet during an interview in 2000, He had dinner with some people from New York Fujianese organizations, and was able to provide us the phone number of the president of the Fuqing association there.

He's attitude toward China is equally contradictory. In private conversations, He pointedly distances himself from the celebratory tone of discussion about the Chinese economy that the Chinese media promotes and many migrants espouse. He also dismisses our comment that Fuqing has recently enjoyed spectacular economic development: "That's [based on] loans. And the government has been cheated a few times: [the developers] take a government loan and then can't repay it and abscond. Or else they purchase the land just to sell it in two or three years to foreigners [ethnic Chinese Indonesians or Malaysians] and are not serious about developing anything."

He expresses pessimism about investing in China, arguing that prospects for profit are bad but also stressing his dislike for bureaucracy and for business that relies on personal connections. He distances himself from the "Chinese style" of business, even though, he points out, the Communist Party secretary of Fuqing is his friend:

Business opportunities in China are few. People don't want to invest there. Most people have lost money. . . . The investment projects the officials put together are unmarketable. And you can't do business in China, because the officials can't guarantee exclusivity.

In China, if you make a lot of money, people get jealous; if you don't, they look down on you. You cannot work over the phone; it takes a lot of traveling, time, and connections. It's very difficult. . . . Over there you need back doors, but we are used to not using back doors here.

He has indeed had negative experiences investing in Fuqing. In 1990, for the first time since leaving in 1981, He went back and, together with his younger brother, who had remained in Fuqing, invested in an electric wire company. He stresses that he was one of the first to invest in Fuqing after the investments made by Liem Sioe Liong, the Indonesian Hokchia tycoon. Yet the company lost money for the first five years. In 1990, He set up the first bathhouse in Fuqing. This business was initially very profitable, but soon lost its customers to fancier, newer bathhouses. He also owns real estate in central Fuqing.

Yet, despite his disparaging statements about Chinese bureaucracy and doing business in China, He has been active in entertaining Chinese delegations, and the Futsing Association's statutes state a commitment to "homeland construction." He met an official of the Fuzhou City Foreign Affairs Office, who later became its director-general, when the latter was studying in England, and helped him to arrange itineraries for visiting official delegations. Apart from the Fuqing city party secretary, He also says he has entertained the former party secretary of Fujian province in London. On some occasions He emphasized that Fujian authorities have been supportive of the association, because of the large amount of money that is remitted to the province through his building society. But at other times He described the hosting of such delegations as a burden and dismissed the conferences organized by authorities in Fujian for overseas Chinese leaders as useless: "We don't have time for this 'you meet me, I meet you.' The more people you meet the more you have to host when they come to England. There are actually very few opportunities to do business with fellow townsmen. We can't even finish with all the business in England."

CHAPTER 5

Fujianese Transnational Practices and Politics

DESPITE OFTEN intense participation in local life, the locality remains, in some sense, incidental to many Fujianese migrants in Europe. Through practice and discourse they are tied to a transnational social space that spans the globe, with nodes in Fujian, New York, and, to a lesser extent, other countries and cities in East and Southeast Asia (Singapore, Hong Kong, Taiwan), North America (Vancouver, Los Angeles, Toronto), and Europe (London, Budapest, Prato). This social space configures the perspective through which migrants look at the geographic locations that migration brings them to, and which is often more meaningful to them than local—British, Hungarian, or Italian—society and institutions. Granted, only Fujianese in privileged positions such as He can fully act out the logic of the transnational geography and move on at the spur of the moment to wherever they please;[1] others are hamstrung by a range of factors, including employment, finances, legal status, gender, or domestic situation. Still, even nonelite Fujianese *are* physically mobile at least in relation to China. And even for illegal migrants in British restaurant kitchens and Italian sweatshops, who appear so subaltern from a local perspective, study in Australia and investment in South America are a regular subject of telephone conversations with relatives in China. Transnational options belong to the mental portfolio of opportunities for these migrants as well.

In this chapter we first review how Fujianese transnational networks affect migration, employment patterns, and entrepreneurship across Europe, Asia, and North America. The rest of the chapter looks at the transnational politics of Fujianese organizations and the discourse of identity underpinning them. That we focus on these issues in the con-cluding part of what is primarily an ethnography of practice stems from our belief that, if transnational is to be used as a meaningful analytical category rather than a loose adjective applied to any cross-border process, it will have to focus as much on processes of identification and the construction of personhood as on processes of structuration.

Living in a Transnational Social Space

Fujianese and other recent Chinese migrants in Europe display both an extraordinary geographic mobility and a high degree of willingness to change social roles. We interviewed people who started trading in Hun-gary, were unsuccessful or lost their money in casinos, and went to Italy or Germany to work in leather workshops or restaurants for three to five years; now they consider using their newly earned money for new investments in Hungary or Romania. Others, whose applications for political asylum in Germany were turned down, chose to reenter Hun-gary illegally because they thought it would be easier to relegalize their status there. Several others who started trading in Russia in the early 1990s went on to Hungary, but as residence permit policies were tight-ened in 1992 went back to Russia or moved on to other countries in eastern Europe. Similarly, in the earlier chapters we documented fre-quent movement between Italy, Spain, and Hungary, between France, the Netherlands, and the UK, and between Europe and North America.

As we pointed out in Chapter 3, migration, even illegal migration, is happening not just from East to West, but also in the opposite direction. Many Fujianese (and Zhejiangese) have family members working in garment or leather workshops in Italy and in restaurants in Spain, Ger-many, or England. A number of entrepreneurs have expanded their im-port or restaurant businesses in several European countries and now circulate among them. Another migratory decision involves education: most Fujianese parents in Hungary wish to send their children to col-lege in the United States or the United Kingdom, and a number have al-ready done so. A few of these children have graduated and joined American companies, some of which have sent them back to Europe.

Transnational Networks and Migratory Decisions

Our research among Fuqing migrants in Szeged, Hungary, shows the strong links among different locations in the logic of transnationalism, and how important it is to use a multisited research strategy to comprehend that logic. There are several hundred Chinese in the city of Szeged, nearly all of whom are from Jiangyin township in Fuqing. Their numbers and the fact that other Chinese in Hungary associate Fujianese, particularly those from Fuqing, with violence, have given Szeged a reputation for being dangerous terrain for a Chinese outsider, and it is somewhat cut off from Chinese elsewhere in Hungary. At the same time, nearly all Fuqingese in Szeged have ties to relatives and friends from Jiangyin elsewhere in China, Europe, or the United States. Such contacts, as well as contacts with non-Chinese locals, are often more important in determining migration strategies and transnational practices, as the case of Yan demonstrates.[2]

Like most Chinese in the southern Hungarian city of Szeged, Yan, in his early 30s, is from Fuqing's Jiangyin county. Yan is the youngest of eight children. He told us: "Our family was poor because my father had died. . . . So when I was 15 I told my mother I was going to find work. I went to Henan, where I had friends." Later Yan went to Jiangxi to join other friends who had migrated there from Fuqing. By that time, Yan says, he had acquired good martial arts skills, and he opened a martial arts school (*wuguan*) in the Jiangxi town where his friends lived and became a popular personality in town. He also married and had two children.

His friends asked him to partner with them in a paper factory, but when it was up and running they tried to push each other out. After the paper plant failed, he applied for a private passport to go to Argentina, where he had a cousin. Meanwhile, he received a phone call from a cousin who lived in Szeged, who said he was being threatened by some Fujianese mobsters led by a man named Li. This was in 1994. Yan's cousin asked him to come urgently to help him. He counted on Yan's reputation as a martial arts master to impress his enemies. According to Yan, Li had been a soldier but had been dismissed from the People's Liberation Army because of theft. But thanks to a high army official who was his fellow townsman, he went unpunished and started a business in Fuzhou. But then he killed someone in a dispute and had to run away. Others in Li's group had similar backgrounds. In Hungary, Li and his group started a company in Budapest that bought merchandise from Chinese importers and sold it to Jiangyin people in Szeged. They did not pay their suppliers and thus made a lot of money. Later they turned to extortion of market traders. Yan says that although there were no real gangs (*bangpai*) in Szeged, what mattered was how many relatives one could rely on locally. "My cousin's family was the weakest. Although he had some relatives, they weren't strong economically."

Yan immediately went to Szeged. It came to a showdown between him and Li, which ended peacefully and without payment. But meanwhile, another relative of Yan's had a fight, which again resulted in threats and demands for compensation between the two families. "I told my relatives to stop doing all this," Yan said, "otherwise I'll leave. . . . But it dragged on until 1996. . . . Later, one of [the mobsters] and his whole family got killed in Budapest." During this period Yan was helping his cousin with his business, selling clothes and shoes at the Szeged market. Later, Yan's cousin returned to China and then went on to South Africa.

In 1995, Yan met Tímea, an ethnic Hungarian woman from Subotica, near the Hungarian border in Yugoslavia, who was then 18. She had fled to Hungary with her family when the war in Yugoslavia broke out. While still studying at a secondary school, she began working part-time at a food stall owned by a friend of her father's at the Chinese market, which, apart from Chinese, also had many traders from Yugoslavia. Tímea found the Chinese customers at her stall nice: they were always polite to her and did not insult her for being a "Yugo." Like the Yugoslavs, they were mistreated by the police, and she would try to help them if they got into trouble. Yan says that friends advised him to marry Tímea; he would thus be entitled to a permanent residence permit because she already had one. They married, and Dennis, their son, was born in 1996.

In 1997–98, Yan had his own wholesale business at the market in Szeged. He got his merchandise from companies in Budapest, and Tímea took orders from Yugoslav customers who came from across the border. Yan sometimes even delivered the goods to Yugoslavia, but usually the customers came to pick them up. Also, they opened a Chinese fast-food outlet at the market. Business was not bad, but in 1998, Yugoslav business dwindled because of the new war in Kosovo.

After Yan got his Hungarian permanent residence permit, the couple successfully applied for a six-month American tourist visa. In 1998 they went to New York. After five months, Tímea went back to pick up Dennis, who had been with her parents. After their visas expired, Yan and Tímea remained in the United States illegally. Yan works in a garment workshop in Brooklyn's Sunset Park, a neighborhood of new immigrants from Guangdong. The workshop is owned by a relative of Yan's first wife who came to New York in the early 1990s. Yan looked him up when he arrived in America, and the man agreed to hire him. Although the working conditions in such Chinese sweatshops in New York are often described as inhumane, Yan is satisfied. His boss allows him to come to work late or stay home if Dennis's nursery school is closed or if he is sick. Usually, Yan works from 9:00 A.M. to 6:00 P.M. and gets paid by the piece, making up to US$3,000 a month.

Tímea works as a cleaner in Manhattan from 6:30 A.M. to 4:00 P.M. She used to work thirteen hours a day for a cleaning company, but then quit and is now her own boss. She is proud of the fact that most of her old customers asked her to continue after she quit the company and that once she rode in the same lift with Harrison Ford: "I couldn't imagine this five years ago, that I would work in the building Harrison Ford and Pavarotti live in." Tímea does not perceive her current status as being lower than that of a prospective law student in Hungary.

Both Tímea and Yan plan eventually to move back to Hungary unless they can legalize their status in the United States, which they consider unlikely. According to Tímea, "The good thing about the U.S. is that incomes are high. You can attain what you want quickly. But I wouldn't like to stay here. As soon as we have made enough money to do something back home, we'll go back, either to China or to Hungary. Both of us are more used to living there and the child can go to a Hungarian school." In Hungary, they would open a shop selling furniture and other home furnishings. Tímea would also like to study law, but she cannot afford to do so in the United States. But before they go back, they want to make more money and to have an American-born child. Tímea said: "Then we'll have four citizenships in the family: Chinese, Yugoslav, Hungarian, and American."

Geographic and Social Mobility

Despite a modest background and limited means, Yan and Tímea were a geographically highly mobile couple, whose mobility was supported by a wide network of kin and friends on at least four continents. Perhaps even more important, to the couple, geographic and social mobility were closely linked. They did not think or talk about their life as rooted in one location, but as the exploration of opportunities around the globe. It is this biographical aspect of transnationalism that makes living in a transnational social space a daily reality, even for people who do not have the money, mettle, or luck to act on it successfully.

In Case 1 we describe the failed migratory experiences in Europe of

Luo Wu: he returned to China without money or a residence permit. In his brother's house in Mingxi he discussed with us the pros and cons of migrating to Australia. Luo Wu, and many others like him we spoke to in Fujian, Italy, Hungary, and Britain, did not have the ability to start an import business in Europe or to study in the United States, but they nevertheless frequently sought and dispensed information about both. An acquaintance of Luo's, Ding, suffered from a chronic illness and was sometimes barely able to make ends meet peddling at the Budapest market, yet he was similarly undeterred. Although he could not afford to pay the middleman's fee believed to be necessary to obtain a visa for his wife and son, he nonetheless said: "Later, when they get residence permits, they can go to western Europe to make more money, even US$1,000. [In] any of the neighboring countries—Austria, the Netherlands, France, Germany—you can make more money. There are many people from Mingxi there." On another occasion, he said that, eventually, his son could also go to the United States because recently some friends had gone from Hungary to the United States with a visa. He said that the pastor at the Chinese church in Budapest, a Taiwanese-American, had promised to help him.[3]

A friend of Ding's had migrated from Hungary to Austria and remained there illegally as an itinerant peddler. His example inspired Ding as he compared their situations: "He says he makes a lot of money; he can save $1,000 a month. He says the police are not like here, they don't check people in the streets, only in the big restaurants. He says it's better than here. Telephone calls to China only cost 80 forints. Here they cost 500! It is true that other expenses are a bit higher, but he makes a lot of money."[4]

As stories of success are circulated globally they turn into the stuff of a transnational social space that is not limited to the elites (see M. Li 1999). Wealthy and well-connected individuals, who rely more on social and economic capital accumulated in China and elsewhere, nevertheless often live in a denser and wider transnational social space. They often move continuously among several countries in which they work, trade, invest, study, educate their children, and network with officials. Because of the nature of entrepreneurial migration to eastern Europe, such practices are more common among migrants there, but they are by no means absent in western Europe as well, as our case study of He shows (see Case 4). For example, a married couple, both former employees of state-owned companies in China, live in Warsaw and Budapest respectively, running import and restaurant businesses and visiting each other once every fortnight. They have companies in Beijing and Fujian that arrange the supply of merchandise from China. They own another company in Hong Kong to take care of financial arrangements. They visit these companies several times a year. Furthermore, they are completing immigration procedures for Canada, where they have opened a business that employs more than ten people, and have already bought a house in Vancouver. The focus of the business in Vancouver is the same as in Warsaw and Budapest: supplying supermarkets and discount stores with low-end garments, shoes, photographic film, and other consumer items. In addition, they supply a German-based furniture maker with raw materials for its plants across eastern Europe. As the wife said, "It doesn't matter where I do my business: I can do the same whether I am in Budapest or in Canada. It's not so much a matter of where you live as of what passport you carry." Another couple, the owners of a warehouse in Hungary, have immigrated to the United States. They settled in Los Angeles, where their son now goes to school, but continue to split their time among Hungary, China, and America.[5]

One reason for the importance of transnational social space in shaping the migratory experience is that it can redraw class boundaries. While there is a clear difference in class between the likes of, say, Yan and He, such differences do not constitute rigid barriers. Peddling at markets in eastern Europe, washing dishes in restaurants in Britain, and sewing clothes in Italy are activities people of diverse backgrounds engage in, from ex-fishermen to full-time students and former government officials. Working alongside each other, they learn about new opportunities and can sometimes benefit from each other's networks. "Benefiting" does not always mean upward mobility, though. Thus a calligrapher struggling to make ends meet in Budapest by making signs for restaurants told us he was considering a move to Britain, where his daughter—financed by his estranged wife—was studying textile engineering at a university while working illegally at a restaurant. Such stories remind us of the ways transnationalism can both separate and reunite families, in ways that can be both liberating and destructive.

In sum, despite their connections to the locality they live in, which are sometimes manifold and successful, one can argue that Fujianese migrants, or at least many of them, live primarily in a transnational social space where flexible accumulation of local—social, cultural, or economic—capital is part of a continuous management of opportunities of geographic and social mobility.

The restlessness of Fujianese migrants is made possible by certain infrastructural factors summed up by Harvey as "time-space compression" (Harvey 1989). But it is also the result of a frame of reference informed by images of global modernity and wealth that today are not only transmitted worldwide on Chinese-language satellite television, but also brought directly to places such as Fuqing. Today's migrants no longer simply switch between the idioms of two localities, but carry with them an idiom that enables them to be self-consciously Fuqingese, Chinese, British, Hungarian, and global all at once. This idiom questions the naturalness of the subordinate position of nonlocal groups in immigrant societies and reinforces in migrants the feeling of legitimacy about manipulating and circumventing immigration and labor regimes of various nation-states. This imaginary, to whose construction and operationalization we now turn, is an essential element of the functioning of Fujianese transnationalism.

Organizations, Politics, and the Operationalization of Identity

The main locus of Fujianese community politics in Europe is the organizations that claim to represent migrants from Fujian or, more narrowly, Fuzhou or Fuqing. At the completion of our research in March 2001, we knew of twelve such organizations in Europe, the first of which was established in 1993. Most of these organizations' leaders also participate in other, non-native-place-based Chinese organizations (such as student associations, women's associations, and chambers of commerce), as well as in umbrella associations uniting various Chinese organizations. All of these organizations share a loyalty to the government of the People's Republic of China. They also are very similar to each other in charter, formal structure, activities, and rhetoric. These associations are more a part of homeland and transnational Chinese politics than of the local political arena in Europe: they very rarely try to make an impact on local politics; indeed, non-Chinese only rarely notice them.

Apart from these, there are a few other outlets for community politics. Chinese missionary churches, Buddhist and syncretic sects, and dissident (with respect to the PRC government) political organizations also shape identity discourses and are potentially lively channels that bring homeland and transnational politics into the host society or transnational politics to the homeland. This section, after discussing the operationalization of identity by organizational elites, their transnational politics, and their relationship with Fujianese outside the elite, also briefly discusses these religious and dissident groups.

Fujianese Organizations in Europe

Most of the associations uniting new migrants from the PRC were founded in the 1980s and 1990s. Many were set up with support from the PRC (although not the Fujianese associations in Britain; see Case 4), and they usually have the promotion of economic and political ties with the PRC as one of their primary goals.

The associations' activities and discourses are remarkably standardized. Association premises are decorated with photographs of Chinese officials and with banners, awards, and mementos received from Chinese government bodies and from each other. Unlike the native-place associations that have been so important historically among the overseas Chinese in Southeast Asia and elsewhere, these organizations appear to emphasize not so much the distinctness as the relatedness of their constituencies: their spaces recall government offices rather than ancestral halls.

Another difference from the traditional native-place organizations is that the territorial definition of Fujianese associations in Europe, except for the UK Fu Tsing Association and the Danish Fuzhou Association (Danmai Fuzhou tongxianghui), does not correspond with dialectal borders, and those associations' business is therefore usually conducted in Mandarin. It is as though the name of the native locality is a mere formality that legitimizes the organization as the representative of a part of the host country's Chinese population to elites of the corresponding administrative unit in China and, conversely, of those territorial units to Chinese elites in the host country. Fujianese organizations in Europe are not primarily interest groups that represent the Fujianese in their relations with other Chinese groups and locals, but associations that strive to gain privileged access to their native province. They then use the status and influence that comes from access to the government of their native province to deal with other local Chinese groups and the government in their place of residence. The associations strive to facilitate relations both between their constituencies and local society and between China and the country of residence. As the statutes of the Fujian Association in the Netherlands (Lü He Fujian tongxiang lianhehui) state: "[The] association is a bridge between fellow provincials in the

Netherlands and at home. This association shall encourage each member and fellow provincial to contribute his efforts to the building of a beautiful homeland at an early date."

The German Fujian Association (Deguo Fujian tongxianghui, Deutsche Fujian Gesellschaft e.V.) specifically proposes to provide services to Fujian province in import and export, joint ventures, organization of trade delegations and visits to fairs, registration of companies in Germany, organization of tours, study in Germany, scholarly and cultural exchange, and translation. Other associations may not be so specific, but their leaders also look for opportunities to act as brokers to bilateral business. Thus our informant He in Britain uses the World Futsing Association's bulletin to recruit investors in Southeast Asia; the head of the Fujian Association in Prato has attempted to get investment from China for a trade company; and the chairman of the Fujian Association in the Netherlands has become an agent for the Fujian Province Travel Agency.

This role of middleman also includes a reverse function, that of conveying requests and policies from the provincial government and the Chinese embassy to their constituencies. The association in the Czech Republic (Jieke Fujian tongxianghui) has enshrined in its statutes that "it shall spread relevant information from the Fujian provincial government and its overseas Chinese affairs office and exit and entry office." In effectively carrying out functions of the Chinese state, the associations resemble early twentieth-century overseas Chinese organizations, which acted as agents of the Qing and Kuomintang governments and were often headed by officials vested with consular powers (M. Li 1995: 12, 141, 267–68).

The motive of patriotism occupies a central place in the statutes of many Fujianese organizations in Europe. Thus, Article 2 (General principles) of the statutes of the Association of Fujian Overseas Chinese in Italy (Fujian sheng lü Yi Huaqiao lianyihui) includes as its second objective "patriotism and love of the native place, concern and support for the project of construction of the fatherland, promotion of Chinese-Italian economic, and cultural contacts." Article 4 further stipulates that the president and vice-presidents must be patriotic and declares that the founders of the association are "Italian Chinese who enthusiastically support all types of development of Fujian Province."

The main activities of Fujianese organizations include receiving and sending delegations, organizing fundraising drives for schools and flood relief in China (the latter also outside the native area), and organizing festivities on traditional Chinese holidays and national holidays in China. They also undertake charitable and mediating functions for the benefit of fellow provincials in the country of residence (such as helping families of murder victims), which was traditionally the main role of overseas Chinese associations. But this function is much less important than catering to objectives tied to China. The vulnerable situation of masses of Fujianese asylum seekers and undocumented migrants in Europe, for instance, is instead attended to by local Chinese and non-Chinese welfare centers, such as the Chinese Information and Advice Center in London and the Immigration Research and Service Center in Prato.[6] As our informant He made clear, the British Fuqing Association does not even allow illegal migrants and asylum seekers to join. Associations elsewhere act similarly. Association leaders in England, Germany, and Holland defend this practice by arguing that representing such people would arouse the suspicion of the local authorities and Chinese alike that the organization abets illegal migration. As our informant He put it, he does not allow illegal migrants and asylum seekers, "not because I want to exclude anyone, but because I dare not. . . . As soon as you help Fujianese, other people will say you are mafia."[7]

Delegations from China are most often made up of officials at the prefecture, county, and sometimes provincial level, mainly those who are in charge of overseas Chinese affairs and foreign economic relations, supplemented by managers of state-owned or private enterprises. Their hosts are organizations and companies that assume responsibility for the arrangements and program. These mid- to low-level delegations do not appear to deal directly with local authorities as partners; in fact, the locals are often unaware of the visit of these delegations, although from the Chinese side the visits are considered official.

According to organization leaders in Britain, Hungary, and Italy, the departments or companies that want to send the delegation usually initiate such events. The account of Mr. Liu, president of the General Federation of Chinese Organizations in Hungary and a native of Xiamen, is typical in this regard: "I don't know how they know about us. They call us and say 'We would like to visit, can you send us an invitation?' They know exactly how many Chinese organizations and newspapers there are in Hungary."[8] In fact, visits of delegations from China became so numerous that they were somewhat of an embarrassment to the central government, which several times between 1993 and 1995 imposed a ban on any further visits (Zhuang 2000b: 48). But both the hosts and the delegations can benefit from the visit. If the delegation is well funded, the hosts stand to gain valuable official connections and can also receive payment from the Chinese restaurants, hotels, and travel agencies that provide their services to the delegation. But if the delegation is short on funding, the hosts may have to absorb substantial losses.

Major festivities organized by the associations often include a performance by a minority arts troupe from China, with speakers of standard Mandarin preferred as hosts. "Pure" Mandarin serves to distance the modernity of the associations and their leaders from the ambivalent image of traditional overseas Chinese with their roots more firmly planted in the past of rural southern China.

The PRC embassy is often involved in planning such activities, which are attended by embassy officials and sometimes serve as occasions to communicate the PRC's political messages, particularly regarding the "unification of the motherland," which is the normal shorthand reference to the solution of the Taiwan issue. In the case of organizations composed of recent migrants from China, the guidance of the embassies is particularly easily traceable. For example, Chinese organizations around the world organized protests against the accidental NATO bombing of the PRC embassy in Belgrade in 1999. One of us (Nyíri) was in Bucharest on the day of such a demonstration and was told by the executive vice-president of the local Fujian association that the embassy had been consulted regarding the protest, in which, he proudly said, his association played a leading role.[9] In the run-up to the presidential elections in Taiwan in 2000, the PRC issued a "white paper" that threatened Taiwan with war if its government declared independence. Embassies organized briefings to explain the white paper to invited representatives of Chinese organizations.[10] Following the briefing, the Hungarian Chinese Association convened a seminar discussing the white paper and condemned pro-independence views.[11] In the same year, Chinese organizations in Hungary convened a "Three Celebrations Committee" in honor of the fiftieth anniversary of the founding of the PRC, the establishment of diplomatic relations between the PRC and Hungary, and the retrocession of Macao to the PRC. Such events should not be seen as orchestrated by PRC authorities; rather, they reflect the willingness of organizations to seek and accept guidance from the former and demonstrate their loyalty.

The organizations do not keep accurate membership lists, but membership often requires paying considerable fees; and the higher the membership level the higher the fee. Therefore formal membership, which ranges from the dozens to the hundreds, is not a good indicator of the influence of the organizations. Their activities, in particular the celebration of major festivals, draw significant numbers of those they claim to represent, including, in western Europe, asylum seekers. Through these events and the media, their construction of a modern, patriotic Chinese and Fujianese identity has an impact beyond the formal membership, but the question remains to what extent these organizations' narratives are internalized by or representative of Fujianese in Europe.

On this point we first have to mention that the claim of the organizations to represent Fujianese does not go unchallenged. One young Paris-born Fujianese, for instance, complained that the Fujian Association in Paris "is gradually degenerating" because, instead of transmitting Fujianese culture to the young, it focuses on business networking to the extent that even non-Fujianese can become members.[12] In Italy, two of the leaders involved in preparing the ground for the Fujianese Association were not born in Fujian but in Zhejiang, and, as some Fujianese pointed out, should thus traditionally be considered Zhejiangese. In addition, the association was headquartered in Rome, a city with only a few Fujianese, but where the Chinese embassy was located, delegations from Fujian tended to arrive in Italy, and, not unimportantly, where the leader of the association himself lived. Fujianese informants in Italy explained that these Zhejiangese became leaders of the association because they had the necessary time and money. The efforts of the leaders to organize a Fujianese association must have been influenced by the fact that, while other Chinese organizations in Italy were already dominated by other Zhejiangese, the Fujian connection was still up for grabs.[13] A student from Fujian in the Netherlands said that the Fujianese Association is useless and only serves people with money who want to make a bit of fame for themselves. An asylum seeker in London agreed: "Those associations have not been recognized so far. Including me, I haven't recognized them either. Ninety percent of the people don't know who the president is. People should be electing those presidents, but they just want to make money."[14]

Second, the instrumental nature of the patriotic commitment of the organizations is sometimes quite clear. A demonstration planned by Chinese organizations in Bucharest against the NATO bombing of the Chinese embassy in Belgrade was called off after the organizations said they had received news that the Romanian government would not allow it. The leaders of the three strongest Chinese associations then decided to hold a demonstration within the confines of the Europe Market, the center of Chinese business. Their argument was that, in any case, they could take photos and send them back to China. Photos with high Chinese officials and newspaper articles commending people for patriotism are assets of considerable importance when doing business or dealing with official procedures back in China. Organization leaders we interviewed, from the president of the Fujian Association in the Netherlands to the president of the Fuqing Association in New York, invariably had such photos exhibited in their offices and showed us such articles. This is what Zhu Dinglong, a Chinese living in Italy, wrote about the Chinese association in Rome:

In Rome, there is a Chinese community association that is supported by our embassy . . . it does not task itself particularly with the affairs of the Chinese that live here. They do one single thing: when delegations from China visit, the association pressures Chinese restaurants in the key cities to offer meals or money to contribute to the costs of the visit or the gifts made to these delegations. But what do all these Chinese that contribute 1 or 2 million lire a head stand to gain? They stand to gain good relations with the embassy, they stand to gain in connections: if one of those Chinese who has put money on the table needs help later, the embassy will certainly be more accommodating of him than of an ordinary Chinese. Furthermore, each time the supporters of the association's activities go to Beijing to take part in a meeting of overseas Chinese associations from all over the world, they may get the chance to have a photo taken with the top leaders and feel closer to power.[15]

According to the president of the Fujian Association in Italy, the establishment of this association was motivated by three factors. First, with so many Fujianese in Italy, the provincial leaders wanted to visit, but there was nobody to receive them. Second, every year there are world Fujianese congresses, and selecting people randomly to attend them became increasingly awkward.[16] Third, a clear representation of the Fujianese to the Chinese embassy in Rome and the provincial authorities in Fuzhou was needed in order to explain what kind of people the Fujianese in Italy were; otherwise they would not know whether the Fujianese were engaged in legal or illegal business. As other migrants from Fujian told us, a particularly important aspect of this was the fact that the embassy was not particularly responsive to individual requests for proof of identity, which was required to apply for legal resident status during the regularization campaigns in Italy. However, the embassy would help when approached through an association.

Similar patterns apply to the development and activities of associations in other countries. The associations have active links with the local Chinese embassy, while the demonstration effect through the infrastructure of world congresses sponsored by the authorities in the areas of origin was often the reason for setting up the association in the first place. The Fujian association in the Netherlands compiled the list of invitees to its opening congress, including leaders of fellow associations from all over the world as well as officials from China, on the advice of the PRC embassy.[17] Leaders of the French, German, and Romanian associations mentioned that their efforts were inspired by seeing, at congresses, how many associations existed in other countries or continents. The French association was founded after the current president's visit to the first World Fujianese Fellowship Conference in the United States.[18] In the United States itself, the symbols of political identification with the PRC—and with the United States—are even more powerful: the flags of the two countries are displayed at association meetings, and both of their anthems are sung.

Despite certain superficial similarities, the creation of new overseas Chinese associations is fundamentally different from the classical segmentary organizational structure of overseas Chinese communities. In the latter structure, native-place and dialect-based organizations represent lower-level territorial units that progressively fit into those representing higher-level units like Russian nested dolls (Crissman 1967). As we have seen, two things differentiate Fujianese associations in Europe from traditional native-place associations. The heavy involvement of Chinese state agencies makes these associations not a recreation of a segmentary structure as described by Crissman; instead they are a co-optation of the traditional notion of native place by the state and migrant elites. There is, for instance, no separate, officially endorsed discourse of "Fujianeseness" or "Cantoneseness" of the kind traditionally encountered among overseas Chinese, especially in Southeast Asia. Furthermore, encouraging the organization of migrants in different host countries along standardized provincial, prefectural, and county identities corresponding to present Chinese administrative divisions—however ahistorical these may be—makes it convenient for the government to arrange and administer its relations with them. Among the new Chinese migrants, the operationalization of the image of the home province and the homeland (*guxiang*) is anchored in the easily understandable myth of the authentic "fatherland" (*zuguo*). Provincial, county, and village identities are firmly subsumed in a single national discourse of patriotism and socialist modernization.

Other Native-Place Associations and Umbrella Organizations

Fujianese associations in Europe are not among the more important Chinese organizations, except in Romania, where the Fujian Association is one of the three most influential organizations. The reason for the marginal position of Fujianese organizations is the smaller number of wealthy Fujianese than of Zhejiangese and Cantonese. In addition, in Russia and the UK, leaders of the Fujianese organizations say they do not want a high profile in order to avoid being accused of having contacts with criminal organizations. That the organization particularly fears scrutiny in Britain is easy to understand, because government and public attention to "snakeheads" has been highest there, especially after the tragedy in Dover. In Russia, the reasons may have more to do with relations with other Chinese migrants. Southerners and particularly Fujianese there have been subjected to hostility from migrants from northern China, who constitute the majority.

The phenomenon of "overlapping leadership" observed in earlier overseas Chinese organizations (Crissman 1967; Skinner 1958) is widespread among Fujianese organization leaders in Europe, although it is more prominent in southern and eastern Europe, Germany, and Denmark, where there are no entrenched overseas Chinese elites that elsewhere often try to exclude Fujianese leaders. It is in Italy, Hungary, and Romania that "overlapping leadership" is most prominent. Officers of the Fujian Association in Hungary have all held numerous other positions in both permanent and ad hoc umbrella organizations. The president of the Fujian Association in Italy is also vice-president of the Rome Overseas and Ethnic Chinese Association (Luoma Huaqiao Huaren lianhehui). In Romania, the executive vice-president of the Fujian Association is also vice-president of the Chinese Chamber of Commerce. In western Europe, though, suspicions that Fujianese associations may be serving as cover for criminal activities add to their citizens' resistance to established Chinese elites. In Great Britain, the leaders of the Fujianese organizations do not occupy any positions in the umbrella organizations; in the Netherlands, only the president of the Fujian Association is one of several dozen board members of the General Chinese Association in the Netherlands (Lü He Huaqiao zonghui, Algemene Chinese Vereniging in Nederland).

Conversely, in Hungary some other Fujianese with ambitions to become overseas Chinese leaders (*qiaoling*) scorn the Fujianese Association and aim straight for broader-based associations. An informant from Fuzhou, who was originally employed by a state enterprise in Sanming and who runs an import-export business and a bar in Budapest, believes that the Fujian association "is useless, they don't even have an office. They have to gain some substance [*benshi*] first."[19] He not only became a vice-president of the oldest Chinese organization in Hungary, the Hungarian Chinese Association (HCA), but was also a vice-chairman of the Budapest congress of the European Federation of Chinese Organizations (EFCO; Ouzhou Huaqiao Huaren shetuan lianhehui) held in August 1998. He also accepted a position from a third, short-lived umbrella organization, the Hungarian Overseas and Ethnic Chinese General Federation (Xiongyali Huaqiao Huaren lianhe zonghui). In 2000 in Berlin, he attended the World Congress of Chinese for the Peaceful Reunification of the Two Sides of the Taiwan Strait as an HCA delegate.

Occasionally, the associations do get involved in local politics in ways that are directly relevant to the local Fujianese population. Most often these activities have to do with economic interests. In September 2000 the management of the Four Tigers Market in Budapest, where many Chinese trade, announced that it would convert approximately 800 stalls to pavilions and simultaneously double or triple rents, depending on the location of the stall. The chairman of the Hungarian Chinese Association and the chairman of the Hungarian Overseas and Ethnic Chinese General Federation appointed themselves vice-heads of a "joint negotiating delegation of Chinese and Vietnamese merchants" that met with the management of the market (the chairman was a Vietnamese former student who spoke good Hungarian). A vice-president of the Fujian association in Hungary accompanied the team.

Dissident and Religious Organizations

The native-place and umbrella organizations described in the preceding section neither have a large active membership nor regularly organize communal activities. In effect, only the leadership meets, while ordinary members, if there are any, participate only as guests at major, formal events. The organizations that actually create functioning social networks available to members, rather than only leaders, are evangelical Christian churches and organizations that promote democracy in China. All of these have successfully recruited among the Fujianese in Europe.

The recently created China Democracy Party (CDP; Zhongguo minzhudang), banned in the PRC, has recruited members among illegal Fujianese migrants with some measure of success. A Chinese restaurant worker illegally present in Germany who himself has joined the party, told us that there were some 1,000 members across the country.[20] One important reason immigrants join dissident organizations is to substantiate their claim for political asylum. The September 23, 2000, issue of *Zhengyi haojue* (Clarion Call of Justice), a publication of the CDP in Germany, claims that New York immigration agencies issued forged CDP or CDJP (China Justice and Democracy Party, a CDP splinter group) documents to help illegal immigrants seeking asylum in the United States, thus doing considerable damage to both organizations. According to the article, the CDP had discovered that some dissidents in New York supported asylum seekers' claims of CDP membership for purely financial reasons. They allegedly issued certificates of membership in phony CDP branches.[21]

In Germany, the July 2000 issue of *Freies China Journal* (Ziyou Huaren bao, Free China Journal),[22] a Chinese-language monthly published by the CDP splinter known as ADC (Alliance for Democracy in China), published an article signed by the German branch of the CDP. The article states:

> Beginning in 1994 . . . a large number of refugees that have come from the Chinese mainland in recent years have joined democratic organizations. But because their level of upbringing is not high, they have had some adverse effects on the democracy movement. They only hope to use the democracy movement to get residence; otherwise they do not care about the democracy movement; after obtaining residence, most no longer participate in democratic activities.[23]

Yet the phenomenon should not be dismissed as just another ploy of "bogus" asylum seekers. It can also be interpreted as attempts by prodemocracy groups to reach beyond the overseas intelligentsia that has turned away from their cause to the nonelite migrants who have experienced hardship themselves. Furthermore, migrants who may have joined dissident activities to lend credence to their asylum claim may, like one informant in Germany, become increasingly attracted to their cause.[24] Conversely, the very fact of their participation may be held against them by the Chinese authorities, putting them in real danger if repatriated.

Evangelical Christian church networks are sometimes strong enough to form the basis of business cooperation, employee recruitment, or even migration routes of Christian Chinese overseas. Numerous organizations, based mainly in the United Kingdom, the United States, Hong Kong, and Taiwan, support missions by ethnic Chinese Christians in territories new to Chinese migration, from Kazakhstan to Italy. The UK-based Chinese Overseas Christian Mission, for example, has helped set up fourteen Christian churches across Italy beginning in the 1990s. Many Fujianese are drawn to these churches: several members of the Fujianese organizational and entrepreneurial elite in Hungary are church members, including the publisher of one of the most popular Chinese papers, *Ouzhou daobao* (Europe Herald), who is also secretary-general of the Fujian association. His paper carries a weekly column entitled "God loves the world." In Moscow the Christian church founded by a Chinese-American missionary has attracted mainly people from Fuqing.

It should be mentioned that other religions have also recruited adherents among Fujianese in Europe, but without creating networks as strong as those of evangelical Christians. Jehovah's Witnesses around Europe who come across Chinese can get language training, literature, and guidance from Chinese-speaking "pioneers" across the continent. In several countries there are Chinese-language study groups and congregations. The active proselytizing of the Jehovah's Witnesses has made awareness of the Witnesses among Chinese high—especially in Italy and Hungary—and many visit the study groups, although very few become regular members. Nonetheless, sometimes personal acquaintanceship with non-Chinese missionaries is formed and maintained (Nyíri 2002).

The Taiwan-based syncretic Buddhist sect Xian Tian Da Dao (banned in the PRC and closely related to the better-known Yiguandao, which is also outlawed in the People's Republic) has established temples and sent missionaries abroad, attracting hundreds of Fujianese. PRC authorities do not take these activities lightly. After a Xian Tian Da Dao temple was established in Hungary, a rival temple was established in the presence of the vice-president of the official Chinese Buddhist Association, holder of various political offices, and with the support of the Hungarian Chinese Association. Now "official" monks from the PRC stay at this temple. Both temples attract crowds of worshippers, especially from Zhejiang and Fujian.[25]

Fujianese Migrants and the Infrastructure of
Chinese Globalization

In Chapter 2, we described the policies and practices of local authorities in sending villages with regard to migration. As we have pointed out in this chapter, though, Fujianese organizations in Europe often deal with Chinese official and quasi-official bodies at the provincial or national level. The contact with higher levels of government is most often initiated by organization leaders when they return home, both to facilitate investment and to source merchandise, and also simply to find reliable business partners. At the same time, officials in Fujian consider it important to monitor the emergence of new Fujianese leaders and organizations abroad and try to keep in touch with them.

As Zhuang Guotu, a leading scholar of overseas Chinese at Xiamen University in Fujian, who is also involved in official overseas Chinese affairs organs and who can be seen as close the official point of view, wrote, "two . . . changes . . . have attracted the attention of the Chinese government from 1978 onward. One is the Overseas Chinese wealth, and the other is the new Chinese emigrants" (Zhuang 2000b: 45).

China's View: New Migrants as Global Patriots

In the 1950s and again briefly in the early 1960s during the moderate interlude between the Great Leap Forward and the Cultural Revolution, the PRC applied preferential policies to the established overseas Chinese, mainly those in Southeast Asia who had left China before 1949 and returned or dependent overseas Chinese in China itself. These policies were aimed at divesting China from diplomatically damaging loyalties of expatriate (former) citizens and insulating the socialist republic from corrupting feudal and bourgeois influences of the overseas Chinese and their home areas. After 1978 many of the old policies were reinstated, but for a radically different purpose: to enlist the influence, capital, and business acumen of the overseas Chinese, particularly those in Southeast Asia and North America, for the new socialist modernization program. No longer principally perceived as a dangerous liability, the overseas Chinese increasingly came to be seen as a prized asset.[26]

In the post-1978 overseas Chinese policy framework, new migrants figured hardly at all. Migrants have only recently been recognized as a useful resource for economic construction in China, attracting foreign investors and business partners, as well as a bridge to overseas Chinese communities in Japan, the United States, and Europe, which are judged to be losing touch with the homeland and Chinese culture. The term "new migrants" (*xin yimin*) was first used in 1995 by the Overseas Chinese Affairs Office of the State Council (Guowuyuan qiaowu bangongshi, Qiaoban for short) in Beijing (Zhuang 2000a: 247, n. 1). A document entitled "Opinion on unfolding new migrant work" (*Guanyu kaizhan xin yimin gongzuo de yijian*) specifies the new policy direction:

> Since reform and opening up, people who have left mainland China to reside abroad (called "new migrants" for short) have continuously become more numerous. They are currently rising as an important force within overseas Chinese and ethnic Chinese communities. In the future they will become a backbone of forces friendly to us in America and some other developed Western countries.[27]

This fresh assessment of new migrants resonates strongly with the efforts in Sanming prefecture to build up a new overseas Chinese area reported on in Chapter 2. As we noted, authorities in Fuqing are generally more low-key about the facts of emigration itself, but they too are much less restrained when it comes to singling out the benefits that new migrants bring to their native place once safely out of the country. A Fuqing county Communist Party deputy secretary, Lin Houxin, called "able-bodied young men who have left the country since reform and opening to settle all over the world . . . an important component of the overseas Chinese force."[28]

Such official endorsements of new migrants are being promoted and amplified by the media. Newspapers and other written media have always played an important role in forging both local community ties and connections with China. And beginning in the second half of the 1990s, television qualitatively changed the equation of Chinese globalization. Commercial television channels and the official China Central Television (CCTV) broadcast via satellite, linking Chinese migrants much more directly and frequently to China and Hong Kong. In Hungary nearly every Chinese we spoke to said they regularly watched CCTV. Through this channel the Chinese government directly tells migrants that they will be given economic privileges if they are "successful"—and success seems to mean the same, money and legal residence, to the state as it does to the overseas Chinese families—and will also be recognized as patriots.

Driven by a desire to manage its increasingly dense web of contacts with new migrants, Chinese state agencies encourage the formation of migrant organizations (Zhuang 2000b: 48–49). They give leaders of overseas Chinese organizations and successful businessmen honorary titles, from membership in government-run associations like the Overseas Exchange Association, which exists in most counties and cities, to overseas membership in the provincial People's Political Consultative Conference. They also organize or endorse frequent and large congresses with thousands of participants to bring together leaders of such organizations. An organization leader may easily go to China two, three, or more times a year to participate in such meetings. These meetings structure the transnational social space of the "new migrant" community, creating a critical density of encounters at which the official discourse on the overseas Chinese is disseminated.

One ongoing project intensively covered in the press has been Project Hope, whose purpose is to build schools in poor rural areas. Schools built with donated funds often bear the names of the individual or organizational donor. Many of the Fujianese we interviewed in Europe, and all association leaders, have donated funds to local projects under this program and said they were informed about the projects by local officials or community elders (clan or temple association leaders) over the phone or during visits to China. All respondents but one said that their contribution was voluntary.

The fact that migrants go abroad with a sense that their migration project is in line with the values of the dominant discourse of Chineseness, rather than violating the national mission of socialist modernization, ties them more firmly to the Chinese nation as defined and led by the Chinese Communist Party. This also adds to pressure from the government to share the fruits of their success (investment, donations) with the homeland. New migrants are also expected to be successful and start contributing to the fatherland within just a few years, rather than given a lifetime or a generation. It is the rapid consummation of the migration project, rather than a change of the project itself, that makes the situation today substantially different from the precommunist period. All associations and their leaders who are regarded as successful Fujianese abroad have donated money to Project Hope, flood relief, and other projects.

Organizational Links among Global Fujianese

The first world organizations aiming to unite overseas Chinese from one sending area or with a particular surname across the globe were formed in the 1960s and 1970s (M. Li 1995: 131). But most date from the 1980s and 1990s, when such associations could gain access to China itself and began to enjoy the support of local governments in China, which recognized their potential to build connections with the overseas Chinese and to attract visitors and investors. Today there are world organizations for many locations, including Fujian. Organization leaders from central Fujian we interviewed mentioned having contacts with two: the World Futsing Association (Shijie Fuqing tongxiang lianyihui, established in 1988) and the Fuzhou Ten Counties World Association (Shijie Fuzhou shi yi tongxianghui, established in 1990). These associations are nodal points of transnational economic, political, and discursive ties to Fujian and China, displaying and creating a transnational social space that accommodates overseas Chinese leaders, local governments in Fujian, and the national government in Beijing (Zhuang 2000b: 48–49). The associations and overseas Chinese leaders use the official idiom of modernization and patriotism of Chinese authorities when speaking about their goals and activities, while the authorities gladly indulge overseas Fujianese by rehearsing the myth of the hardy pioneers.

The World Futsing Association was founded in Singapore at the initiative of Liem Sioe Leong, one of Indonesia's richest men and a famous overseas Chinese tycoon. Now over the age of 80, Liem is honorary president. Most of the member organizations—and thus most of the seventy vice-presidents—are from Indonesia; the only Europeans among them are He from England (see Case 4) and Cao Yanling from Denmark. There are also member organizations in North America, Argentina, South Africa, and Australia. In 2000 the seat of the association—which by then included member organizations in several Chinese cities—was moved to Hong Kong, which in 1997 had become a special administrative region of the PRC.

According to the executive vice-president's report at the association's third congress in 2000, the work of the World Futsing Association is conducted under four headings.[29] The first is promoting unity among Fuqing people and contacts between their organizations around the world. The second is supporting the founding and development of Fuqing organizations. The third is "vigorously support[ing] new overseas Chinese [*xin qiaomin*] from Fuqing; enthusiastically [inducing] the second and third generations of Chinese descent to deepen their understanding and feeling for the homeland." The organization "attributes great importance to supporting and cultivating new overseas Chinese [from Fuqing] and vigorously supports them in establishing their enterprises overseas." These aims resonate with official national statements on new migrants.[30] The fourth area is promoting the participation in "homeland construction" and recruiting investors "for the government of the homeland."

In September 1989, in the wake of the Tian'anmen crackdown, when contacts with overseas Chinese became especially important to a China shunned by Western powers, the Fuqing county head sent a telegram congratulating the World Futsing Association on the the launch of its bulletin *Rongqing*. Five days later he sent another congratulatory telegram to a meeting of the association's presidency in Singapore. In the same year, Liem Sioe Liong led the first delegation of the association to Fujian and was met by the provincial party secretary at the airport. In 1990, Liem led another delegation to Fuqing, where he worshipped his ancestors.[31]

After the founding congress of the World Futsing Association in 1988, the second congress in 1993 was again held in Singapore, but the third one, in 2000, was convened in Fuqing itself under the slogan "Unity, love for one's native area [*ai 'xiang*], development." It hosted more than a thousand participants from eleven countries plus Taiwan, Hong Kong, Macao, and six Chinese cities. According to the association's report, the total cost of the meeting was RMB 2,238,350 (US $270,000), of which Liem Sioe Liong's group donated RMB 1 million.[32] Although formally it was an unofficial event organized by the World Futsing Association, the Fuzhou party secretary and other leaders personally "inspected and guided" preparations.[33] Indeed, as the local newspaper *Fuqing shibao* commented, this was "far more than an event organized by NGOs; the great importance of the enthusiastic response it elicited for . . . a high-level united front should not be underestimated."[34] During the congress, the mayor of Fuzhou together with the executive vice-president of the association, also an Indonesian ethnic Chinese, unveiled a local water regulation plant, with Liem Sioe Liong personally pressing the button that started the water flow. Fuqingese all over the world had raised funds for this project, in Indonesia alone to the tune of RMB 200 million (US$24 million). The director of the Overseas Chinese Affairs Office of the State Council, Guo Dongpo, and the governor and party secretary of Fujian Province attended the congress, which passed detailed proposals "for the economic and social development of the homeland in the twenty-first century."[35]

Public statements by the leaders of the World Association display an almost single-minded focus on modernizing China as a goal of the organization, phrased as gratitude, love, and contribution to the homeland and its construction and development; these statements were primarily for the benefit of the central and provincial leadership, though they also acknowledged the locals in Fuqing.[36] But although resolutions of the organization sound almost as if they have been taken from a five-year plan, their details are not likely to have been unilaterally dictated by the authorities' interests; they are more likely intended to help shape government decisions in a way advantageous to overseas businessmen.

The official media in China eagerly echo the rhetoric of the association and its leaders. After the 2000 congress, the *Fuqing shibao* (Fuqing Times) commented: "Holding this congress in the proper way has very important contemporary and historical significance for further opening up domestic and foreign economic and trade relations, and for promoting even better the development of Fuqing and even Fuzhou and Fujian." The author insisted that Fuqing has become a famous overseas Chinese home area not just because its overseas Chinese are numerous, but more important, because they are all patriotic. Fuqingese are "industrious, frugal, and rich in the pioneering, fighting spirit"; their "determination" and "vitality" have left "courageous traces" around the globe; despite their outstanding achievements wherever they were, they wanted to "repay" the homeland.[37] This description of the "Fuqing spirit" is similar to that of Fuqing Party Secretary Song Kening, who at the congress said this spirit was one of "united team players, realistic pioneers, resilient entrepreneurs, courageous trailblazers."[38] The article continues with stock metaphors that celebrate the unbreakable tie of the overseas Chinese with the homeland, which saturate writings, speeches, and even informal conversations about and by overseas Chinese. Crucially, these metaphors conflate ties with the native area and with China as a whole. They laud the untiring national spirit of the descendants of the Yellow Emperor and Emperor Yan. The celebration of history and roots points directly to the future as well: Fuqingese abroad want to make their homeland "march in pace with the times and join the mainstream of the world."[39]

Going beyond the generalities pronounced by the party secretary, another commentator wrote that at the congress, along with overseas Chinese leaders from the old generation, "the elite of the second and third generations and the best of new overseas migrants from Fuqing" met with high-tech leaders and scientists from Fuqing living in China. This was important, he wrote, because it manifested "the transmission of the sense of the homeland" "to a new generation of overseas compatriots" and signified hope that "the association, in supporting homeland construction, will take a step from purely attracting investment and donations to attracting investment and knowledge."[40]

The Fuzhou Ten Counties World Association was founded in Malaysia, and it held its sixth World Congress in 2000 in Australia. The historical designation "Ten Counties" indicates the Fuzhou dialect area, which includes Fuqing.[41] As for the World Futsing Association, the drive behind this association comes from Southeast Asia, although there are many North American member organizations as well. The fifth congress of the association, with more than three thousand participants present, was held in 1998 in the Great Hall of the People in Beijing. The program of the convention was similar to that of the Fuqing congress of the World Fuqing Association, but, perhaps because it was held in Beijing, had higher-level officials in attendance. It featured the PRC anthem, addresses by provincial and city leaders from Fujian, the reading of congratulatory telegrams, and a dance performance. Vice-Premier Qian Qichen, Director of the National Overseas Chinese Affairs Office Guo Dongpo, and United Front Department Director Wang Zhaoguo all gave addresses, and Li Ruihuan, chairman of the National People's Political Consultative Conference, received a delegation of congress participants.[42]

Another regular event, not tied to a permanent organization, is the World Fujianese Fellowship Conference (Shijie Fujian tongxiang kenqin dahui). The first such congress was organized by the Fujian association in southern California. One of us (Nyíri) attended the third congress, held in Quanzhou, a large, historical city in southern Fujian, on September 5–7, 1999. The organizing committee of the congress consisted of provincial government and party leaders and was chaired by Vice-Governor Wang Yifu. This event, too, was dominated by 340 delegations of native-place, surname, and other associations. Other participants were invited individually if they were considered particularly important by the organizers. Most of the 2,638 delegates were from Taiwan and Hong Kong, followed by Macao and Southeast Asia.[43] From Europe, the Fujian associations of Italy, France, the Czech Republic, Romania, and Hungary were represented by small delegations.[44]

Various administrative regions in Fujian organized seminars during the congress to promote investment. The event was in fact scheduled immediately before the popular Xiamen International Trade Fair. While the rhetoric of the congress celebrated fellowship and patriotism—according to one newspaper, "Participants expressed their wish to contribute further to the great enterprise of unifying the motherland and to the construction of the homeland"[45]—for the participants from Europe with whom we stayed in touch throughout the event, it was primarily an opportunity to mill about in hotel lobbies and make potentially useful contacts with officials and businessmen from everywhere. The president of the Fujian Association in the Czech Republic said: "We will use the contacts we made at this congress to spread information about investment in the Czech Republic to Singapore, Japan, the U.S., and so on." Yeung Pak Kan, the president of the Fuzhou Ten Counties Hong Kong Association, told us that the only way he met Fujianese who live in Europe was through world associations and international meetings: "If people living in those countries don't visit back home, we won't know about them." Yeung was impressed with the president of the Romanian Fujian Association, whom he met in Quanzhou for the first time: "He has done very well with shoes; he also has a plant in Fuzhou."[46]

It appeared that the recommendation of officials present played a role in forming an opinion of a potential business partner. People considered to be "overseas Chinese leaders," either because they held honorary positions in the PRC or were mentioned by officials or in the press, were often better known to participants than than they were in their own country, indicating that the network brokered by officials was becoming a more important source of information than the native-place and kin network. For example, most of our interviewees at the congress knew about the chairman of the Fujian Association in Hungary from reports in the *Fujian qiaobao* (Fujian Overseas Chinese Journal) and about another resident of Hungary from Putian who is a member of the Fujian Province People's Political Consultative Conference. But they did not know about two other equally successful businessmen in the UK and Russia who could not boast such accolades. Both of the latter two individuals also head their newly established local Fujianese associations, but their activities had not yet been reported in the media or noted by officials.

Most association leaders in Europe know at least a few other association leaders in other countries, having met at one of the earlier Fujianese congresses. In Romania, Hungary, the Czech Republic, and Russia, many association leaders were acquainted before the organizations were established or because they served in an association in one country before moving to another. This feature of the transnationalization of the organizational structure suggests that the organizations in various places have a common standard and draw their membership from a single elite operating across eastern Europe.

The British, Dutch, and French associations have floated the idea of organizing a European Fujianese association.[47] Associations in different countries often send delegations to each other's founding meetings and other major celebrations, or send congratulatory letters or little banners, which are read during meetings or displayed at the association premises. Some association leaders, generally through higher-level Chinese organizations in their countries of residence, have been involved in the European Federation of Chinese Associations, which also serves as a conduit of information and coordination. The overseas Chinese affairs bureau at the provincial and lower levels also serves to bring associations into contact with each other.[48] Such mediation serves a useful role as a matchmaking service between new and still weakly organized associations, but also makes sure that no one whose views are at odds with those of the PRC is invited.

This class of transnational leaders is the main vehicle of PRC authorities for gaining control of aspects of Chinese globalization processes relevant to the government. It is state agents who do the most to institutionalize Chinese globalization, organizing holiday celebrations, exhibitions, arts festivals, and sports contests, handing out awards, congratulating each other with them, and then reporting on them. It should be emphasized, though, that the Chinese state does not wish to gain full control, let alone sovereignty, over overseas Chinese and their associations. Realizing full well that they are operating in a situation where state power is multicentered and has to be negotiated, the PRC authorities at the local and national levels have taken great care in setting their priorities and policy goals. The overseas Chinese elites are actively tied into an imagined "deterritorialized" nation and their cooperation is recruited for the project of socialist modernization. At the same time, these same Chinese associations and elites noticeably steer clear of active involvement in local ethnic politics in their countries of residence, preferring to leave this role to Chinese and non-Chinese organizations without ties to the PRC authorities. This is clearly illustrated by the seeming anomaly that the PRC embassy in London has been against setting up a Fuqing association in the UK (see Case 4). There were at least two good reasons for this. Fujianese—particularly those from Fuqing—were tainted by the politically sensitive issues of illegal immigration and asylum seeking. Moreover, and relatedly, more established local Chinese elites and associations distrusted the Fujianese and blocked the entry of their leaders and associations into the Chinatown inner circle. Under these conditions, the PRC's diplomatic interests were considered to be ill served by recognizing the UK's Fujianese associations.

Chinese Media and Migration

Driven by higher education levels as well as greater access to news and multimedia, the growth of media run by Chinese migrants in Europe has been much more rapid than in earlier periods. Owners of Chinese newspapers in Europe, all of whom once worked for state-owned newspapers, often invite editors from China to edit them. New migrant media have a remarkably standard content, style, and layout. Their reliance on the same stories from the Internet is in part a technical necessity because newspapers usually have small staffs. The range of opinions expressed in reporting on sensitive political issues—including any coverage of Chinese or American politics, and particularly issues such as Taiwan or NATO's bombing of the Chinese embassy in Belgrade—follows closely the line of the CCP's official newspaper, *The People's Daily* (*Renmin ribao*). The more specifically overseas Chinese content falls in two categories: the reproduction of the discourse of Chineseness of the PRC (focusing on cultural heritage and Chinese virtues), and overseas Chinese affairs around the world. The latter frequently depict the dynamic, resourceful, transnational Chinese businessman, portray the experiences of Chinese in their countries of residence in a humorous way, or report on atrocities or injustices committed against Chinese. In this way, the papers continually reproduce the Chinese / foreign dichotomy, thus reinforcing the perception of the countries of residence as foreign and other. The papers also report on contributions to Project Hope and other donation drives in China intended to build schools, bridges, roads, and other public projects, and on visits to China by local Chinese organizations to participate in congresses and state celebrations. All of these are heavily couched in the official discourse on patriotism and modernization.

Both narratives of belonging and the standardization of migrant media contribute to the construction of a global Chinese identity with shared values and raise cultural Chineseness and transnational modernity in importance to the reader. New migrant media are a two-way communication tool: they are used to convey messages from China to the diaspora and the reverse. Chinese state media regularly pick up stories from these publications, a relatively easy task because they are written against a background of the same assumptions, in the same style, and sometimes even by the same people as their own. New migrant media form a contiguous narrative space with the official media in China, amplifying their impact among the Chinese populations abroad.

Shijie rongyin (World Fuqing voice), a quarterly magazine published in Hong Kong since 2000 by the World Futsing Association, illustrates particularly well the extent to which the media space of mainland Chinese and overseas Chinese have merged. Many issues of the magazine start with articles by Fuqing officials reprinted from newspapers in Fuqing or their speeches in praise of the association. The magazine reports on historical and contemporary "patriotic overseas Chinese" from Fuqing and their efforts to contribute to the betterment of Fuqing. Another part includes reports on activities of Fuqing associations around the world, mostly in Indonesia. Each issue reports on the visits to Fuqing of leaders of some member organization and / or the visits of Fuqing officials to member organizations. Between *Shijie rongyin* and the mainland media there is continuous recycling of text (e.g., facts and figures on economic development, essays on "the Fuqing spirit" and "the World Association spirit," resolutions of the association). The party secretary quotes "overseas Chinese leaders" (*qiaoling*), and the qiaoling quote the party secretary, reproducing normative statements about what kind of people Fuqingese are. Indeed, the supposedly distinguishing traits of Fuqing people—that they are industrious and thrifty and have an eye for the market—are also supposedly distinguishing traits of all Chinese, so the claim is not that Fuqing people are different from other Chinese, but that they are the most quintessentially Chinese of all.

Conclusion

The current migration from the PRC supports and is supported by an infrastructure of transnationalism that strengthens both nationalism and state-building. New migrants from China are instrumental in state-building overseas, accompanied by the state's promotion of Chinese identities that are both global and grounded in the concept of the native place and the nation. Indeed, as in Mingxi county (see Chapter 2), the image of the global Chinese migrant has become such a symbol of authenticity and modernity that the ability of a homeland to create or support its own migrants or diaspora boosts its claim to modernity and historical authenticity. This "secondary nationalism" (Yoshino 1999: 11) is focused less on historical memory and ancestral myth—which are taken for granted—than on essentialized character traits and patterns of behavior to which people can relate in their everyday lives. Global Chinese media play an active role as producers of this discourse.[49]

It is a crucial question to what extent such patriotic narratives are consumed and internalized by those beyond organization elites. Aihwa Ong has captured the way migrants from Hong Kong selectively mobilize elements of various identities to cope with competing regimes of family, capitalist workplace, and nation (see Ong 1999). In our own research, we found very similar strategies for juggling conflicting identities at work. In many conversations, migrants used elements of the patriotic discourse and talk about Chinese being industrious and "an outstanding people" (*youxiu minzu*). They also commonly observed that China's problem is that people are of "lower quality" than citizens of other nations. Both kinds of statements fit into the speakers' agenda of picturing themselves as embarking on a modernizing project having to do with opening China to the world, but nonetheless carrying an intrinsic value that cannot be found in non-Chinese. In other words, to be a truly modern Chinese, international exposure is a precondition; conversely, this modernity hinges on a Chinese essence that continues to inform Chinese patterns of being in the world beyond China.

CHAPTER 6

Conclusion: Rethinking Chinese Migration
and Globalization

THE RECENT FLOW of Fujianese migrants to Europe is inextricably linked to the three events that arguably have contributed most to the fundamental changes in the world over the past twenty-five years. First, and perhaps most obvious, Fujianese emigration has been made possible by the reforms and opening up to the outside world in the People's Republic of China. In the twenty-five years since 1978, China has transformed itself from a hermetic communist state to a major playing field for—and increasingly also a prominent player in—international political, economic, and social events. In Fujian, the reforms upset the artificially privileged position of the province's interior, revitalized the links with Taiwan and between the overseas Chinese and their native places, boosted foreign investment and foreign trade, and enabled a much freer mobility of people, both internally and internationally.

Second, the further integration and expansion of the European Union, coupled with the transition of southern European societies from countries of net emigration to countries of net immigration, has made it easier for migrants to explore opportunities across the length and breadth of the continent. The increased freedom of movement has amplified the long-established pattern of Chinese settlement in Europe that saw Chinese migrants fan out from a few metropolitan core areas (London, Paris, and the western part of Holland) to ever more distant areas and countries in search of opportunities, markets, and jobs not yet taken up by other Chinese.

Third, the fall of the Soviet bloc opened up a vast frontier that was rapidly explored by Chinese traders, investors, workers, and (in the

Russian Far East) farmers. In Europe, direct migration to Russia and eastern Europe strengthened and linked up with the ongoing expansion of Chinese migrants across western, northern, and southern Europe. As a result, in the 1990s and 2000s the whole of Europe from Moscow to Dublin and Lisbon has become a playing field for Chinese migrants with networks and migratory flows that connect Budapest and Prato as closely as they connect London and Rotterdam.

Migration and Fujianese Home Communities

Migration is the dominant locally available opportunity of advancement in many sending areas in Fujian. Migration often features as a dominant strategy in local discourses on social mobility that prescribe what constitutes success and how to attain it; those same discourses proscribe (or simply ignore) others that locally are not considered an option. In the source areas of Fujianese mass migration a culture of migration has taken root that prepares all able-bodied men and women for their eventual departure. The culture of migration stigmatizes local alternatives to emigration as second-rate or even a sign of failure. Such a culture of migration can and often does persist even after the opportunity structure in the destination countries or the home areas has changed. The sediment of past rational choices, a culture of migration often renders current emigration decisions unintelligible in terms of a narrow cost-benefit analysis. Migratory flows from Fujian are therefore sensitive to factors (including policies) that change the cost-benefit calculation of emigration, but, once started, such flows can never be fully contained by government policies. In this respect, Fujianese migration is no different from migration from many other parts of the world.

With the onset of the reforms in 1978, strict controls on population mobility that had been put in place from the mid-1950s onward were relaxed significantly; by the mid-1990s, ideological and administrative barriers had ceased to significantly restrict both the internal and the international mobility of Chinese. This is not to say that the Chinese administration is no longer a factor. But preventing population mobility beyond what the plan ordains is no longer a policy goal, particularly in overseas Chinese home areas, where contact with the overseas Chinese populations is a cornerstone of local development strategies.

Migration as a Biographical Event

Currently, the chief factors constraining population movement from China are the immigration regimes of transit and receiving countries. The nature and degree of the enforcement of immigration controls determine how and how many Chinese seek entry. In the UK, this has led to the preponderance of asylum and illegal immigration of Fujianese; in Hungary, Chinese immigrants are mainly legal as registered entrepreneurs; in Italy, many immigrants from Zhejiang and Fujian enter illegally, usually with the intention of gaining legal status during one of the periodic regularizations.

Migration facilitators play a crucial role in the emigration project of many migrants. Obtaining permissions, passports, and visas is a highly specialized and often risky task. This is true even where legal entry into the destination country is sought, and is further complicated where there is a need for illegal transit or entry. Facilitators or "snakeheads" are therefore best seen not as hardened criminals, but as professionals who offer a range of services, some of which may be in breach of law, while others may be perfectly aboveboard.

Fujianese emigrate and continue to move after first touching base in Europe as part of a family strategy for advancement. Each migrant's core objective is to generate savings and remittances for his or her natal or nuclear family, or both. Migrants thus do not measure their earnings abroad by their local purchasing power, but by how much they can save and how much that money will be worth back home. Major decisions such as through-migration to a third country, extension of the time abroad, investment in an enterprise, and the emigration of additional family members usually take place in consultation with the other members of the transnationally dispersed family, which remains the core reference group for the migrant. We should not be under the mistaken impression, though, that Chinese simply surrender their personal ambitions and desires to the interests of the family. As in other contexts, Chinese migratory behavior often entails emotionally difficult decisions and conflicting claims; at the end of the day, each individual decides what he or she wants to do. Migration in Fujian is couched as much in the language of self-sacrifice for the family's survival and prosperity as in terms of personal ambition, adventurism, and success.

Despite experiences of suffering and persecution in China, Fujian migrants come to Europe with one overriding motive: making money by working as hard as they can. In making their migratory decisions, they evaluate the costs and possible risks of transit, their expected income, employment opportunities, and the chances of gaining legal residence. They are, on the whole, neither hapless victims of unscrupulous smugglers nor political refugees fleeing political persecution; neither are they attracted by the spoils of the western welfare state. They are, and should be treated as, immigrants who generate their own employment and, ultimately, wealth.

Work in Europe and Transnational Connections

In Europe, the overwhelming majority of Fujianese workers are employed in a Chinese segment of the economy that produces for the non-Chinese economy, although non-Chinese employers very recently also have begun to hire Fujianese immigrants in the UK and particularly in Italy. In Italy, larger and more successful Chinese employers also hire Italian workers. Despite these developments in the direction of a fuller integration, Fujianese migrants predominantly operate in a local Chinese labor market that straddles the interface of the general local labor market and a transnational Chinese labor market. The wages and work of local Chinese can therefore only be understood by taking the impact of both the local and the transnational Chinese labor markets into account. To Chinese transnationals, the wage differentials and possible level of savings in the Chinese labor market around the globe are as important as pay and conditions offered by non-Chinese employers, if not more so. Chinese labor continues to flow from the home communities, and just as important, Chinese migrants easily move from country to country in Europe and even beyond in search of better-paying jobs, more favorable immigration policies, or better investment opportunities.

As migration from Fujian increased in the 1980s and 1990s, both in the number of migrants and the number of areas of origin and destination, limited and often incidental connections between overseas Chinese and kin or friends in China strengthened and multiplied, tying home areas, long-established overseas Chinese communities, and new international migrants in transnational networks fully specialized in migration, charitable fundraising, return investment, and much more tentatively, international trade and investment. Equally important, many levels and agents of the Chinese state have become increasingly involved in nurturing overseas Chinese transnational networks for their own purposes of nation-building and economic development. Many ethnic Chinese from long-established overseas Chinese communities are actively engaged in networks and identity formation transnationally within the context of their own nation-states in Southeast Asia and in North America and Europe, independent from any residual connections to China or the Chinese government. Yet with the surge in Chinese emigration, these efforts will increasingly have to meet the challenge of new migrants to whom firm ties to China and its nationalistic discourse are much less problematic and are often even considered desirable.

Fujianese Migrants and Chinese Globalization

Our study of Fujianese migration highlights some of the consequences of the fact that both China and Europe have become major sites and players in the global arena. Chinese migration to Europe has increased in both scale and degree of professionalization, in the range of origins, destinations, and social backgrounds of the people involved, and in the types of activities pursued in Europe. Fujianese migration to Europe is thus a small but significant part of the globalization of capital flows, ideas, and people that create, in Manuel Castells's words, a "network society" (Castells 1996).

Yet our study also shows that the term *globalization* is too sweeping to be of much value in analyzing specific phenomena such as Chinese migratory flows and the transnational social spaces they have opened up. In this book we did not approach globalization as a set of processes that forge a structural transformation of the world order. Globalization processes do not produce an increasingly homogenized world exclusively dominated by global—and particularly American—capitalism in its many forms: economic, political, technological, and cultural. Without wishing to deny the reality of a certain amount of structural change, we would argue that phenomenological and situational approaches to globalization are equally important, because they highlight the fact that the opportunities and spaces opened up by the network society often are and look very different for Chinese migrants than for Western cosmopolites.

In the introductory chapter we coined the phrase "Chinese globalization" to look at the increasingly interconnected world through Chinese eyes. We realize that this term can easily be misinterpreted as overessentializing Chineseness and Chinese separateness. We therefore want to emphasize that we do not wish even to suggest that a parallel process of globalization is taking place that is accessible only to Chinese or is uniquely Chinese. Quite the contrary, this book shows that Chinese migratory flows can only be understood in the context of global processes that affect all people.

However, we do with the term "Chinese globalization" wish to convey that much of globalization theory suffers from the assumption that the natural nodes of globalization processes are the large "global cities": New York, Los Angeles, London, Paris, and perhaps Tokyo, Hong Kong, Singapore, and Mexico City. Globalization theory carries over from its predecessor, center-periphery theory, a spatial projection of differences of power and wealth that perhaps reveals more of the world that we academics live in than of the reality inhabited by the people we study. Most mobility of people takes place between peripheral areas rather than from a periphery to a center, a mobility that cannot immediately be grasped when looking at the periphery from the vantage point of the center. The centrality of the eastern and southern European frontier in Fujianese migratory flows in Europe illustrates rather nicely that for Chinese migrants the map of the world looks distinctly different from what we ourselves would assume, with centers and peripheries in some unexpected places.

Furthermore, while exploring the opportunities and constraints of Chinese globalization, Chinese also have to negotiate a world made up of social actors and institutions that appear to them very different from how they appear to the settled population in Europe. "Snakeheads" are not "the people traffickers who use the misery of others for their own gain,"[1] but are professional service providers, or perhaps even respected community members. Conversely, law firms are not integral parts of a precious legal system that upholds the equality of all citizens before the law, but gatekeepers for a highly peculiar immigration arrangement who require you to lie.

This brings us to the second and perhaps more fundamental point that we want the phrase "Chinese globalization" to convey. It will be some considerable time still before Chinese globalization reaches the point that flows of Chinese goods, capital, knowledge, or culture have become ubiquitous enough to say in a diffusionist fashion that the world is becoming more Chinese.[2] Currently, the flows described by Chinese globalization continue to operate within parameters set by a world order still dominated by mainly Western capitalism. Yet these

flows are at the same time distinct and distinctive, which becomes particularly clear when one focuses, as we have done in this book, on
global flows of people rather than goods, capital, or knowledge. Migrants are not mere commodities, but social actors in their own right,
and control over them will always be negotiated and tentative. Moreover, as social actors, migrants are vectors of capital, ideas, and goods:
gaining control over Chinese migrants is one of the key ways also to
gain control over other aspects of Chinese globalization.

Chinese globalization is, in the final analysis, a politically charged
process. Social spaces opened up by international migrants are therefore sites and modalities for the contestation (and sometimes resolu-
tion) of conflict. Such contestations involve a range of stakeholders,
none of whom can fully control the outcome, including agents of nation-states and the migrants themselves. When studying international
migration from the perspective of Chinese globalization, we wish to
understand how Chinese people, society, and culture become part of
the world, and how competing powerful actors (the Chinese national
and local state, states of receiving countries, overseas Chinese tycoons,
ethnic Chinese organizations and lobbies) seek to gain control over this
process.

This perspective has led our investigations in directions we did not
anticipate when we commenced the research. Highlighting the fractured, discontinuous, multicentered, yet interconnected nature of Chinese globalization has enabled us to steer clear of the evolutionist
assumption that globalization has somehow created a novel (postmodern?) form of social organization that transcends the conventional
fetters of modern life: nations, states, local communities, and perhaps
even class, race, gender, and family. Instead, our research has shown
how these familiar forms of social organization and the connectivity
forged by Fujianese transnationalism have begun to shape and alter
each other, sometimes simply reaffirming conventions, at other times
spawning mixed or indeed altogether new events and institutions,
which have at least one thing in common: no single party, no matter
how powerful, has as yet managed fully to control them.

Multiple Moves

Our study of Fujianese migration and transnational connections has
yielded an understanding of the dynamics of the surge in Chinese emigration that has increasingly profound implications for China itself, for

receiving and transit countries, and for the world order. In the previous section, we highlighted the connections between the new Chinese emigration and global transformations, while cautioning that such a macro view carries the risk of teleology: by framing the many changes taking place in the world order in terms of an evolutionary transformation, such a view can easily gloss over the many fissures, discontinuities, and unexpected developments that are most clearly revealed by a close-up view of the subaltern perspective of those at the periphery.

More concretely, in our study we have tried to do so by unpacking the image of the monolithic threat of Chinese international migration. We found that even a highly specific category of migrants such as the Fujianese is made up of different flows, each embedded in its own migration configuration with its own migratory routes, arrangements, destinations, and history. Furthermore, such migration configurations are tied to migration systems in sending, transit, and receiving countries consisting of multiple migratory flows to, from, and through any of these countries. But we also found Chinese migration to be a cumulative process, both within the established sending areas and far beyond them. The demonstration effect of the real or imagined achievements of international migrants tempts individuals and even governments to find ways to imitate this success.

Migration for our Fujianese informants was not a simple move from permanent settlement in one country to permanent settlement and full integration in another. Each migratory move was usually part of a longer career of geographic and social mobility consisting of several long-term or short-term moves, sometimes and sometimes not entailing a change in permanent residence. Before their own first moves, to most of our informants the facts and consequences of mobility were a normal aspect of life in a transnational social space, connecting their home communities with migrants (or their descendants) around the globe. International migration propelled only a minority of informants into a more truly cosmopolitan way of life, particularly the more successful entrepreneurs and those who had pioneered their own migration rather than following the paths across transnational social space carved out by others. Similar to (and in fact often joining) the entrepreneurial and professional Chinese elites living in societies along the Pacific Rim, these informants permanently negotiated and lived in multiple societies and cultures (Mitchell 1995, 1998, 2001; Ong 1999; Skeldon 1994).

Fujianese Transnationalism and Migration: Policy Considerations

The heterogeneity and transnationalism of Chinese migration do not add up to an unequivocal picture. On closer inspection, the category of "Chinese migration" gives way to a kaleidoscope of flows, biographies, and ambitions. More and more people are moving about the planet in more ways and for more reasons. Some of these people are Chinese; others are not. Chinese and other migrants are not all seeking to immigrate to centers of the world system in the United States or Europe, but simply have become much more mobile as part of their life in transnational social spaces. They are indeed moving to the United States and western Europe, but they are also moving to much less obvious places such as eastern Europe, Siberia, Central Asia, and Africa. Moreover, frequently a central objective of their migration is not permanent settlement elsewhere, but the ability to move freely when and where they want to go, including elsewhere in China.

Like many conventional theories of international migration, migration policies of national governments in receiving and sending countries are still overwhelmingly informed by the assumption that international migration severs migrants from their country of origin and permanently inserts them into the society of destination. From this it follows that the ultimate objectives of such policies should be to select only desirable candidates for future permanent settlement, to minimize the disruptions caused by the insertion of alien elements into host societies, and to facilitate the speedy and full integration of immigrants, ultimately turning them into citizens of their new nations who are fully conversant in the language and culture of their new fatherland, which itself is considered unproblematic and unaffected by the inflow of migrants.[3]

Our findings indicate that permanent residency continues to be important to transnational migrants such as the Fujianese, but often for fundamentally other reasons than is normally assumed. We found that only migrants who, for example, had a child or who fell seriously ill after migrating wished to gain residency in order to claim public housing or medical care (benefits were almost never an issue). Permanent residency was vital to the majority of our informants because it would give them the right to find employment and make possible free (or at least freer) movement in and out of the country for themselves and their families. Countries that issue long-term multi-entry visas with the right to seek employment to such migrants will not open the floodgates, but will remain internationally competitive and connected to the flows of transnational labor, entrepreneurship, and capital. Individual countries, no matter how robust or powerful they may be, cannot and should not try to seal themselves off from these connections. Following the experiences of more traditional immigration countries such as Canada, the United States, and Australia, several European countries (Germany, the UK) have pioneered schemes to admit migrants with skills or qualifications in especially short supply. We believe that such schemes should not necessarily be limited to skilled migrants. Unskilled migrants, like many of the Fujianese we interviewed, likewise do not easily fit the stereotype of a traditional immigrant who wishes to settle permanently; many arrive in Europe simply as highly mobile workers exploring employment opportunities in multiple countries.

Equally important, aiming for the legalization and regulation of Fujianese and other migratory flows is the only way to fundamentally address the current asylum crisis in Europe and the serious abuses that are currently part of the migration trade and the exploitation of cheap and disposable immigrant laborers. Although our research has not focused explicitly on the migration trade itself, we conclude from the evidence collected in the course of our interviews that debt bondage, violence, and abuse by brokers and enforcers are the exception rather than the rule. Having said that, the Dover incident in 2000 and recent police investigations in the UK have shown that criminal negligence, extortion, and even hostage-taking do occur. But we believe that pushing the migration trade even further underground will very likely only raise the risk and price of transit and with it the likelihood that irregular migrants will suffer even more.

Similarly, irregular migrants employed in the ethnic Chinese sector and elsewhere are without legal protection and are fully exposed to the rigors of the labor market. This may work to their advantage when the economy of the ethnic sector is booming, with workers frequently changing jobs in pursuit of better work or pay. However, when there are no longer plenty of jobs around, agents who can introduce jobs, landlords, and employers face few restrictions. Migrants may end up being unable to pay off their migration debts and may even continue needing subsidies from their family and friends back home. Such migrants often put up with considerable hardship in the form of low pay, poor living conditions and food, and even disease before contemplating return migration.[4]

The kaleidoscopic nature of Chinese international migration means it presents many challenges, in particular to receiving societies. The strongly cumulative nature of migration from China that we found evidence for will bring the option of international migration within reach of an increasing number of regions and people. If this trend continues, international mobility of ever-larger numbers of Chinese may put considerable strain on the international migration order. Managing these flows must be a high priority, but should not, in view of the observations in the preceding paragraph, be predicated on the assumption that it is possible to stop or cap the inflow at the receiving end. Migration management cannot be done unilaterally, but should involve sending, receiving, and transit societies in equal measure. *When governments consider measures that could help manage a particular migratory flow, they need to consider both their own goals and the interests of others involved in the particular migratory flow, including the governments of sending areas, coethnics already resident in receiving areas, and the migrants themselves.* Migration management entails close cooperation between multiple actors and finding acceptable trade-offs between conflicting interests rather than unilateral measures. Such cooperation may not be easy to achieve, but will enlist the considerable influence and power of all of the players involved in formulating and achieving a key joint policy aim: the creation and management of a sustainable level of migration.

Sending countries in particular play a pivotal role, and without their cooperation any attempt at migration management is doomed to fail. In this context the fact that the government of the People's Republic of China is beginning to free itself from the straitjacket of its own long-established overseas Chinese policies is especially important. In Chapters 2 and 5, we discussed how in the course of the 1990s the Chinese government gradually moved to the position that certain types of international mobility, of certain types of people, from certain origins to certain destinations are desirable. Increased talk about "new migrants" in the media and in official documents signals the beginning of a much broader approach that considers emigration potentially beneficial to China, thus paving the way for a future national standardization of scattered local practices that are now merely condoned. Yet at this writing in 2003, the national government has only very recently begun to put the policy apparatus in place to deal with emigration routinely and systematically.[5] Importantly, this also means that there is room for governments of the destination countries to help the Chinese administration regulate and streamline its emerging national emigration policies, opening a window of opportunity that neither the Chinese government nor the governments of receiving countries can afford to miss.

Notes

CHAPTER 1. INTRODUCTION

1. The term *snakeheads* (*shetou*) derives from the term *human snakes* (*renshe*) and refers to irregular, or illegal, migrants. Although in Chinese snakehead is commonly used by our informants without any strong negative overtones, we resist this usage in this book. The word as adopted in English both orientalizes "exotic" Chinese practices and highlights the criminal aspects of the migratory process. We also do not use the English terms *human smuggler* and *human trafficker*, which are similarly negatively charged, but instead use the more neutral terms *migration facilitator* and *migration broker*, which draw attention to the fact that such people are professional providers of services, only some of which are illegal.

2. The working title of the project was "At the Margin of the Chinese World System: The Fuzhou Diaspora in Europe." This project was funded by the Economic and Social Research Council of England and Wales (ESRC grant number L214252012) under its program on transnational communities. The research staff on the project included Antonella Ceccagno of the University of Bologna, Mette Thunø of the University of Copenhagen, and Pál Nyíri and Frank Pieke of the University of Oxford. The analysis and conclusions of this book represent a collective effort of all members of the research staff.

3. A case in point are the data on the overseas Chinese and migrants collected by the Fujianese Office of Overseas Chinese Affairs (Qiaoban). In most places we were prevented from using the data because they were confidential; where we did gain access (for instance, in villages that we visited or studied) we found the data to be woefully incomplete anyway.

4. Such concepts originate as much from the West (mainly the United States) as from Asia itself. They are based on the view that different modernities have emerged in Asia that conflict with the dominant Western modernity. Aihwa

Ong has written a very useful critique of these orientalizing and self-orientalizing constructions and the interests that they serve in the West and in Asia itself (Ong 1997).

5. See, for instance, Adam McKeown's brilliant overview of overseas Chinese transnationalism and diaspora between 1842 and 1949. Many of his observations and conclusions are highly relevant to our own study of the new migration from China since the 1980s (McKeown 1999).

6. When we first started thinking about ways of conceptualizing the connections between the many Chinese things that exist the world over, we did use these very two concepts. Subsequent analysis of our material, reflection, and discussions during team meetings convinced us that such structuralist concepts would lead us to an analytical dead end and force our research findings into a mold that did not really fit.

7. China is by no means unique in this respect, although it can be argued that its overseas Chinese policies are much more explicit and detailed than, for instance, those affecting India's nonresident Indians or Germany's *Aussiedler*. However, it should be stressed that the Chinese state does allow a considerable degree of choice in its relationships with overseas Chinese. China in this respect is very different from countries such as the Philippines and Eritrea that require a much more binding and material commitment from their emigrant populations.

8. The issue of Chinese outward investment became increasingly important in the 1990s and is key evidence that China is no longer a peripheral area at the receiving end of the global system, but is becoming much more fully integrated in the world economy (Cai 2000a; Slater 1998). Outward foreign investment is by no means limited to large state organizations or enterprises. Anecdotal evidence of outward investment from Chinese villages was found in fieldwork conducted by Pieke in Shanxi and Jiangsu province in 1998 and by Nyíri in Hungary in 1999.

9. Since the 1980s many developed and urbanized counties in China have received municipal status from the national government, giving them greater autonomy in a range of policy fields (Chan 1994: 20–33). In Chinese, such municipalities are officially referred to as "county-level cities" (*xianji shi*). Since this is a bit of a mouthful, in this book we refer to all counties and county-level cities as "county."

CASE 1

1. This is village B, which is discussed in detail in Chapter 2. This composite case study is based on interviews and conversations put together as case files aN01003C6 and aN01219C2.

2. The first man from Mingxi to settle in the Prato area, Hu Zhiming, was also a schoolmate of Ding's. He had migrated to Mingxi from Zhejiang in 1987, joining relatives who had migrated from Zhejiang to Italy. For further details, see Case 3 and Chapter 2.

CHAPTER 2. OLD AND NEW TRANSNATIONAL VILLAGES IN FUJIAN

1. Interview with a migrant family in village A, September 5, 2000 (filename Z000905i1).

2. Wu Xiafeng, "Duowei'er can'an weijie" (The conclusion of the tragic case of Dover), *Nanfang zhoumo*, December 28, 2000.

3. A voluminous literature exists on the history of Fujian and the overseas Chinese. An introduction to the history of Fujian can be found in Wei 1996. For further information the reader is advised to consult Tan and Zhang 1999 and Pan 1998. Studies on the history of central Fujianese emigration can be found in Yang, Wang, and Tong 1992, esp. T. Wu 1992 and Lin and Lin 1994.

4. In the 1840s and 1850s, French and British ships only occasionally had called on Fuzhou to recruit contract laborers (T. Wu 1992: 148).

5. All figures in the paragraph are from D. Wu 1994, pp. 148–52. Wu does not give an exact date for the figures, but they seem to be from the late 1980s. Such figures should in any case be treated with care. They amount to both a serious understatement because they do not take into account much recent, irregular migration, and an overstatement because they include every person of Chinese extraction, even those whose links with central Fujian are tenuous at best. The figure of 35,000 central Fujianese in the United States, for instance, is likely to consist mainly of ethnic Chinese U.S. residents from Southeast Asia who have no connections with the recent migrants directly from central Fujian.

6. Lyons 1998. Statistical data in this section are indicators of diversity rather than exact data owing to chronic uncertainties in Chinese statistical reporting at the grassroots level; on this point, see Cai 2000.

7. Interview with party secretary of village B, June 24, 2000 (filename Z00624i1); interview with director of the branch of the Federation of Returned Overseas Chinese at the township of village A, August 21, 2000 (filename Z00082i1).

8. For more details on wages in Europe see Chapter 4.

9. Interview with the deputy director of the Fuqing city branch of the Federation of Returned Overseas Chinese, December 24, 1999 (filename Z91224i1).

10. Rongqiao Economic and Technical Development Zone (Rongqiao jingji jishu kaifaqu); Yuanhong Investment District (Yuanhong touziqu).

11. Subsequently, five industrial villages were selected as main producers of industrial export products (electronics, plastic, glass, food, garments, shoes, and aluminum products). Finally, in the late 1990s, Jiangyin peninsula was approved as a key provincial open economic zone. The peninsula will focus on the production of basic industrial coast-related products, energy, steel, and transportation (Fujiansheng jihua weiyuanhui and Fujiansheng tongjiju 1999: 180–81).

12. A preference for employing outsiders is widespread in China; see Woon 1997: 9; Huang 2000: 190–209; A. Chan 2001: 7–10; C. Lee 1998: 109–36. Local workers are difficult to control because they have their own land, family networks, and commitments, and quite often also have connections with local cadres. In fieldwork carried out near Shanghai one of the authors (Pieke) found

that outside investors often only hired the number of local workers as so-called *tudigong* (work-for-land employees) required by their lease or purchase of land-use rights from the township or village leadership.

13. Group interview with women in village A, December 28, 2000 (filename Z001228i1).

14. Interview with director of the township branch of the Federation of Returned Overseas Chinese where village A is located, August 21, 2000 (filename Z000821i1); Fujiansheng tongjiju 2000: 406–7.

15. Local official statistics for migration in the early twentieth century and after 1979 provided by the township branch of the Federation of Returned Overseas Chinese, June 1, 2000 (filename Z000601i1); August 25, 2000 (filename Z000825i1); interview with the director of the township branch of the Federation of Returned Overseas Chinese where village A is located, August 21, 2000 (filename Z000821i1). Donations come largely from relatives of former coolie workers, who at the beginning of the twentieth century went to Singapore, where they prospered in the car business; see F. Wang 1994.

16. Interviews with the party secretary of village A, August 22, 2000 (filename Z000822i1) and September 7, 2000 (filename Z000907i1); and Yu 1994.

17. See "A cun qiaojuan jiben qingkuang" (Basic situation of overseas Chinese dependants in village A), photocopied document collected on August 25, 2000.

18. Interview with the director of the branch of the Federation of Returned Overseas Chinese in the township of village A, August 21, 2000 (filename Z000821i1).

19. Interview with retired party secretary of village A, August 21, 2000 (filename Z000821i1).

20. Interview with migrant family in village A, December 12, 2000 (filename Z001228i1).

21. Michael Szonyi's research has documented how kinship, temple affiliation, village membership, and adherence to the official regulations and tax system became increasingly intertwined in the Fuzhou area during the Ming and Qing dynasties (Szonyi 2000).

22. Local official statistics for migration in the early twentieth century and after 1979 provided by the township branch of the Federation of Returned Overseas Chinese on June 1, 2000; local official statistics for donations from overseas Chinese provided by township branch of the Federation of Returned Overseas Chinese on August 26, 2000. Donations were made throughout the collective period, although both their frequency and the sums involved increased greatly from 1979 on, when a RMB 60,000 donation was made for the restoration of the village temple.

23. Interview with the head of village A middle school, September 4, 2000 (filename Z000904i2).

24. The importance of communal ancestor worship practices for the reinforcement of lineage and village identity is well documented in anthropologi-

cal studies of Hong Kong, Taiwan, and pre-1949 southeastern China. See Ahern 1973; Baker 1968; Freedman 1958; J. Watson 1976; R. Watson 1985.

25. Interview with the retired party secretary of village A, December 27, 2001 (filename Z001227i1). For a fuller study of the role of overseas Chinese in recreating ancestor worship and popular religion in their ancestral village in southern Fujian, see Kuah 1998, 1999, 2000. For other examples of the revival of ancestor worship and popular religion in rural China, see, for instance, Anagnost 1997; Brandtstädter 2001; Dean 1986, 1989, 1998; Feuchtwang 1998; Flower and Leonard 1998; Jing 1996; Litzinger 2000; Pieke 2003; Schein 2000; Siu 1989, 1990.

26. Interview with migrant families, September 5, 2000 (filename Z000905i1); interview with the retired party secretary of village A, September 7, 2000 (filename Z000907i1).

27. Interview with retired party secretary of village A, August 22, 2000 (filename Z000822i1); interview with migrant families, September 5, 2000 (filename Z000905i1).

28. A migrant from village A remits on average RMB 50,000–80,000 per year after having paid off traveling debts. Interview with village A retired party secretary, August 22, 2000 (filename Z000822i1); group interview with women in village A, December 28, 2000 (filename Z001228i1).

29. Interview with retired truck driver from village A and retired party secretary of village A, September 4, 2000 (filename Z000904i1).

30. Interview with retired truck driver from village A, September 4, 2000 (filename Z000904i1).

31. Fuzhou: RMB 6,600; Quanzhou: RMB 6,922; Jinjiang: RMB 6,898.

32. Conversation with cadre from the Mingxi county forestry department, August 1, 1999 (filename Z90915I1).

33. Interview with deputy party secretary of Mingxi county, January 29, 2000 (filename Z00129i1).

34. On the prospects and problems associated with China fir forestry in the Jiangxi-Fujian border region, see Tapp 1996.

35. Since the late 1990s, deforestation in China has been officially recognized as an acute ecological problem. Legislation was strengthened to protect natural forests by amending the 1984 Forestry Law of the People's Republic of China (Zhonghua Renmin Gongheguo senlin fa) on April 29, 1998 (*Renmin ribao*, May 4, 1998), and subsequently by documents such as "Guowuyuan guanyu baohu senlin ziyuan zhizhi huilin kai he luanzhan sendi de tongzhi" (Circular by the State Council on protecting forest resources by preventing burning trees to reclaim wasteland and randomly occupying timberland), *Renmin ribao*, September 13, 1998; "Guanyu yanli daji pohuai senlin ziyuan weifan fanzui huodong de tongzhi" (Circular on severely striking back at illegal activities destroying forest resources), *Renmin ribao*, October 29, 1998; "Zhonghua Renmin Gongheguo senlinfa shishi tiaoli" (Regulations on the implementation of the forestry law of the People's Republic of China), *Renmin ribao*, February 4, 2002. In Fujian, the media have reported on several court cases involving persons ac-

cused of illegally cutting down or burning trees (see *Mingxi ribao*, October 7, 2002; January 16, 2002; April 4, 2002).

36. Interview with cadre from the Forestry Department in the township of village B, September 15, 1999 (filename Z90915i1); interview with the township party secretary, the township deputy head, and the township chairman of the branch of the Federation of Returned Overseas Chinese of the township of village B, January 29, 2000 (filename Z00129i1).

37. Interview with chairman of the Mingxi County Federation of Returned Overseas Chinese, August 2, 1999 (filename Z90915i1) and June 23, 2000 (filename Z00623i1).

38. Interview with chairman of Mingxi County Federation of Returned Overseas Chinese, June 23, 2000 (filename Z00623i1).

39. Mingxixian difangzhi bianzuan weiyuanhui 1997: 116–18. In fact, village B contains one hamlet of about fifty migrants from southern Zhejiang, who had settled in the village in the early 1960s; see below (interview, village head of village B, January 31, 2000, filename Z00131i1).

40. On ethnic enclaves, see Portes and Bach 1985; Portes, Guarnizo, and Landolt 1999; Portes and Jensen 1987; Zhou 1992; Zhou and Logan 1989.

41. We consider this account to be the most plausible reconstruction of the facts, which had to be pieced together from several sources that partly contradict each other. These sources are an interview with the chairman of the Mingxi branch of the Federation of Returned Overseas Chinese, September 18, 1999 (filename Z90918I1); *Fujian qiaobao*, November 5, 1999, p. 1; interview with a schoolteacher, January 30, 2000 (filename Z00130i1); interview with former emigrants, January 31, 2000 (filename Z00131i1). A slightly different account of the commencement of migration from village B is presented in Case 3. Unfortunately, none of these accounts specifies the exact nature of kinship connections between Hu Zhiming (whose father was from Qingyuan county in Zhejiang) and Zhejiangese in Europe (who are from the adjacent county of Wencheng).

42. Interview with migrant family, January 30, 2000 (filename Z00130i1).

43. Although this particular link was incidental, the fact that such links existed was no accident at all. Sanming / Mingxi migration as a whole was much facilitated by connections with a variety of Zhejiangese who either had migrated to Sanming, or whom Sanming migrants encountered en route or after arriving in Europe.

44. Mingxixian difangzhi bianzuan weiyuanhui 1997: 117; interview with the chairman of the Mingxi county Federation of Returned Overseas Chinese, June 23, 2000 (filename Z00623i1); interview with the party secretary of village B, June 24, 2000 (filename Z00624i1).

45. Interview with chairman of Mingxi county Federation of Returned Overseas Chinese, June 23, 2000 (filename Z00623i1); interview with party secretary of village B, June 24, 2000 (filename Z00624i1); interview with village head of village B, January 31, 2000 (filename Z00131i1); interview with deputy head of village B, August 2, 1999 (filename Z91108i1); *Fujian ribao*, April 17, 2002.

46. Village B survey, 2000. Chain migration based on kinship or coethnic ties

has in many contexts been shown to reduce the costs of traveling, to raise the benefits upon arrival, and to mitigate the risks on the journey to the destination areas; see Massey et al. 1994.

47. Interview with the party secretary of village B, June 24, 2000 (filename Z00624i1).

48. Village B survey, 2000; interview with party secretary and deputy head of village B, June 24, 2000 (filename Z00624i1).

49. Interview with the deputy head of village B, August 12, 1999 (filename Z91108i1). On house-building as conspicuous consumption more generally in Fujian, see Knapp 1996.

50. Interview with chairman of Mingxi county branch of the Federation of Returned Overseas Chinese, August 2, 1999 (filename Z90915i1); interview with chairman of Mingxi county branch of Federation of Returned Overseas Chinese, June 23, 2000 (filename Z00623i1).

51. Interview with peasant in charge of maintaining local temple, January 29, 2000 (filename Z00129i1); interview with migrant families, January 31, 2000 (filename Z00131i2).

52. The modernity of "traditional" practices has been highlighted in ethnographic work in a range of settings in rural China; see the references in n. 24.

53. This often is less of a blessing than it seems. Agricultural land in China is not owned, but is held under long-term responsibility contracts. This means that landholders are responsible for keeping their land under cultivation, which may be very difficult for migrant families that lack sufficient labor.

54. *Fujian qiaobao*, November 5, 1999, p. 1.

55. Interviews in Beijing on July 29, 1999, with the director of the Sanming City Government Liaison and Trade Office, Beijing (filename N90729i1) and in Fuzhou on August 4, 1999, with the head of the Sister Cities Division, Fujian Province Foreign Affairs Office (filename N90804L1).

56. Interview with the chairman of Mingxi branch of the Federation of Returned Overseas Chinese, August 1, 1999 (filename Z90915i1).

57. Interview with the chairman of Mingxi branch of the Federation of Returned Overseas Chinese, September 18, 1999 (filename Z90918i1). Despite the assertion of this informant, we found that the government is in fact openly involved in financing individual migrants (see below).

58. Interview with village B party secretary, August 2, 1999 (filename Z91108i1).

59. Interview with village B party secretary, August 2, 1999 (filename Z91108i1); interview with another village party secretary and returned migrants, January 29, 2000 (filename Z00129i1).

60. Interview with the chairman of the Mingxi branch of Federation of Returned Overseas Chinese, June 23, 2000 (filename Z00623i1); *Fujian qiaobao*, April 18, 2002; *Fujian ribao*, April 17, 2002.

61. Xinhua News Agency, "Jiang Zemin on Rights of Returned Overseas Chinese," Translated in FBIS-CHI-1999-1104 (November 4, 1999), p. 1.

62. Interview with chairman of the Mingxi county branch of Federation of

Returned Overseas Chinese, August 1, 1999 (filename Z90915i1). According to official records, annual remittances from overseas migrants have reached US$10 million in Mingxi county (the average since 1995). *Fujian ribao*, April 17, 2002.

63. Interview with migrants' wives in village A, December 27, 2000 (filename Z00122711).

64. Interviews with Ninghua contract farmers, January 30, 2000 (filenames Z00130i1 and Z00130i2).

CASE 2

1. This case study is based on case file No1118C1.

CHAPTER 3. GETTING OUT, GETTING IN, AND MOVING ON

1. Field notes, December 17, 2001 (file N11217L1).

2. The main exception throughout this period was the largely illegal emigration to Hong Kong.

3. Contrary to popular belief, considerable population mobility did occur throughout the collective period, most of it through a form of unified planning by the state or involving individual bureaucratic units. The evidence on this point is ably collected in Lary 1999.

4. The three following paragraphs provide only the barest outline of the history of Europe's Chinese. Fuller accounts are given in Pieke 1998; Pieke forthcoming.

5. On Chinese migration to Africa, see A. Li 2000. Li's book is mainly historical, but also contains a brief section on recent developments.

6. Xiao Feng, "Shei shi Duofo'er can'an sinanzhe" (Who are the victims of the Dover tragedy). *Nanfang Zhoumo*, June 30, 2000, p. 1.

7. Little research has been done on this important topic, but data provided to us by the British Home Office reveal that between 1998 and 2000 the rise in the absolute number of student visas issued to PRC nationals (excluding Hong Kong) was the highest in the category "remainder of Asia," roughly coterminous with East and Southeast Asia. In 1998 the number of visas issued to Chinese was 5,400, or 7.3 percent of the total of 53,500 for the category "remainder of Asia." In 1999 the figure was 11,000 (13.4 percent) of 82,100; in 2000 it was 18,900 (19.1 percent) of 99,100.

8. Interview with a recruiter for David Game College in China, London, September 22, 1999 (file N90922L1). During a conversation in July 2002 with a teacher at a private high school in Oxford we were told that Chinese had become the school's largest ethnic group and that the school had started turning down large numbers of Chinese applicants in order to preserve the pluralistic nature of its student body.

9. Data provided by the British Home Office, April 2001. For details, see Pieke 2002: 24–25.

10. Since 2001, British authorities have increasingly processed asylum claims

from Chinese within six months, thus depriving them of the work permit. It remains to be seen whether this will have a significant impact on the mechanisms of migration.

11. For a review of British immigration history and policy, see Glover et al. 2001.

12. "UK, Ireland: Asylum," *Migration News* 7, no. 4 (April 2000); http://migration.ucdavis.edu.

13. "Begging For It," *The Economist*, March 25, 2000, p. 38.

14. "UK: Migrants, Asylum," *Migration News* 8, no. 1 (January 2001); http://migration.ucdavis.edu.

15. "UK: Elections, Asylum, Smuggling," *Migration News* 8, no. 5 (May 2001); http://migration.ucdavis.edu.

16. "UK: Asylees, Chinese," *Migration News* 7, no. 9 (September 2000); http://migration.ucdavis.edu.

17. "UK: Migrants, Asylum," *Migration News* 8, no. 1 (January 2001); http://migration.ucdavis.edu.

18. "UK, Ireland: Asylum," *Migration News* 7, no. 4 (April 2000); http://migration.ucdavis.edu.

19. Although sponsors were supposed to facilitate migrants' entry into the labor market, they were not required to provide jobs themselves.

20. See, for example, *Il sole 24 ore*, July 12, 2002.

21. http://www.stranieriinitalia.it/business18nov.htm.

22. Data courtesy of Endre Sik of TÁRKI (Union for Informatics in the Social Sciences) in Budapest.

23. Data from the Hungarian Ministry of the Interior.

24. United States Department of State, "Hungary: Country Reports on Human Rights Practices—2000," released by the Bureau of Democracy, Human Rights, and Labor, U.S. Department of State, February 23, 2001; http://www.state.gov/g/drl/rls/hrrpt/2000/eur/774pf.htm. For a review of Hungarian immigration and integration policies, see Nyíri 2001.

25. *China Daily* (Hong Kong ed.), November 23, 2001.

26. Chinese tourism in Europe is possible only to countries that have concluded a bilateral agreement with China to that effect. Visas valid for the whole Schengen area are not issued to Chinese tourists, which is a major inhibiting factor for the development of Chinese tourism and an issue high on the agenda in ongoing negotiations between China and the European Commission. The Schengen area, named for the city in Luxembourg where a 1985 agreement to reduce cross-border controls was signed by seven European countries, now includes fifteen countries: Austria, Belgium, Denmark, Finland, France, Germany, Iceland, Italy, Greece, Luxembourg, the Netherlands, Norway, Portugal, Spain, and Sweden. All except Norway and Iceland are members of the European Union.

27. Interview in Moscow, June 20, 1999 (file N90620L1).

28. The work unit (*gongzuo danwei*) or place of work is the backbone of the urban administrative structure. The work unit is a person's normal point of

contact with the state administration and its permission is required for most public or private matters. For further details, see Pieke 1996, chap. 2; Lü and Perry 1997; Walder 1986.

29. Telephone conversation in Budapest, November 17, 1999, file N90928L1.

30. Telephone conversation in Budapest, December 24, 1999, file N91224L1.

31. Meeting with the family, Budapest, summer 2001.

32. Yang's own parents had gone to Southeast Asia in the 1930s. When World War II broke out, his father was working on a Dutch ship that was recalled to the Netherlands for six years, where he settled in Rotterdam. Yang, a native of Fuzhou, left the Netherlands in the 1970s for Hong Kong to work in the business of an uncle. Around 1980, he returned to the Netherlands. The father of Mr. Chen, president of the Fujian association in the Netherlands, left his native Zeli village, Tantou township, for Hong Kong in the 1960s, where he found employment as a sailor. In 1967 he jumped ship in the Netherlands and became a cook in a Chinese restaurant. In 1975, Chen's mother, wife, and brother joined him (interview in Sneek, Netherlands, February 1999, Field Report 4). A paternal uncle of Hao's, president of the UK Futsing Association, moved to England from Singapore. Male members of Hao's family from Fuqing had migrated to Singapore for several generations. Hao's father was born there but returned in 1958 to China "to contribute to socialist construction." In 1981, after graduating from upper secondary school in China, Hao went to London as a student, financed by his uncle (see Case 4 for further details). The uncle of Zheng Chun, a 2000 economics graduate of Amsterdam University, went to the Netherlands in the early 1970s as a sailor; he had gone to Hong Kong at the age of 11. They are the only family in the Netherlands from Yutian Village in Changle. Zheng Chun himself migrated to the Netherlands at age 15 on a family reunification visa permitting permanent residence. His parents moved to Hong Kong in 1990 (interview with Chen in Amsterdam, February 1999).

33. Field notes, March 7, 2001 (file N10307L1)

34. Conversation in Budapest, summer 2000.

35. Conversation in Mingxi, August 11, 1999 (filename N90811L1).

36. Information about a migrant from Tianjin collected during a conversation with his relative, a shopkeeper in Budapest, during the summer of 2000.

37. Information as reported to us in an interview with an informant from Qingdao, Budapest, April 14, 2000.

38. Ibid.

39. This is called *gong fei zi pai*, carrying a private passport but using public funds.

40. Pu met his fate in the form of five brothers from Fujian, who had paid RMB 60,000 each for passports and spent a further RMB 40,000 on the road, intending to get to western Europe. They first got to Russia, from which a broker took them to Hungary, but there told them that the route via Yugoslavia was closed because of the war there; instead, he took them to Romania. The broker eventually abandoned them, and the brothers decided to go back to China and settle accounts with the broker's representative. On their way back, however,

they met Pu in Moscow. When they discovered that Pu's company was the one that had issued their employment invitations, they killed Pu and his girlfriend.

41. Interview in Moscow, June 19, 1999 (filename N90619L1).

42. Ibid.

43. "Feifa chuguo zhongjie jigou jian cai hei zhao da jiemi" (Revealing the secrets of the black money illegal migration brokerages make), *Lianhe Shangbao* (Budapest), November 17–23, 2000.

44. "Zhongguoren jia liuxue feifa yimin Yingguo" (Chinese fake students illegally immigrate to Britain), *Lianhe Shangbao* (Budapest), November 10–16, 2000.

45. Ibid.

46. Interview in London on November 28, 2001 (filename N01128I3).

47. Case file 7 (filename N01003C7).

48. As we show in Chapter 4, nominal wages of Fujianese migrants in Britain are higher than in Italy, which looks attractive from China; however, living in and getting to Britain are also more expensive than in Italy or elsewhere on the continent.

CASE 3

1. This case study is based on interviews and conversations put together as case file N01012C1.

2. This is village B, described in Chapter 2.

3. The case of Hu Zhiming is discussed in more detail in Chapter 2. Note that the story as presented here is slightly different from the story that we reconstructed of Hu Zhiming's pioneering migration to Italy in that in Yi's version Zhiming is not the first, but the second migrant to Italy from village B.

CHAPTER 4. WORK AND LIFE IN EUROPE

1. As in Europe, only estimates of absolute numbers of migrants from individual source areas are available. However, a reasonably reliable indicator of the relative unimportance of Fuqing migrants in the United States is the fact that only one out of a total of forty-three Fujian organizations represents Fuqing. Interview with Noon Ling Chen, vice-chairman, World Futsing Association, chairman, Fu Tsing American Association (Meiguo Fuqing Lianhui), vice-chairman, Fukien American Association (Meidong Fujian Tongxianghui), March 2, 2001, file N10302L1.

2. Marlowe Hood, "Dark Passage," *Los Angeles Times Magazine*, June 13, 1993, pp. 12–17.

3. See Chapter 3, n. 7.

4. *Xin jiexian (Zoneast)*, November 2000, pp. 10–14. Although a sergeant of the Chinatown Unit of the Metropolitan Police denied that gangs had been involved in the attack on the martial arts master or in street hawking, he confirmed that Fujianese "gangs" were attempting to take over Chinatown. His

suspicion was reinforced by the discovery of an arms cache belonging to mainland Chinese in the spring of 2002. Interviews in London, June 1999, November 2000, and Oxford, December 2001; telephone interview, March 2002.

5. Interview in London, June 2, 1999 (file N90602I3).

6. Interview in London, June 1, 1999 (file N90601I1).

7. Ibid.

8. Comment made to representatives of the British Home Office during discussions at the second user group workshop of our ESRC project, Oxford, December 11, 2001.

9. Interview on June 1, 1999 (file N90601I1).

10. Interviews in New York, March 2001 (files N10316I1, N10307L1).

11. Interviews with the owner of a Fujianese employment agency in London, June 1999–October 2001 (file N01107C1).

12. Interview with the owner of a Fujianese employment agency in London, June 5, 1999 (file N90605I1).

13. Interviews in Prato, May 25, 2001 (filename C01052511), June 1, 2001 (filename C01060113).

14. Interviews with workers in New York, March 2001.

15. Interview with a sergeant of the London Metropolitan police, London, June 1, 1999.

16. *Xin jiexian (Zoneast)*, November 2000, p. 14.

17. Interview in London, November 19, 2000 (file N01119C4).

18. Ibid.

19. Interviews in London, November 2000–March 2001 (file N01122C1).

20. Interviews with workers in New York, March 2001. See also Wang Kaijie [Jack Wang], "Fuzhouren zai Niu Yue" (Fuzhounese in New York), *Shijie ribao/World Journal* (New York), March 8–14, 2001.

21. Interview in New York, March 1, 2001.

22. This opinion was voiced to us by both Fujianese and non-Fujianese Chinese in New York in March 2001. See, for instance, N10304L1.

23. This company is headed by Mr. He, who also is the chairman of the UK Futsing Association. For more details on Futsing Finance and Mr. He, see Case 4.

24. Interview with a non-Fujianese Chinese migrant in New York, March 1, 2001 (file N10301L1).

25. Interview in London, January 19, 2000 (file N01107C1).

26. Interview in London, February 2001.

27. Caritas analysis of World Bank data, Central Intelligence Agency, United Nations Development Programme (Caritas di Roma 2001, p. 121).

28. Interviews in Prato, May 1, 2001 (filename C01050111), May 20, 2001 (filename C01052011), and July 8, 2001 (C01070811). Similar information was also provided in interviews for another research project on Chinese businesses in Prato in November 2001 by Antonella Ceccagno and Mo Dongke.

29. Data for Milan from Regione Lombardia and Fondazione I.S.M.U. 2002, and for Prato from Centro Ricerche e Servizi per L'Immigrazione 2000.

30. "Da immigrati ad artigiani, i cinesi al primo posto" (From immigrants to entrepreneurs: the Chinese on top), *La Repubblica*, August 6, 2000, p. 24.

31. Interview with Francesco Toccafondi, head of the Prato branch of CGIL, Prato, March 2001.

32. Centro Ricerche e Servizi per L'Immigrazione 2001, p. 46.

33. Interviews in Prato, May 1, 2001 (filename C010501i1), May 15, 2001 (filename C010506i2), May 20, 2001 (filename C010520i1), and July 8, 2001 (filename C010708i1). The same information was also provided during a subsequent research project of Antonella Ceccagno and Mo Dongke on Chinese businesses in Prato: interviews in Prato, November 15, 2001 (file AC / MDK 1) and March 26, 2002 (file AC / MDK 4).

34. Sometimes the needs of the workers and not the slim profit margins granted by the suppliers are seen as obstacles that prevent the owner from paying the proper tax and pension contributions for his dependent workers. This is related to the perception that the payment of contributions is the employee's responsibility.

35. Since the police have become aware of this, applicants for legalization have sometimes had to prove payment of taxes over a period of, for example, six months. The Chinese, however, perceive this situation as harassment and not as the enforcement of the obligation to pay the taxes that are due.

36. *In nero* or irregularity is not a clearly defined category and can refer to any, a few, or all of the following practices: businesses that are registered but do not pay tax or only part of the taxes, businesses that are simply not registered, or businesses that employ workers without paying social security for them.

37. "Luoma Weiduoli'ao diqu jumin kangyi Huashang" (Residents of Rome's Piazza Vittorio area protest Chinese businesses), *Il Tempo Europa-Cina/ Ouhua Shibao* (Rome), September 5, 2000, p. 1.

38. In some places, Chinese middlemen reportedly have begun to run their own network of African peddlers whom they supply with goods; Karin Hough, personal communication, 2002.

39. Interviews in the San Giuseppe Vesuviano and Terzigno, Campania, October 1999.

40. Interviews in Treviso and Montebelluna, June 18, 2000, and October 12, 2001 (files N01003C4, N01003C6, N01003C8). Interviews in Prato, May 1, 2001 (file AC 3), May 6, 2001 (file AC 5), May 27, 2001 (file AC 10), June 1, 2001 (file AC 13), June 26, 2001 (file AC 18), July 8, 2001 (file AC 19).

41. Interview in Empoli, June 26, 2000 (file N01002C1).

42. Interviews in Prato, May 27, 2001 (filename C010527i2), and June 17, 2001 (filenames C010617i1 and C010617i2).

43. Both men said there were only a few hundred people from Lianjiang and Changle in Italy, mostly in Milan and Turin rather than in Prato. But the Fujianese Association is constituted in such a way as to have vice-presidents representing each area of Fujian from which there are migrants (presumably of sufficient economic standing).

44. This association is locally known as the Associazione Culturale Cinese di Fu Jian, Toscana / Yidali Fujian Huaqiao Huaren Zhongxibu Lianyihui (the Chinese name actually translates as Association of Overseas Chinese from Fujian in West-Central Italy), but vis-à-vis the Rome-based Fujian Sheng Lü Yi Huaqiao

Lianyihui (Association of overseas Chinese from Fujian province in Italy) and Chinese authorities, it acts as the branch of the latter. For further discussion of this point, see Chapter 5.

45. The Prato workshop owner left home in 1959 at the age of 13 to escape starvation, and went to Fujian because village elders advised him that Fujian had lots of land and needed labor. He got off the train at the first stop in Fujian, which was Guangze Brigade in Nanping, the prefecture bordering on Sanming to the north. Later, he graduated as a railway mechanic and worked as a mechanic and electrician until 1983, when he started his own spare parts business. In 1986 he moved to Italy, where he obtained legal residency in the 1987 regularization. He had migrated to Italy to join two uncles who had gone there from Zhejiang in 1943 and 1957; the first of them was part of the original flow of Wenzhou migrants who had specialized in selling stone carvings (interview in Rome, September 5, 1999, filename N90905L1).

The story of the workshop owner in Rome was very similar: born in Wenzhou, he moved to rural Nanping at age 7 with his parents, who were sent down to the countryside during the Cultural Revolution. He went to Italy in 1987, joining several relatives who had moved there from Zhejiang in the 1940s and 1950s (interview in Prato, October 1999, filename N00928C5). See Chapter 2 for more details on the connection between Zhejiang and Fujian migration to Europe.

46. Interview in Prato, June 17, 2001 (filename C010617i1).

47. The Association of Chinese Merchants of the Komondor Trade Center (also known as the Four Tigers Market, the center of the Chinese economy in Hungary) conducted a survey asking merchants from different Chinese provinces to estimate the number of traders from their provinces; the figures added up to about 8,000. If one adds around 2,000 Chinese shops with an average of two Chinese employees, and 300 restaurants and fast-food outlets with an average of four employees, one arrives at a total of 13,200; in addition, a few hundred Chinese work in the ethnic service sector.

48. The criteria for inclusion in the database do not appear reliable, but its size minimally allows the conclusion that there are a considerable number of Chinese in Hungary with professional and business backgrounds.

49. "Cipot a cipoboltból" (Shoes from the shoe shop), *Népszabadság*, April 18, 2002, p. 32.

50. Interviews with migrants from Shandong, Gansu, and Beijing in Hungary, 2000–2001.

51. One example of this strategy involved Hai'er, a Chinese manufacturer of air conditioners (interviews with Zhao Luoyan, Budapest, 2000).

52. The project managers have been elusive about the source of funding and have issued no written statements about it. At one press conference, they referred to the project as being cofinanced by "the Chinese side" and an Austrian bank loan.

53. This practice is common in Hungary and by no means limited to Chinese employers.

54. Interviews in Rome, October 1999; Treviso, June 18, 2000; Freiburg im Breisgau, August 21, 1999; and New York, March 5, 2001 (files N01004C1, N01003C4, N10306C1).

55. Interviews in Moscow, June 22, 1999 (file N90623I1).

56. Two former factory buildings opposite the market were leased or purchased by entrepreneurs, who rent them out to hawkers without a stall at the main Four Tigers. Leases there are much cheaper than at the more established Four Tigers.

57. Interview in Budapest on April 18, 2001 (file N10418L1).

58. Interview in Budapest on December 1, 1999 (file N91201L1).

59. Interview in Budapest on May 2, 2000 (N00502L1).

60. The inflation rate of the forint has been around 10 percent a year since the late 1980s, but there was sharp change in 2000, from 250 to 320 forint to the U.S. dollar.

61. www.sandic.hu.

62. One mu is 0.067 hectares.

63. Interviews in Budapest on December 12, 2000, and February 28, 2001 (files N01212L2, N10228I1, N01215C1).

64. Interview in Budapest on February 28, 2001 (file N10228I1).

65. Ibid.

66. Interview in Putian on August 22, 1999 (file N90822I1).

67. Interview in Putian on August 22, 1999 (file N90822I2).

68. During a visit to Chen on August 21, 1999 (file N90821I1).

69. Interview on February 19, 2001 (file N01227C2).

70. Interview on January 1, 2001 (files N10101L1, N01226C1).

71. Interview on May 18, 2000 (files N00518L1, N01219C1).

72. Interview on September 25, 2000 (files N00925L1, N00924C1).

73. Interviews with managers at Las Vegas, Grand, and Várkert casinos, Budapest, December 1999.

74. Interviews with a gambler from Shandong and his relatives in Budapest, 2000; with a croupier from Zhejiang at a gambling club, Budapest, 2001; and with the relative of a Fujianese debt enforcer, Szeged, 2000.

75. Interview at the World Fujianese Fellowship Conference, Quanzhou, September 5, 1999 (file N90905L1).

76. Interview in San Giuseppe Vesuviano, October 1999 (file N01003C5).

77. Interview in London, June 2, 1999 (file N90602I2).

78. Interview in London, February 3, 2001 (file N10203C1).

79. The main exception is the majority of *peranakan* Chinese from Indonesia in the Netherlands, whose ancestors often migrated to Indonesia several centuries ago.

80. Such views are, of course, typical of the exoticized imaginary of the Other and closely parallel popular views of Chinese immigrants in local societies. And they are not limited to the Fujianese: northern Chinese tend to offer such observations on Zhejiangese as well, while Fuzhounese themselves say similar things about migrants from Fuqing.

81. Interview in Budapest, November 2001.

82. Interview in Prato, June 28, 2000 (files N00628L1, N00928C9).

83. Interview in Terzigno, October 1999.

84. In Italy, migrants from Putian are mainly from its northernmost townships bordering on Fuqing, many of whom speak the Fuqing dialect. Interview in Terzigno, October 1999.

CASE 4

1. This case study draws on the following files: N01105C1, N01119C2, N01107C1, N01119C1, N01126C3, N01107C2. As an association leader, He is a public figure in the UK and China, and we have decided to use his real name rather than a pseudonym here.

2. See Chapter 5 for a more detailed discussion of the World Futsing Association.

CHAPTER 5.   FUJIANESE TRANSNATIONAL PRACTICES AND POLITICS

1. See Case 4.

2. Case file N10306C1.

3. Case file N01222C1.

4. Ibid.

5. Case file N01219C1.

6. This is the overwhelming trend, though not universally true: the German association has at least had plans for setting up German-language classes and a legal aid and translation service for asylum seekers.

7. Case file N01105C1.

8. Case file N00924C1.

9. Interview with Mr. Chen in Bucharest, May 1999 (Nyíri field report 8).

10. Communication by Mr. Liu, president of the General Federation of Chinese Organizations in Hungary, May 2001.

11. *Lianhe shangbao* (Budapest), February 25–March 2, 2000, p. 1.

12. Interview in Paris, March 1999 (Nyíri field report 4).

13. Interviews in Campania in April 1999 and June 2000 (Nyíri field report 6, case file N00930C8).

14. Case file N01124C1.

15. D. Zhu 1995.

16. We discuss these congresses in more detail below. For an earlier study of these congresses, see H. Liu 1998.

17. Interview with the president of the Dutch Fujianese Association, Sneek, the Netherlands, March 1999 (Nyíri field report 3).

18. This section is based on interviews with organization leaders as well as charters of the Romanian, Czech, Italian, Dutch, and German associations. The interviews were with honorary president of the Hungarian Fujianese Association, Budapest, February 1999 (case file N01215C1); the president and executive

vice-president of the Dutch Fujianese Association in Rotterdam, March 1999 (Nyíri field report 3); the president of the German Fujianese Association in Mainz, March 1999 (Nyíri field report 3); the interim president of the Italian Fujianese Association, Rome (case file N00928C1); the president of the Prato-Tuscany Fujian Association, Prato, April 1999 (case file N00928C5); the president of the French Fujianese Association, Paris, March 1999 (Nyíri field report 4); the president of the Fujian Chamber of Commerce (UK); and the president of the UK Futsing Association, London, June 4 1999 (case files N01105C1, N90602I2); the executive vice-president of the Romanian Fujianese Association, Bucharest, June 1999 (Nyíri field report 8); leaders of the Russian Association, Moscow, June 23, 1999 (N90623I1); and the first president of the Fujianese Association of the Czech Republic, Quanzhou, China, September 5, 1999 (N90905L1).

19. Case file N00920C1.

20. Case file N01004C1.

21. Jiang Xiaodong, "Zhongguo Minzhu Zhengyidang jianjie" (Introduction to the Chinese Democracy and Justice Party), *Zhengyi haojue*, 2000, no. 6, p. 12.

22. Not to be confused with the *Free China Journal* published by the government of the Republic of China on Taiwan.

23. "Zhongguo nanmin zai Deguo gaikuang" (The general situation of Chinese refugees in Germany), *Freies China Journal* (Ziyou Huaren bao), July 2000, pp. 30–31.

24. Case file N01004C1.

25. In contrast, the Falungong, made famous outside China when the PRC government banned it as a counterrevolutionary organization in 1999, held no public activities in Hungary before the ban, although its flyers circulated among those Chinese interested in Buddhism. Since the ban, there has been only a single occurrence of a Chinese man distributing Falungong literature at the Four Tigers Market, which was followed by meetings of Chinese organizations condemning the event.

26. For an overview of China's overseas Chinese policies in the 1950s and 1960s, see Fitzgerald 1972; for post-1978 developments, see Thunø 2001.

27. The statement goes on to say: "Strengthening new migrant work has an important real meaning and a deep, far-reaching significance for promoting our country's modernizing construction, implementing the unification of the motherland, expanding our country's influence, and developing our country's relations with the countries of residence." This passage is quoted not from Zhuang's article, but directly from the document; see Shanghai shi xin yimin yanjiu ketizu (Shanghai new migrants research project team) 1997, p. 36. Although the document does not carry a number or even a date, and Zhuang in turn does not give the exact title, the content of the the two quotations makes it likely that they come from the same source.

28. *Shijie rongyin*, 2000, no. 4 (December), pp. 36–37.

29. Lin Wenjing 2000, "Man huai hao qing yujin ershiyi shiji" (Entering the twentieth century with one's bosom full of lofty emotions), *Shijie rongyin*, 2000, no. 2 (May), pp. 7–9.

30. See, e.g., the 1999 work report of Guo Dongpo, the chairman of the China Overseas Exchange Committee, who wrote: "Especially throughout the 1990s, the extra strengthening of determined work . . . has vigorously improved and increased the contact to 'new migrants,' overseas Chinese and second and third generation ethnic Chinese" (Thunø 2001: 925).

31. Chen Xuanrong, ed., "Shijie Fuqing Tongxiang Lianyihui da shi ji" (Major activities of the World Futsing Association), *Shijie rongyin*, 2000, no. 1 (January), pp. 20–22.

32. *Shijie rongyin*, 2000, no. 4 (December), inside back cover.

33. "Man tang gong hua zhanxing shi, yurong qiao xian qu Yuanxiao" (In a full hall, speaking together of moving things forward: overseas worthies of Fuqing gather on Yuanxiao day), *Shijie rongyin*, 2000, no. 2 (May), pp. 4–5.

34. "Guan shan nan zu, xiangqng yong xu" [Passes and mountains are hard to block: feelings for the homeland continue forever], *Shijie rongyin*, 2000, 2 (May), p. 26.

35. *Shijie rongyin*, 2000, no. 2 (May), pp. 2–4.

36. Thus, Liem Sioe Liong began his speech at the third congress of the association by addressing first Guo Dongpo, national Returned Overseas Chinese Federation Chairman Lin Taoban, provincial Party Secretary Chen Mingyi, Governor Xi Jinping, Fuzhou prefecture Party Secretary Zhao Xuemin, and Prefect Weng Fulin, and only then "all esteemed leaders of Fujian province, Fuzhou prefecture, and Fuqing city." Similarly, the photos in *Shijie rongyin* tend to feature association leaders in the company of national or provincial leaders.

37. "Shu gao qian li ye wangbuliao gen" (Although a tree may be a thousand miles high, it still cannot forget its roots), reprinted in *Shijie rongyin*, 2000, no. 2 (May), p. 3.

38. "Qingji guyuan shu fengbei, zai zao huihuang xiang weilai" (Pay homage to the monumental trees of the ancestral land; recreate the glory for ages to come), *Shijie rongyin*, 2000, no. 2 (May), p. 10.

39. "Shu gao qian li ye wangbuliao gen," *Shijie rongyin*, 2000, no. 2, p. 3.

40. "Guan shan nan zu, xiangqing yong xu," *Shijie rongyin*, 2000, no. 2 (May), p. 26.

41. See Chapter 1.

42. Fukien American Association, 1999, booklet commemorating the association's fifty-seventh anniversary, pp. 62–64.

43. "Jiabin yunji, chengkuang kongqian" (Guests of honor assemble like clouds; line-up is a record), *Quanzhou wanbao*, September 4, 1999, p. 2.

44. Field notes N90905L1.

45. "Xiangqin changxu nongnong xiangqing; tong gen shou-zu gong hua sangzi" (Chatting freely, feelings of fellowship run high; sharing common roots, brothers talk about their native place), *Quanzhou wanbao*, September 7, 1999.

46. Interview in Hong Kong on September 10, 1999 (N90910L1).

47. Interview with Mr. He, president of the UK Futsing Association, case file N01105C1.

48. Interview with Huang Qingpo of the Overseas Section of the Fujian Overseas Chinese Affairs Office, Fuzhou, August 5, 1999, file N90805I1.

49. See Barmé's *In the Red* (Barmé 2000: 255–80) for a discussion of the role of the state and cultural producers in the domestic rise of that discourse.

CHAPTER 6. CONCLUSION

1. David Blunkett, Home Secretary, Foreword to *Secure Borders, Safe Haven* (Home Office 2002: 6).

2. See Hannerz 2000 for an enlightening discussion of the overlap and differences between the recent wave of globalization theories and diffusionism in anthropology a century ago.

3. For a similar criticism of conventional conceptualizations of international migration, see Mitchell 1997: 103; and Mitchell 1998: 730–31.

4. In a 2001 study of recent immigrants in New York City's Chinatown, who were mainly from Fujian, Ming-jung Ho found strong evidence that poor living conditions and long workdays contribute to the high incidence of tuberculosis among this group (Ho 2001).

5. The diplomatic fallout after the July 2000 Dover incident, for instance, forced the government to impose a blanket ban on the issuance of passports to any male applicant under 35 years of age in Fuzhou prefecture. This was a clear sign of a government at a loss how to manage the huge demand for emigration in this part of China.

Chinese Names and Terms

ai xiang	love for ones native area, local patriotism	爱乡
bangpai	criminal gang	帮派
benshi	ability, competence	本事
Changle	Changle	长乐
chegong	lathe worker, skilled tailor in workshop	车工
da gong huzhao	big service passport	大公护照
Danmai Fuzhou tongxianghui	Danish Fuzhou Association	丹麦副州同乡会
Deguo Fujian tongxianghui	German Fujian Association	德国福建同乡会
Fahuoshang, baohuoshang	supplier (fahuoshang: as importer; baohuoshang: as middleman)	发货商；包货商
fan ren	to trade people	贩人
fenxiang	dividing the incense; ritual transfer of temple ashes	分香
Fujian sheng lü Yi Huaqiao lianyihui	Association of Fujian Overseas Chinese in Italy	福建省旅意华侨联谊会
Fuqing	Fuqing	福清
Fuzhou	Fuzhou	福州

gao yimin	"to do migration"; to work in the migration business	搞移民
gong fei zi pai	to carry a private passport but use public funds	公费自派
gongwu huzhao	(big) service passport	公务护照
gongzuo danwei	work unit	工作单位
guangtoudang	"Bald Party," skinheads	光头党
Guiqiao	returned overseas Chinese	归侨
Guowuyuan qiaowu bangongshi	Overseas Chinese Affairs Office of the State Council	国务院侨务办公室
guxiang	Native place, homeland	故乡
Huamei Yimin Ruji Gongsi	Chinese American Immigration and Naturalization Company	华美移民入籍公司
jie	to receive, to sponsor somebody's migration	接
Jieke Fujian tongxianghui	Czech Fujian Association	捷克福建同乡会
keren	Guest, client, customer	客人
Lianjiang	Lianjiang	连江
Lü He Fujian tongxiang lianhehui	Fujian Association in the Netherlands	旅荷福建同乡联合会
Lü He Huaqiao zonghui	General Chinese Association in the Netherlands	旅荷华侨总会
Luoma Huaqiao Huaren lianhehui	Rome Overseas and Ethnic Chinese Association	罗马华侨华人联合会
Mingxi	Mingxi	明溪
Mosike huaqiao huaren lianhehui	Moscow Association of Overseas Chinese	莫斯科华侨华人联合会
Nanping	Nanping	南平
Ningde	Ningde	宁德
Ouzhou Huaqiao Huaren shetuan lianhehui	European Federation of Chinese Organizations (EFCO)	欧洲华侨华人社团联合会
Putian	Putian	莆田

Qiaoban	Overseas Chinese Affairs Office	侨办
qiaojuan	dependents of overseas Chinese	侨眷
qiaoling	overseas Chinese leaders	侨领
qiaomin	overseas migrants	侨民
qiaoxiang	overseas Chinese home area	侨乡
Renmin ribao	*People's Daily*	人民日报
renqing	human obligations, human feelings	人情
renshe	"human snakes," smuggled migrants	人蛇
rentou shengyi	people trade	人头生意
Sanming	Sanming	三明
Shaowu	Shaowu	邵武
shetou	"snakehead," human smuggler, migration broker	蛇头
Shijie Fujian tongxiang kenqin dahui	World Fujianese Fellowship Conference	世界福建同乡垦亲大会
Shijie Fuqing tongxiang lianyihui	World Futsing Association	世界福青铜像联谊会
Shijie Fuzhou Shi Yi tongxianghui	Fuzhou Ten Counties World Association	世界福州十邑同乡会
Shougong	manual worker	手工
Shunchang	Shunchang	顺昌
toudu	to smuggle across a border; to cross a border illegally	偷渡
wuguan	martial arts school	武馆
xiagang	to leave one's post, to be made redundant	下岗
xiangzhen qiye	township and village enterprise (TVE)	乡镇企业
xianji shi	county-level municipality, county with city status	县级市
Xianyou	Xianyou	仙游
xiao gong huzhao	little service passport	小公护照
xin qiaomin	new overseas Chinese	新侨民
xin yimin	new migrants	新移民

Xiongyali Huaqiao Huaren lianhe zonghui	Hungarian Overseas and Ethnic Chinese General Federation	匈牙利华侨华人联合总会
yang lanka	"to feed the blue card," to pay taxes in order to extend one's residence permit	养兰卡
yimin guwen gongsi	migration service company	移民顾问公司
yimin shiwusuo	migration service company	移民事务所
yingong putong huzhao	ordinary passport for public business, little service passport	因公普通护照
yinsi (putong) huzhao	(ordinary) passport for private business, private passport	因私护照
youshen	parading the god	游神
youxiu minzu	outstanding race or people	优秀民族
zagong	odd jobs, odd jobs worker	杂工
Zhongguo minzhudang	China Democratic Party (CDP)	中国民主党
Zhonghua dangdai wenxue yishupin zhanzangguan	Treasury of the Works of Contemporary Chinese Literature and Art	中华当代文学艺术品展赃馆
zou xiang shijie	march toward the world, to be cosmopolitan	走向世界
zuguo	fatherland	祖国
zuo huo	to trade goods	作货
zuo ren	to trade people	作人

References

Ahern, Emily M. 1973. *The Cult of the Dead in a Chinese Village*. Stanford: Stanford University Press.

Ambrosini, Maurizio. 2001. "Il lavoro" (Work). In I.S.M.U., ed., *Sesto rapporto sulle migrazioni 2000* (Sixth report on migration 2000), pp. 91–101. Milan: FrancoAngeli.

Ambrosini, Maurizio, and Eugenio Zucchetti. 2002. "Il lavoro" (Work). In I.S.M.U., ed., *Settimo rapporto sulle migrazioni 2001* (Seventh report on migration 2001), pp. 117–31. Milan: FrancoAngeli.

Anagnost, Ann. 1997. *National Past-times: Narrative, Representation, and Power in Modern China*. Durham, N.C: Duke University Press.

Appadurai, Arjun. 2000. "Grassroots Globalization and the Research Imagination." *Public Culture* 12: 1–19.

Archaimbault, Charles. 1987. "Boeren en landlopers: migranten uit Oost China" (Peasants and tramps: migrants from East China). In Gregor Benton and Hans Vermeulen, eds., *De Chinezen* (The Chinese), pp. 22–26. Muiderberg: Coutinho.

Baker, Hugh D. R. 1968. *A Chinese Lineage Village: Sheung Shui*. London: Frank Cass.

Barmé, Geremie. 2000. *In the Red: On Contemporary Chinese Culture*. New York: Columbia University Press.

Basch, Linda G., Nina Glick Schiller, and Cristina Szanton-Blanc. 1994. *Nations Unbound: Transnational Projects, Postcolonial Predicaments, and Deterritorialized Nation-States*. Amsterdam: Gordon and Breach.

Beltrán Antolín, Joaquín. 1998. "The Chinese in Spain." In Gregor Benton and Frank N. Pieke, eds., *The Chinese in Europe*, pp. 211–37. Basingstoke: Macmillan.

Blangiardo, Giancarlo. 2002. "La presenza straniera in Italia" (The foreign presence in Italy). In I.S.M.U., ed., *Settimo rapporto sulle migrazioni 2001* (Seventh Report on Migration 2001), pp. 17–26. Milan: FrancoAngeli.

Blangiardo, Giancarlo, and Patrizia Farina. 2001. "La presenza regolare e irregolare" (The regular and irregular presence). In I.S.M.U., ed., *Sesto rapporto sulle migrazione 2000* (Sixth report on migration 2000), pp. 11–23. Milan: FrancoAngeli.

Brandtstädter, Susanne. 2001. *Redefining Place in Southern Fujian: How Ancestral Halls and Overseas Mansions Re-appropriate the Local from the State.* Max Planck Institute for Social Anthropology Working Paper no. 30. Halle, Germany: Max Planck Institute for Social Anthropology.

Burawoy, Michael. 2000. *Global Ethnography: Forces, Connections, and Imaginations in a Postmodern World.* Berkeley: University of California Press.

Cai, Kevin G. 2000a. "Outward Foreign Direct Investment: A Novel Dimension of China's Integration into the Regional and Global Economy." *The China Quarterly* 160: 856–80.

————. 2000b. "Between State and Peasant: Local Cadres and Statistical Reporting in Rural China." *The China Quarterly* 163: 783–805.

Campani, Giovanna, and L. Maddii. 1992. "Un monde à part: les Chinois en Toscane" (A world apart: The Chinese in Tuscany). *Revue Européenne des Migrations Internationales* 8: 51–72.

Carchedi, Francesco, and Marica Ferri. 1998. "The Chinese Presence in Italy: Dimensions and Structural Characteristics." In Gregor Benton and Frank N. Pieke, eds., *The Chinese in Europe*, pp. 261–77. Basingstoke: Macmillan.

Carfagna, Massimo. 2002. "I sommersi e i sanati. Le regolarizzazioni degli immigrati in Italia" (Clandestines and those regularized through amnesty: the regularization of immigrants in Italy). In Asher Colombo and Guiseppe Sciortino, eds., *Stranieri in Italia. Assimilati ed esclusi* (Foreigners in Italy: assimilated and excluded), pp. 53–87. Bologna: Il Mulino.

Caritas di Roma. 2001. *Dossier statistico immigrazione, 2001* (Statistical dossier on immigration, 2001). Rome: Anterem.

Castells, Manuel. 1996. *The Rise of the Network Society.* Oxford: Basil Blackwell.

Ceccagno, Antonella. 1998. *Cinesi d'Italia* (Chinese in Italy). Rome: Manifestolibri.

————. 2001a. "Nei-Wai: interazioni con il tessuto socioeconomico e autoreferenzialità etnica nelle comunità cinesi in Italia" (Nei-wai: interaction with the socioeconomic fabric and ethnic self-reference in Chinese communities in Italy). *Mondo Cinese* 101: 75–93.

————. 2001b. "Preliminary Considerations on the Economic and Social Mobility of the Chinese in Prato." In Renzo Rastrelli, ed., *European Dynamics of the Chinese Diaspora: The Future for Prato*, pp. 140–56. Prato, Italy: Provincia di Prato.

————. 2003a. "Changing Times: Recent Trends in the Relationship between Chinese Businesses and the Local Market in Italy." In Giusi Tamburello, ed., *L'Invenzione della Cina* (The invention of China). Lecce: Congedo (forthcoming).

————. 2003b. "Le migrazioni dalla Cina verso l'Italia e l'Europa nell'epoca della globalizzazione" (Migrations from China to Europe and Italy in the era of globalization). In Antonella Ceccagno, ed., *Migranti a Prato. Il distretto tessile multietnico* (Migrants in Prato: the multi-ethnic textile district), pp. 25–68. Milan: FrancoAngeli.

Centro Ricerche e Servizi per L'Immigrazione. 2000. *Prato multietnica* (Multiethnic Prato), 2001 ed. Prato, Italy: Prato Centre for Immigration Research and Services.

———. 2001. *Prato multietnica* (Multiethnic Prato), 2001 ed. Prato, Italy: Prato Centre for Immigration Research and Services.

Cesareo, Vincenzo. 2002. "Editoriale" (Editorial). In I.S.M.U., ed., *Settimo rapporto sulle migrazioni 2001* (Seventh report on migration 2001), pp. 7–14. Milan: FrancoAngeli.

Chan, Anita. 2001. *China's Workers under Assault: The Exploitation of Labor in a Globalizing Economy.* Armonk, N.J.: M. E. Sharpe.

Chan, Kam Wing. 1994. *Cities with Invisible Walls: Reinterpreting Urbanization in Post-1949 China.* Hong Kong: Oxford University Press.

Cheng, Lim-Keak. 1985. *Social Change and the Chinese in Singapore: A Socio-Economic Geography with Special Reference to Bang Structure.* Singapore: Singapore University Press.

Cheng, Xi. 2002. "Non-Remaining and Non-Returning: The Mainland Chinese Students in Japan and Europe since the 1970s." In Pál Nyíri and Igor R. Saveliev, ed., *Globalising Chinese Migration*, pp. 158–172. Aldershot: Ashgate.

Chin, James. 2002. "Gold from the Lands Afar: New Fujianese Emigration Revisited." In Pál Nyíri and Igor R. Saveliev, eds., *Globalising Chinese Migration*, pp. 242–53. Aldershot: Ashgate.

Chin, Ko-lin. 1999. *Smuggled Chinese: Clandestine Immigration to the United States.* Philadelphia: Temple University Press.

Chin, Ung-Ho. 1997. *Chinese Politics in Sarawak: A Study of the Sarawak United People's Party.* Kuala Lumpur: Oxford University Press.

City of Budapest. 1997. *Jelentés a Budapesten élo kínaiakról* (Report on the Chinese living in Budapest). City of Budapest.

Crisp, Jeff. 1999. "Policy Challenges of the New Diasporas: Migrant Networks and Their Impact on Asylum Flows and Regimes." Transnational Communities Programme Working Paper Series WPTC-99-05. http:// www.transcomm.ox.ac.uk/.

Crissman, Lawrence W. 1967. "The Segmentary Structure of Urban Overseas Chinese Communities." *Man*, n.s., 2: 185–204.

de Tinguy, Anne. 1999. "Chinese Immigration to Russia: A Variation on an Old Theme." In Gregor Benton and Frank N. Pieke, ed., *The Chinese in Europe*, pp. 301–19. Basingstoke: Macmillan.

Dean, Kenneth. 1986. "Field Notes on Two Taoist Jiao Observed in Zhangzhou, December 1985." *Cahiers d'Extreme-Asie* 2: 191–209.

———. 1989. "Revival of Religious Practices in Fujian: A Case Study." In Julian F. Pas, ed., *The Turning of the Tide: Religion in China Today*, pp. 51–78. Hong Kong and New York: Royal Asiatic Society, Hong Kong Branch and Oxford University Press.

————. 1998. "Transformations of the *She* (Altars of the Soil) in Fujian." *Cahiers d'Extreme-Asie* 10: 19–75.

Department of Social Security. 2000. *Productive Activities and Occupational Levels in the Province of Prato, Year 2000.* Unpublished report, Prato, Italy: City of Prato.

DeStefano, Anthony M. 1997. "Immigrant Smuggling through Central America and the Caribbean." In Paul J. Smith, ed., *Human Smuggling: Chinese Migrant Trafficking and the Challenge to America's Immigration Tradition,* pp. 134–55. Washington, D.C.: Center for Strategic and International Studies.

Eberstein, Bernd. 1988. *Hamburg–China: Geschichte einer Partnerschaft (Hamburg–China: history of a partnership).* Hamburg: Christians.

Edmonds, Richard Louis. 1996. "Geography and Natural Resources." In Brian Hook, ed., *Fujian: Gateway to Taiwan,* pp. 63–94. Hong Kong: Oxford University Press.

European Federation of Chinese Organisations (EFCO). 1999. *The Chinese Community in Europe.* Amsterdam: EFCO.

Farina, Patrizia. 2002. "La presenza straniera in Europa" (Foreigners in Europe). In I.S.M.U., ed., *Settimo rapporto sulle migrazioni 2001* (Seventh report on migration 2001), pp. 27–35. Milan: FrancoAngeli.

Fasano, Luciano, and Francesco Zucchini. 2002. "L'implementazione locale del testo unico sull'immigrazione" (Local implementation of the immigration law). In I.S.M.U., ed., *Settimo rapporto sulle migrazioni 2001* (Seventh report on migration 2001), pp. 61–74. Milan: FrancoAngeli.

Feuchtwang, Stephan. 1998. "What Is a Village?" In Eduard B. Vermeer, Frank N. Pieke, and Woei Lien Chong, eds., *Cooperative and Collective in China's Rural Development: Between State Organization and Private Interest,* pp. 46–74. Armonk, N.J.: M. E. Sharpe.

Fitzgerald, Stephen. 1972. *China and the Overseas Chinese.* London: Cambridge University Press.

Flower, John, and Pamela Leonard. 1998. "Defining Cultural Life in the Chinese Countryside: The Case of the Chuanzhu Temple." In Eduard B. Vermeer, Frank N. Pieke, and Woei Lien Chong, eds., *Cooperative and Collective in China's Rural Development: Between State Organization and Private Interest,* pp. 273–90. Armonk, N.J.: M. E. Sharpe.

Freedman, Maurice. 1958. *Lineage Organization in Southeastern China.* London and New York: Athlone Press and Humanities Press.

Fujian sheng difangzhi bianzuan weiyuanhui (Editorial Committee of the local gazetteer of Fujian province). 1992. *Fujian shengzhi: Huaqiaozhi* (Provincial gazetteer of Fujian: overseas Chinese volume). Fuzhou: Fujian Renmin Chubanshe.

Fujiansheng jihua weiyuanhui (Fujian planning committee) and Fujiansheng tongjiju (Fujian province statistical bureau), ed. 1999. *Fujiansheng duiwai kaifang ershi nian* (Two decades of opening up to the world in Fujian province). Beijing: Zhongguo Tongji Chubanshe.

Fujiansheng renmin zhengfu bianzuan weiyuanhui (Fujian provincial government editorial committee), ed. 1999. *Fujian nianjian, 1999* (Fujian yearbook, 1999). Fuzhou: Fujian Renmin Chubanshe.

Fujiansheng tongjiju (Fujian province statistical bureau), editor. 1997. *Fujian tongji nianjian* (Fujian statistical yearbook). Beijing: Zhongguo Tongji Chubanshe.

———. 2000. *Fujian tongji nianjian* (Fujian statistical yearbook). Beijing: Zhongguo Tongji Chubanshe.

Giddens, Anthony. 1990. *The Consequences of Modernity*. Stanford: Stanford University Press.

Giese, Karsten. 1999. *Irreguläre Migration vom chinesischen Festland nach Taiwan* (Irregular migration from the Chinese mainland to Taiwan). Berlin: UniTerra.

Glick Schiller, Nina, Linda Basch, and Cristina Blanc-Szanton. 1995. "From Immigrant to Transmigrant: Theorizing Transnational Migration." *Anthropological Quarterly* 68: 48–63.

Glover, Stephen, Cerei Gott, Anaïs Loizillon, Jonathan Portes, Richard Price, Sarah Spencer, Vashanti Srinivasan, and Carole Willis. 2001. *Migration: An Economic and Social Analysis*. Home Office Research, Development and Statistics Directorate Occasional Paper no. 67.

Griffin, Nicholas John. 1973. "The Use of Chinese Labor by the British Army, 1916–1920: The 'Raw Importation,' Its Scope and Problems." Ph.D. thesis, University of Oklahoma.

Guarnizo, Luis Eduardo, and Michael Peter Smith. 1998. "The Locations of Transnationalism." In Michael Peter Smith and Luis Eduardo Guarnizo, eds., *Transnationalism from Below*, pp. 3–34. New Brunswick, N.J.: Transaction.

Gupta, Akhil, and James Ferguson. 1997. "Beyond 'Culture': Space, Identity, and Politics of Difference." In Akhil Gupta and James Ferguson, eds., *Culture, Power, Place: Explorations in Critical Anthropology*, pp. 33–51. Durham, N.C.: Duke University Press.

Gütinger, Erich. 1998. "A Sketch of the Chinese Community in Germany: Past and Present." In Gregor Benton and Frank N. Pieke, eds., *The Chinese in Europe*, pp. 197–208. Basingstoke: Macmillan.

Hannerz, Ulf. 1987. The World in Creolisation. *Africa* 57.

———. 1988. "American Culture: Creolized, Creolizing." In Erik Åsard, ed., *American Culture: Creolized, Creolizing and Other Lectures from the NAAS Biennial Conference in Uppsala, May 28–31, 1987*. Uppsala: Swedish Institute for North American Studies.

———. 1992. *Cultural Complexity: Studies in the Social Organization of Meaning*. New York: Columbia University Press.

———. 2000. *Flows, Boundaries and Hybrids: Keywords in Transnational Anthropology*. Oxford: Transnational Communities Programme Working Paper WPTC-2K-02.

Harvey, David. 1989. *The Condition of Postmodernity: An Enquiry into the Origins of Cultural Change*. Oxford: Blackwell.

Hatton, Timothy J., and Jeffrey G. Williamson. 1998. *The Age of Mass Migration: Causes and Economic Impact.* Oxford: Oxford University Press.

Held, David, Anthony McGrew, David Goldblatt, and Jonathan Perraton. 1999. *Global Transformations: Politics, Economics and Culture.* Cambridge, Eng.: Polity Press.

Ho, Ming-jung. 2001. "Discourses on Immigrant Tuberculosis: A Case Study of New York City's Chinese Laborers." D.Phil. thesis, Institute of Social and Cultural Anthropology, University of Oxford.

Home Office. 2002. *Secure Borders, Safe Haven: Integration with Diversity in Modern Britain.* Home Office.

Hood, Marlowe. 1998. "Fuzhou." In Lynn Pan, ed., *The Encyclopedia of the Chinese Overseas,* pp. 33–35. Singapore: Archipelago Press and Landmark Books.

Hu, Xuwei, and Hu, Tianxin. 2000. "Trends and Patterns of Foreign Direct Investment." In Y. M. Yeung and David K. Y. Chu, eds., *Fujian: A Coastal Province in Transition and Transformation,* pp. 212–30. Hong Kong: The Chinese University Press.

Huang, Cen. 2000. "The Dynamics of Overseas Chinese Invested Enterprises in South China." In Cen Huang, Guotu Zhuang, and Tanaka Kyoko, eds., *New Studies on Chinese Overseas and China,* pp. 190–209. Leiden: International Institute for Asian Studies.

Huntington, Samuel P. 1998. *The Clash of Civilizations and the Remaking of World Order.* London: Touchstone.

Jin, Liangjun. 2000. *Deguo* (Germany). Beijing: Lüyou Jiaoyu Chubanshe.

Jing, Jun. 1996. *The Temple of Memories: History, Power, and Morality in a Chinese Village.* Stanford: Stanford University Press.

Knapp, Ronald G. 1996. "Rural Housing and Village Transformation in Taiwan and Fujian." *The China Quarterly* 147: 779–94.

Kuah, Khun Eng. 1998. "Rebuilding Their Ancestral Villages: The Moral Economy of the Singapore Chinese." In Gungwu Wang and John Wong, eds., *China's Political Economy,* pp. 249–75. Singapore: University of Singapore Press and World Scientific.

———. 1999. "The Changing Moral Economy of Ancestor Worship in a Chinese Emigrant District." *Culture, Medicine and Psychiatry* 23: 99–132.

———. 2000. *Rebuilding the Ancestral Village: Singaporeans in China.* Aldershot: Ashgate.

Kwong, Peter. 1997. *Forbidden Workers: Illegal Chinese Immigrants and American Labor.* New York: New Press.

Kyle, David, and John Dale. 2001. "Smuggling the State Back In: Agents of Human Smuggling Reconsidered." In David Kyle and Rey Koslowski, eds., *Global Human Smuggling: Comparative Perspectives,* pp. 29–57. Baltimore: Johns Hopkins University Press.

Larin, Alexander G. 1998. "Chinese in Russia: An Historical Perspective." In Gregor Benton and Frank N. Pieke, eds., *The Chinese in Europe,* pp. 281–300. Basingstoke: Macmillan.

Lary, Diana. 1999. "The 'Static Decades': Inter-provincial Migration in Pre-reform China." In Frank N. Pieke and Hein Mallee, eds., *Internal and International Migration: Chinese Perspectives*, pp. 29–48. Richmond: Curzon.

Lee, Ching Kwan. 1998. *Gender and the South China Miracle: Two Worlds of Factory Women*. Berkeley: University of California Press.

Lee, Leo Ou-fan. 1994. "On the Margins of the Chinese Discourse: Some Personal Thoughts on the Cultural Meaning of the Periphery." In Tu Wei-ming, ed., *The Living Tree: The Changing Meaning of Being Chinese Today*, pp. 221–38. Stanford: Stanford University Press.

Levitt, Peggy. 2001. *The Transnational Villagers*. Berkeley: University of California Press.

Li, Anshan. 2000. *Feizhou Huaqiao renshi* (A history of the overseas Chinese in Africa). Beijing: Zhongguo Huaqiao Chubanshe.

Li, Minghuan. 1995. *Dangdai haiwai Huaren shetuan yanjiu* (Research on contemporary overseas Chinese associations). Xiamen: Xiamen Daxue Chubanshe.

———. 1999. "'To Get Rich Quickly in Europe!'—Reflections on Migration Motivation in Wenzhou." In Frank N. Pieke and Hein Mallee, eds., *Internal and International Migration: Chinese Perspectives*, pp. 181–98. Richmond: Curzon.

———. 2001. "'Fei jingying yimin' zhi lu: 20 shiji moye Xi'ou yimin zhengce yu Zhongguo xin yimin" (The road of "non-economic migration": immigration policies in western Europe at the end of the twentieth century and China's new migrants). Paper presented at the 2001 ISSCO conference, Taipei.

Li, Victor Hao. 1994. "From *Qiao* to *Qiao*." In Tu Wei-ming, ed., *The Living Tree: The Changing Meaning of Being Chinese Today*, pp. 213–20. Stanford: Stanford University Press.

Liang, Zai. 2001. "The Demography of Illicit Emigration from China: A Sending Country Perspective." In David Kyle and Rey Koslowski, eds., *Global Human Smuggling: Comparative Perspectives*. Baltimore: Johns Hopkins University Press.

Liang, Zai, and Wenzhen Ye. 2001. "From Fujian to New York: Understanding the New Chinese Immigration." In David Kyle and Rey Koslowski, eds., *Global Human Smuggling: Comparative Perspectives*, pp. 187–215. Baltimore: Johns Hopkins University Press.

Lieberthal, Kenneth G., and David M. Lampton, ed. 1992. *Bureaucracy, Politics, and Decision Making in Post-Mao China*. Berkeley: University of California Press.

Lieberthal, Kenneth G., and Michel Oksenburg. 1988. *Policy Making in China: Leaders, Structures, and Processes*. Princeton, N.J.: Princeton University Press.

Lin, Jiazhong, and Enyan Lin. 1994. "Gudai chuguo de Fuzhouren" (Emigrant Fuzhounese of antiquity). In Jiazhou Tong, ed., *Fuzhou diqu Huaqiao chuguo shi lunwenji* (Collection of studies on the history of overseas Chinese migration from Fuzhou prefecture), pp. 157–67. Fuzhou: Fuzhou Shi Huaqiao Lishi Xuehui.

Litzinger, Ralph A. 2000. *Other Chinas: The Yao and the Politics of National Belonging*. Durham, N.C.: Duke University Press.

Liu, Hong. 1998. "Old Linkages, New Networks: The Globalization of Overseas Chinese Voluntary Associations and Its Implications." *The China Quarterly* 155: 582–609.

Liu, Ningrong. 1996. *Zhongguo "renshe" chao* (The tide of Chinese "human snakes"). Hong Kong: Jiushi Niandai Zazhishe.

Live, Yu-Sion. 1998. "The Chinese Community in France: Immigration, Economic Activity, Cultural Organization and Representations." In Gregor Benton and Frank N. Pieke, eds., *The Chinese in Europe*, pp. 96–124. Basingstoke: Macmillan.

Lü, Xiaobo, and Elizabeth Perry. 1997. *Danwei: The Changing Chinese Workplace in Historical and Comparative Perspective.* Armonk, N.J.: M. E. Sharpe.

Lyons, Thomas P. 1998. Interprovincial Disparities in China: Fujian Province, 1978–1995. *Economic Geography* 74: 405–33.

———. 2000. "Regional Inequality." In Y. M. Yeung and David K. Y. Chu, eds., *Fujian: A Coastal Province in Transition and Transformation*, pp. 327–51. Hong Kong: Chinese University Press.

Mabogunje, Akin. 1970. Systems Approach to a Theory of Rural-Urban Migration. *Geographical Analysis* 2: 1–17.

Mao, Chun. 1992. *Zhongguoren zai Dong'ou (90 niandai xin rechao chuguo taojin jishi)* (Chinese in eastern Europe: A chronicle of the new boom of gold-digger migrants of the 1990s). Beijing: Lüyou Jiaoyu Chubanshe.

Marazzi, Antonio. 2002. "La famiglia immigrata" (The immigrant family). In I.S.M.U., ed., *Settimo rapporto sulle migrazioni 2001* (Seventh report on migration 2001), pp. 213–23. Milan: FrancoAngeli.

Marcus, George E. 1995. "Ethnography in / of the World System: the Emergence of Multi-Sited Ethnography." *Annual Review of Anthropology* 24: 95–117.

Massey, Douglas S. 1988. "Economic Development and International Migration in Comparative Perspective." *Population and Development Review* 14: 383–413.

Massey, Douglas S., Joaquin Arango, Graeme Hugo, Ali Kouaouci, Adela Pellegrino, and J. Edward Taylor. 1993. "Theories of International Migration: A Review and Appraisal." *Population and Development Review* 19: 431–66.

———. 1994. "An Evaluation of International Migration Theory: The North American Case." *Population and Development Review* 20: 728–33.

———. 1998. *Worlds in Motion: Understanding International Migration at the End of the Millennium.* Oxford: Oxford University Press.

McKeown, Adam. 1999. "Conceptualizing Chinese Diasporas, 1842 to 1949." *Journal of Asian Studies* 58: 306–37.

Medved, Felicita. 2001. "Trafficking—Smuggling—'Illegal' Migration: Dichotomy or Continuum?" Paper presented at the conference Migration and Asylum: Policies in Countries on the "Schengen Periphery" and the Balkans, Ljubljana, November 30—December 1.

Mingxixian difangzhi bianzuan weiyuanhui (Editorial committee of the Mingxi county local gazetteer). 1997. *Mingxi xianzhi* (Mingxi county gazetteer). Beijing: Beijing: Fangzhi Chubanshe.

Mitchell, Katheryne. 1995. "Flexible Circulation in the Pacific Rim: Capitalisms in Cultural Context." *Economic Geography* 71: 364–82.

———. 1997. "Transnational Discourse: Bringing Geography Back In." *Antipode* 29: 101–14.

———. 1998. "Reworking Democracy: Contemporary Immigration and Community Politics in Vancouver's Chinatown." *Political Geography* 17: 729–50.

———. 2001. "Transnationalism, Neo-liberalism, and the Rise of the Shadow State." *Economy and Society* 30: 165–89.

Myers, William H. 1997. "Of *Qinqing, Qinshu, Guanxi,* and *Shetou*: The Dynamic Elements of Chinese Irregular Population Movement." In Paul J. Smith, ed., *Human Smuggling: Chinese Migrant Trafficking and the Challenge to America's Immigration Tradition,* pp. 93–133. Washington, D.C.: Center for Strategic and International Studies.

Naughton, Barry. 1991. "Industrial Policy during the Cultural Revolution: Military Preparation, Decentralization, and Leaps Forward." In William A. Joseph, Christine P. W. Wong, and David Zweig, eds., *New Perspectives on the Cultural Revolution.* Cambridge, Mass.: Council on East Asian Studies / Harvard University.

Nyíri, Pál. 1998a. "Létezik-e kínai maffia?" (Is there a Chinese mafia?). *Belügyi Szemle.*

———. 1998b. "New Migrants, New Community: The Chinese in Hungary, 1989–1995." In Gregor Benton and Frank N. Pieke, eds., *The Chinese in Europe,* pp. 350–79. Basingstoke: Macmillan.

———. 1999. *New Chinese Migrants in Europe: The Case of the Chinese Community in Hungary.* Aldershot: Ashgate.

———. 2001a. "Expatriating Is Patriotic? The Discourse on 'New Migrants' in the People's Republic of China and Identity Construction among Recent Migrants from the PRC." *Journal of Ethnic and Migration Studies* 27: 635–53.

———. 2001b. "Hungary's Treatment of Immigrants: EU Expectations as Cause and Pretext for Improvement or Worsening." Paper delivered at the conference "Migration and Integration in Europe," Seeon, Germany, July 6–8.

———. 2003. Moving Targets: Chinese Christian Proselytism among Transnational Migrants from the PRC: Introductory Thoughts. *European Journal of East Asian Studies,* 2: 59–97 .

Omodeo, Maria. 1997. "Studenti cinesi nella scuola italiana: ritardo scolastico ed obiettivi limitati" (Chinese students in Italian schools: educational lag and limited objectives). In Antonella Ceccagno, ed., *Il caso delle comunità cinesi* (The case of the Chinese community), pp. 193–205. Rome: Armando.

Ong, Aihwa. 1997. "Chinese Modernities: Narratives of Nation and of Capitalism." In Aihwa Ong and Donald Nonini, eds., *Ungrounded Empires: The Cultural Politics of Modern Chinese Transnationalism,* pp. 171–202. New York: Routledge.

———. 1999. *Flexible Citizenship: The Cultural Logics of Transnationality.* Durham, N.C.: Duke University Press.

Organisation for Economic Cooperation and Development (OECD). 2001. *Migration Policies and EU Enlargement: The Case of Central and Eastern Europe.* OECD.

Pan, Lynn, ed. 1998. *The Encyclopedia of the Chinese Overseas.* Singapore: Archipelago Press and Landmark Books.

Pang, Ching Lin. 1993. *Tussen inpassing and identiteit: de Chinese gemeenschap in België (Between integration and identity: the Chinese community in Belgium).* Louvaine: Steunpunt Migranten, Hoger Instituut voor de Arbeid, Catholic University of Louvaine.

Parker, David. 1998. "Chinese People in Britain: Histories, Futures and Identities." In Gregor Benton and Frank N. Pieke, eds., *The Chinese in Europe,* pp. 67–95. Basingstoke: Macmillan.

Paul, Marc. 2002. "The Dongbei: The New Chinese Immigration in Paris." In Pál Nyíri and Igor R. Saveliev, eds., *Globalising Chinese Migration,* pp. 120–28. Aldershot: Ashgate.

Pieke, Frank N. 1987. "Four Models of China's Overseas Chinese Policies." *China Information* 2: 8–16.

———. 1996. *The Ordinary and the Extraordinary: An Anthropological Study of Chinese Reform and the 1989 People's Movement in Beijing.* London: Kegan Paul International.

———. 1998. "Introduction." In Gregor Benton and Frank N. Pieke, eds., *The Chinese in Europe,* pp. 1–17. Basingstoke: Macmillan.

———. 1999. "Introduction: Chinese Migration Compared." In Frank N. Pieke and Hein Mallee, eds., *Internal and International Migration: Chinese Perspectives,* pp. 1–26. Richmond: Curzon.

———. 2002. *Recent Trends in Chinese Migration: Fujianese Migration in Perspective.* IOM Migration Research Series No. 6. Geneva: International Organization for Migration.

———. 2003. The Genealogical Mentality in Modern China. *Journal of Asian Studies* 62: 101–28.

———. Forthcoming. "Past and Present Chinese Migration to Europe." *Studi Emigrazione.*

Pieke, Frank N., and Gregor Benton. 1998. "The Chinese in the Netherlands." In Gregor Benton and Frank N. Pieke, eds., *The Chinese in Europe,* pp. 125–67. Basingstoke: Macmillan.

Portes, Alejandro. 2001. "Introduction: The Debates and Significance of Immigrant Transnationalism." *Global Networks* 1: 181–93.

Portes, Alejandro, and Robert L. Bach. 1985. *Latin Journey: Cuban and Mexican Immigrants in the United States.* Berkeley: University of California Press.

Portes, Alejandro, and Leif Jensen. 1987. "What's an Ethnic Enclave? The Case for Conceptual Clarity." *American Sociological Review* 52: 768–71.

Portes, Alejandro, Luis E. Guarnizo, and Patricia Landolt. 1999. "Introduction: Pitfalls and Promise of an Emergent Research Field." *Ethnic and Racial Studies* 22: 217–37.

Portyakov, V. 1996. "Are the Chinese Coming? Migration Processes in Russia's Far East." *International Affairs: A Russian Journal of World Politics, Diplomacy and International Relations* 41: 132–40.

Regione Lombardia, and Fondazione I.S.M.U. 2002. *Osservatorio regionale per l'integrazione e la multietnicità. Rapporto 2001* (Regional Monitoring Institute on Integration and Mutliethnicity. Report 2001). Fondazione I.S.M.U.

Reyneri, Emilio. 2000. "Il mercato del lavoro. L'integrazione nell'occupazione dipendente" (The work market: integration into dependent employment). In Giovanna Zincone, ed., *Secondo rapporto sull'integrazione degli immigrati in Italia* (Second report on the integration of immigrants in Italy), pp. 331–65. Bologna: Il Mulino.

Sassen, Saskia. 1991. *The Global City*. Princeton, N.J.: Princeton University Press.

———. 1996. *Losing Control? Sovereignty in an Age of Globalization*. New York: Columbia University Press.

Schein, Louisa. 2000. *Minority Rules: The Miao and the Feminine in China's Cultural Politics. Body, Commodity, Text*. Durham, N.C.: Duke University Press.

Schloenhardt, Andreas. 1999. "Organized Crime and the Business of Migrant Trafficking." Paper presented at the Australian Institute of Criminology, November 10, 1999. http://www.aic.gov.au/conferences/occasional/schloenhardt.html.

Shanghai shi xin yimin yanjiu ketizu (Shanghai new migrants research project team). 1997. Shanghai shi xin yimin yanjiu (Shanghai new migrants research). *Zhongguo Renkou Kexue* 1997, 3: 36–41, 52.

Shen, Jianfa, Xiaohua Tang, and Zhong Lin. 2000. "Population Growth and Mobility." In Y. M. Yeung and David K. Y. Chu, eds., *Fujian: A Coastal Province in Transition and Transformation*, pp. 455–85. Hong Kong: Chinese University Press.

Shi, Xueqin. 2000. "Gaige kaifang yilai Fuqing qiaoxiang de xin yimin: jiantan feifa yimin wenti" (New migrants since the beginning of the reform period from migration areas in Fuqing, Fujian: the problem of illegal migration). *Huaqiao huaren lishi yanjiu* 4: 26–31.

Shieh, Shawn. 2000. "Centre, Province and Locality in Fujian's Reforms." In Y. M. Yeung and David K. Y. Chu, eds., *Fujian: A Coastal Province in Transition and Transformation*, pp. 83–117. Hong Kong: Chinese University Press.

Shirk, Susan. 1993. *The Political Logic of Economic Reform in China*. Berkeley: University of California Press.

Shkurkin, Anatoly M. 2000. "Chinese on the Labour Market in Eastern Siberia and the Russian Far East." Paper presented at the workshop "The Last Decade of Migration from the People's Republic of China to Europe and Asia," Budapest, May 26–27.

Siu, Helen F. 1989. "Recycling Rituals: Politics and Popular Culture in Contemporary Rural China." In Perry Link, Richard Madsen, and Paul G. Pickowicz, eds., *Unofficial China: Popular Culture and Thought in the People's Republic of China*, pp. 121–37. Boulder, Colo.: Westview Press.

————. 1990. "Recycling Tradition: Culture, History, and Political Economy in the Chrysanthemum Festivals of South China." *Comparative Studies in Society and History* 32: 765–94.

Skeldon, Ronald. 1994. "Reluctant Exiles or Bold Pioneers: An Introduction to Migration from Hong Kong." In Ronald Skeldon, ed., *Reluctant Exiles? Migration from Hong Kong and the New Overseas Chinese*, pp. 3–18. Armonk, N.Y.: M. E. Sharpe.

Skinner, G. William. 1958. *Leadership and Power in the Chinese Community of Thailand*. Ithaca, N.Y.: Cornell University Press.

Slater, Jim. 1998. "Outward Investment from China." In Roger Strange, Jim Slater, and Limin Wang, ed., *Trade and Investment in China: The European Experience*, pp. 269–83. London: Routledge.

Smith, Paul J., ed. 1997. *Human Smuggling: Chinese Migrant Trafficking and the Challenge to America's Immigration Tradition*. Washington, D.C.: The Center for Strategic and International Studies.

Summerskill, Michael. 1982. *China on the Western Front: Britain's Chinese Work Force in the First World War*. London: Michael Summerskill.

Szonyi, Michael. 2000. "Local Cult, *Lijia*, and Lineage: Religious and Social Organization in the Fuzhou Region in the Ming and Qing." *Journal of Chinese Religions* 28: 93–126.

Tan, Chee-Beng, and Xiaojun Zhang. 1999. *Bibliography of Studies on Fujian with Special Reference to Minnan*. Hong Kong: Institute of Asia-Pacific Studies, Chinese University of Hong Kong.

Tapp, Nicholas. 1996. "Social Aspects of China Fir Plantations in China." *Commonwealth Forestry Review* 75: 302–8.

Teixeira, Ana. 1998. "Entrepreneurs of the Chinese Community in Portugal." In Gregor Benton and Frank N. Pieke, eds., *The Chinese in Europe*, pp. 238–60. Basingstoke: Macmillan.

Thunø, Mette. 1997. "Chinese Migration to Denmark: Catering and Ethnicity." Ph.D. thesis, University of Copenhagen.

————. 1998. "Chinese in Denmark." In Gregor Benton and Frank N. Pieke, eds., *The Chinese in Europe*, pp. 168–96. Basingstoke: Macmillan.

————. 1999. "Moving Stones from China to Europe: The Dynamics of Emigration from Zhejiang to Europe." In Frank N. Pieke and Hein Mallee, eds., *Internal and International Migration: Chinese Perspectives*, pp. 159–80. Richmond: Curzon Press.

————. 2001. "Reaching Out and Incorporating Chinese Overseas: The Transterritorial Scope of the PRC by the End of the Twentieth Century." *The China Quarterly* 168: 939–58.

Tu, Wei-ming. 1994a. "Cultural China: The Periphery as the Center." In Tu Wei-ming, ed., *The Living Tree: The Changing Meaning of Being Chinese Today*, pp. 1–34. Stanford: Stanford University Press.

————, ed. 1994b. *The Living Tree: The Changing Meaning of Being Chinese Today*. Stanford: Stanford University Press.

United Nations. 2001. *Replacement Migration: Is It a Solution to Declining and Ageing Populations?* United Nations ST / ESA / SER.A / 206.

Walder, Andrew G. 1986. *Communist Neo-Traditionalism: Work and Authority in Chinese Industry.* Berkeley: University of California Press.

Wallace, Claire, Vasil Bedzir, and Oksana Chmouliar. 1997. *Spending, Saving or Investing Social Capital: The Case of Shuttle Traders in Post-Communist Central Europe.* East European Series, no. 43. Vienna: Institute for Advanced Studies.

Wang, Furui. 1994. "XX qiaoxiang shilüe" (A short history of the overseas Chinese village of XX). In Yang Yinxian, Wang Shuyu, and Tong Jiazhou, eds., *Fuzhou diqu Huaqiao chuguo shi lunwenji* (Collection of studies on the history of overseas Chinese migration from Fuzhou prefecture), pp. 140–43. Fuzhou: Fuzhou Shi Huaqiao Lishi Xuehui.

Wang, Gungwu. 1994. "Among Non-Chinese." In Wei-ming Tu, ed., *The Living Tree: The Changing Meaning of Being Chinese Today*, pp. 127–47. Stanford: Stanford University Press.

Wang, L. Ling-chi. 1994. "Roots and the Changing Identity of the Chinese in the United States." In Wei-ming Tu, ed., *The Living Tree: The Changing Meaning of Being Chinese Today*, pp. 185–212. Stanford: Stanford University Press.

Watson, James L. 1976. *Emigration and the Chinese Lineage: The Mans in Hong Kong and London.* Berkeley: University of California Press.

———. 1977. "The Chinese: Hong Kong Villagers in the British Catering Trade." In James L. Watson, ed., *Between Two Cultures: Migrants and Minorities in Britain*, pp. 181–213. Oxford: Basil Blackwell.

Watson, Rubie S. 1985. *Inequality among Brothers: Class and Kinship in South China.* Cambridge, Eng.: Cambridge University Press.

Wei, Wou. 1996. "History and Culture." In Brian Hook, ed., *Fujian: Gateway to Taiwan*, pp. 1–29. Hong Kong: Oxford University Press.

Woon, Yuen-fong. 1997. "Economic Development and Family Patterns: A Comparative Study of the Peasant Family in Two Overseas Chinese Homelands in South China." *China Information* 12: 1–27.

Wu, David Yen-ho. 1994. "The Construction of Chinese and Non-Chinese Identities." In Tu Wei-ming, ed., *The Living Tree: The Changing Meaning of Being Chinese Today*, pp. 148–67. Stanford: Stanford University Press.

Wu, Tongyong. 1992. "Fuzhou diqu Huaqiao chuguo shilüe." In Jiazhou Tong, ed., *Fuzhou diqu Huaqiao chuguo shi lunwenji* (Collection of studies on the history of overseas Chinese migration from Fuzhou prefecture), pp. 146–53. Fuzhou: Fuzhou Huaqiao Lishi Xuehui.

———. 1994. "Fuzhou diqu Huaqiao chuguo shilüe." In Jiazhou Tong, ed., *Fuzhou diqu Huaqiao chuguo shi lunwenji* (Collection of studies on the history of overseas Chinese migration from Fuzhou prefecture), pp. 146–53. Fuzhou: Fuzhou Huaqiao Lishi Xuehui.

Wubben, Henk J. J. 1986. *"Chineezen en ander Aziatisch ongedierte": Lotgevallen van Chinese immigranten in Nederland, 1911–1940* ("Chinese and other Asian vermin": The vicissitudes of Chinese immigrants in the Netherlands, 1911–1940). Zutphen: De Walburg.

Xinjing, Yi-er-san. 1995a. "Fuzhou touduke zai Niuyue" (Fuzhou illegal immigrants in New York). *Jiushi Niandai* 1995: 68–75.

———. 1995b. "Jinse maoxian de daijia" (The price of taking the golden risk). *Jiushi Niandai* 1995: 80–85.

———. 1995c. "Niuyue Tangrenjie qitan" (Strange tales from New York Chinatown). *Jiushi Niandai* 1995: 86–92.

Yang, Li, and Xiaodun Ye. 1993. *Dongnanya de Fujianren* (The Fujianese in Southeast Asia). Fuzhou: Fujian Renmin Chubanshe.

Yang, Yinxian, Shuyu Wang, and Jiazhou Tong. 1992. *Fuzhou diqu Huaqiao chuguo shi lunwenji* (Collection of studies on the history of overseas Chinese migration from Fuzhou prefecture). Fuzhou: Fuzhou Shi Huaqiao Lishi Xuehui.

Yeung, Y. M. 2000. "Introduction." In Y. M. Yeung and David K. Y. Chu, eds., *Fujian: A Coastal Province in Transition and Transformation*, pp. 1–24. Hong Kong: Chinese University Press.

Yoshino, Kosaku. 1999. "Rethinking Theories of Nationalism: Japan's Nationalism in a Marketplace Perspective." In Kosaku Yoshino, ed., *Consuming Ethnicity and Nationalism*, pp. 8–28. Honolulu: University of Hawai'i Press.

Yu, Jianlong. 1994. "Fuqing Gaoshan diqu lüri xin huaqiao de diaocha he sikao" (Investigation and thoughts on new Chinese migrants to Japan from the Gaoshan area in Fuqing). In Yang Yinxian, Wang Shuyu, and Tong Jiazhou, eds., *Fuzhou diqu Huaqiao chuguo shi lunwenji* (Collection of studies on the history of overseas Chinese migration from Fuzhou prefecture), pp. 119–23. Fuzhou: Fuzhoushi Huaqiao Lishi Xuehui.

Zanfrini, Laura. 2001. "La programmazione dei flussi per motivi di lavoro" (The planning of waves for work purposes). In I.S.M.U., ed., *Sesto rapporto sulle migrazioni 2000* (Sixth report on migration 2000), pp. 181–210. Milan: FrancoAngeli.

———. 2002. "La programmazione dei flussi per motivi di lavoro" (The planning of waves for work purposes). In I.S.M.U., ed., *Settimo rapporto sulle migrazioni 2001* (Seventh report on migration 2001), pp. 225–52. Milan: Franco Angeli.

Zhang, Sheldon, and Ko-lin Chin, eds. 2001. "Task Force Orientation and Organizational Efficacy in Transnational Human Smuggling Activities." Unpublished paper.

Zhou, Min. 1992. *Chinatown: The Socioeconomic Potential of an Urban Enclave.* Philadelphia: Temple University Press.

———. 1998. "'Parachute Kids' in Southern California: The Educational Experience of Chinese Children in Transnational Families." *Educational Policy* 12: 682–704.

Zhou, Min, and John R. Logan. 1989. "Returns on Human Capital in Ethnic Enclaves: New York City's Chinatown." *American Sociological Review* 52: 768–71.

Zhu, Dinglong. 1995. "Dinamiche all'interno della comunità cinese a Roma" (Internal dynamics of the Chinese comminity in Rome). In Antonella Ceccagno, ed., *Il caso delle comunità cinesi: communicazione interculturale ed istituzioni*, pp. 37–44. Rome: Armando Editore.

Zhu, Yu. 2000. "*In Situ* Urbanization in Rural China: Case Studies from Fujian Province." *Development and Change* 31: 413–34.

Zhuang, Guotu. 2000a. "The Case of Jinjiang in South Fujian: An Introduction to a Current Research Project on *Qiaoxiang* Overseas Relations." In Cen Huang, Zhuang Guotu, and Tanaka Kyoko, eds., *New Studies on Chinese Overseas and China*, pp. 239–48. Leiden: International Institute for Asian Studies.

———. 2000b. "Policies of the Chinese Government toward Overseas Chinese Since 1978." *Ajia Taiheiyô Sekai to Chûgoku: Kaihatsu no naka no ningen* (The Asia-Pacific world and China: Human development), Shirizu Chugoku Ryoiki kenkyu (China Area Studies Series), no. 10. Tokyo: Ministry of Education, Science, Sports, and Culture, Scientific Research in Priority Areas 113: Structural Change in Contemporary China.

Zlotnik, Hania. 1992. "Empirical Identification of International Migration Systems." In Mary M. Kritz, Lin Lean Lim, and Hania Zlotnik, eds., *International Migration Systems: Global Approach*, pp. 19–40. Oxford: Clarendon Press.

religion: Falungong, 22, 221n25; organizations, 178–80; popular religion and ancestor worship, 58, 208–9n24
rentou shengyi (people business), *see* migration brokers or snakeheads *(shetou)*
residences, *see* living arrangements
residency, permanent, 201–2
restaurant business in Britain, 112–14, 115–17
Romania, 4, 84, 132, 174, 176, 177, 188
rural vs. urban migration, 54
Russia: brain drain to, 75; early hub of Chinese migration, 128; ethnographic methodologies, 4, 5; historical background of Chinese migration to, 71; Hungarian migrants, 134; labor export companies, 95; Luo family case study (Italy and Hungary), 30–31; Mingxi county (Village B), 54; native-place organizations, 177, 188; reasons for Chinese migration to, 72; Soviet bloc, effect of fall of, 193–94; travel agencies, 95–96; Wu siblings case study, 103

Sanming prefecture, Village B in, *See* Mingxi county (Village B)
Scandinavia, 7, 71, 170
scholars as emigrants, 74–75
self-employment and entrepreneurship, 141–44; Britain, 78; Hungary, 130–33, 135–41; Italy, 81–82, 83, 121–22
self-perpetuating and self-stimulating nature of migration, 61–63
sending communities, *see* origin / source / sending communities
sending money home, 25, 26, *see also* foreign investment projects; A Yong case study, 68; Fuqing municipality, 44, 45, 48–50, 64–65; He case history (Britain), 153, 160–61; Luo family case study, 36; Mingxi county, 56–57; native-place organizations, 171–72
service agencies, 142
service passports, 87, 96
shetou, see migration brokers or snakeheads *(shetou)*
Shijie rongyin (World Fuqing Voice), 191
shuttle traders, 54, 75, 84, 91, 128, 130, 132, 138

Singapore, *see* Southeast Asia
smuggling trade with Taiwan, 44, 47
snakeheads, *see* migration brokers or snakeheads *(shetou)*
social acceptance of immigrants: Britain, 77; Hungary, 85–86; Italy, 82
social mobility, 166–69, 200; culture of migration and, 194; family strategy for, 195; He case history (Britain), 153–61; Hungary, 129
social relationships of Fujianese migrants, 144–46, 148
social services in Italy, 120, 125–26, 217n34
source communities, *see* origin / source / sending communities
Southeast Asia: A Yong case study, 66–67; alien fifth column fears, 22; Britain, migrants to, 109–12; Chinese migration to Europe from, 71, 73; Fujian migrations to, 40; Fuqing area migration to, 25, 45–46, 48, 50–51; He case study, 153; migrant sources, 1; the nation-state's role, 14; native-place associations, 170; social relationships between Fujianese migrants and migrants from, 145–46
southern Europe, Fujianese migration to, 2, 4, 71, 72, 99–100, *see also* specific countries
Spain, 4, 5, 134, 142
sponsors, 33, 73, 80, 82
student migrants, 74–75, 212n7–8

Taiwan: Fujian's proximity to, 42, 43; Japanese colony, 40; Luo family case study, 30; rivalry with PRC, 14, 22; smuggling trade, 44, 47
tax and social insurance payments in Italy, 120, 217n34
taxes on migrant communities by home states, 20–21
textile workers in Italy, 118–21, 150
Thailand, *see* Southeast Asia
Third Front policy, 25, 41
Thunø, Mette, 7–8, 9
Tian'anmen crackdown, 46, 90, 185
tourism, 86–87, 96, 213n26
transit countries, 18, 99–100
transnationalism, 162–92, 196–97; Chinese globalization spawning, 12–15, 38;